Understanding Korean Public Administration

Although much has been written about Korean public administration, the international academic community has little knowledge about it as most of the literature has been written in Korean. This book aims to make this knowledge more accessible internationally by filling that gap, covering both the history and the current status of the Korean public administration. This book is a collaboration of many Korean public administration scholars and would appeal to those interested in the secrets of Korea's rapid development in such a short span of time.

Each chapter covers historical contexts, key to understanding Korean public administration and an important aspect as Korea is a fast-changing society. The book takes a more pragmatic approach than putting the Korean experience into Western theories. Each chapter, therefore, provides an extensive discussion on the lessons learned and practical implications.

Kwang-Kook Park is Professor at the Department of Public Administration, the Catholic University of Korea. His research focuses on organizational theory, government innovation, and cultural policy. He served as the President of the Korean Association of Public Administration in 2013. He has been the President of Korea Environment Institute since 2014. He has published numerous articles that have appeared in the *International Review of Public Administration*, the *Korean Public Administration Review*, the *Korean Policy Studies Review*, and others.

Wonhee Lee is Professor of Public Administration and Public Policy at Hankyong National University and also Executive Director at the Research Center on State Owned Enterprises, Korea Institute of Public Finance.

Seok-Hwan Lee is Dean of the Graduate School of Public Administration and Professor of Public Administration and Public Policy at Kookmin University, Seoul, Korea where he specializes in public performance measurements and management.

T0393981

Routledge Advances in Korean Studies

Understanding Korean Public Administration

Lessons learned from practice

Edited by Kwang-Kook Park,
Wonhee Lee, and Seok-Hwan Lee

Routledge
Taylor & Francis Group

LONDON AND NEW YORK

First published 2016 by Routledge

2 Park Square, Milton Park, Abingdon, Oxfordshire OX14 4RN
711 Third Avenue, New York, NY 10017

Routledge is an imprint of the Taylor & Francis Group, an informa business

First issued in paperback 2018

British Library Cataloguing in Publication Data
A catalogue record for this book is available from the British Library

Library of Congress Cataloging-in-Publication Data
Names: Pak, Kwang-guk, editor. | Yi, Wæon-hæui, 1962– editor. | Yi, Sæok-hwan, 1968– editor.
Title: Understanding Korean public administration : lessons learned from practice / edited by Kwang-Kook Park, Wonhee Lee and Seok-Hwan Lee.
Description: Abingdon, Oxon ; New York : Routledge, 2016. | Series: Routledge advances in Korean studies ; 32 | Includes bibliographical references and index.
Identifiers: LCCN 2015042286 | ISBN 9781138902596 (hardback) | ISBN 9781315668031 (ebook)
Subjects: LCSH: Public administration—Korea (South) | Political planning—Korea (South)
Classification: LCC JQ1725 .U54 2016 | DDC 351.5195—dc23
LC record available at http://lccn.loc.gov/2015042286

ISBN: 978-1-138-90259-6 (hbk)
ISBN: 978-1-138-31799-4 (pbk)

Typeset in Galliard
by Apex CoVantage, LLC

Contents

Figures

Tables

Contributors

Chad Anderson (PhD, University of Incheon; Masters of Labor and Industrial Relations, Rutgers University–New Brunswick) is Associate Professor of Public Administration at the Incheon National University, South Korea. He researches urban administration, cultural administration, education, and human and labor relations.

Kyung-Ho Cho (PhD, University of Georgia) is Professor of Public Administration and Public Policy at Kookmin University, Seoul, Korea, where he teaches organization theory and public personnel administration. He was an LG Yonam Research Professor at the University of Georgia and served as an Adjunct Professor at California State University at East Bay. His research has focused on identifying the distinctive features of organizations and personnel management in the public sector, especially as contrasted with business organizations, and on leadership, motivation, performance, commitment, and organizational changes and innovation in the Korean government. He serves as President of the Korean Society for Public Personnel Administration (2016).

Young-Chool Choi (PhD, Newcastle University, UK) is Professor of Public Administration at Chungbuk National University, Korea. He obtained his PhD from the University of Newcastle upon Tyne, UK. He is currently the Editor-in-Chief of the *Korea Local Administration Review*. He is also currently President of the Korean Association for Comparative Policy Studies. His main research interests include local government policy, decentralization, local governance, and social economy.

Keunsei Kim (PhD, Syracuse University) is Professor of Public Administration, Graduate School of Governance, Sungkyunkwan University, Seoul, Korea. His research interests include public organization theory, state administration apparatus, and public management.

Kilkon Ko is Associate Professor at the Graduate School of Public Administration, Seoul National University. He is also an Editor-in-Chief of the *Asian Journal of Political Science*. He earned his PhD in public and international affairs from the University of Pittsburgh.

Jong Youl Lee (PhD, The City University of New York) is Professor of Public Administration and former Dean of the College of Social Sciences at Incheon National University, Incheon, Korea, as well as past President of the Seoul Association for Public Administration and current president of the Korean Association for Cultural Policy Studies. He researches urban administration, policy studies, cultural administration, and risk management.

Sang Cheoul Lee is Professor at the Department of Public Policy and Management of Pusan National University. He is President of the Korean Association for Local Government Studies and a member of the Committee for the Management of Public Institutions.

Seok-Hwan Lee (PhD, Rutgers University–Newark) is Dean of the Graduate School of Public Administration and Professor of Public Administration and Public Policy at Kookmin University, Seoul, Korea, where he specializes in public performance measurements and management. He formerly taught in the Doctor of Public Administration program at the University of Illinois at Springfield. His research interests include strategic performance management in the public sector and organizational theory and behavior.

Wonhee Lee (PhD, Seoul National University) is Professor of Public Administration and Public Policy at Hankyong National University and also Executive Director at the Research Center on State Owned Enterprises, Korea Institute of Public Finance. His research interests include budgeting, public finance management, and strategic planning and management of SOEs. He co-authored *Open Budget* published by Harvard University Press.

M. Jae Moon is the Underwood Distinguished Professor of Public Administration at Yonsei University. He is currently Editor-in-Chief of the *International Review of Public Administration* (IRPA). He also chairs the Section of Korean Public Administration since 2012. Earning his PhD from the Maxwell School at Syracuse University in 1998, he previously taught at the University of Colorado at Denver, Texas A&M University, and Korea University. His research interests include e-government, public management, information technology, and development administration.

Seunghwan Myeong (PhD, Syracuse University) is Professor of Public Administration in Social Science at Inha University, Incheon, Korea. His research focuses electronic government and governance, government organization innovation, social networks, information technology management, IT project strategy, policy analysis and evaluation, the digital divide, Big Data management, and future studies.

Sung-Jun Myung (PhD, University of Pittsburgh) is Associate Professor at the department of Public Administration at Gyeongsang National University, Jinju, Korea, where he specializes in regional development and sustainable development.

Hyunshin Park (PhD, Sungkyunkwan University) is Assistant Professor of the Division of General Studies and the Teaching Profession at Dongduk Women's University, Seoul, Korea, where he lectures on public administration. His research interests include civic service, public service delivery, and public organizational theory.

Jin Park (PhD, University of Pennsylvania) is Professor at the KDI School of Public Policy and Management. He formerly served as Executive Director of the Research Institute for State-Owned Entities at the Korea Institute for Public Finance and as Director of Administrative Reform Team in the Ministry of Planning and Budget. His research interests include public-sector reform, development economics, conflict resolution, and the north Korean economy.

Kwang-Kook Park (PhD, University of Georgia) is Professor of the Department of Public Administration at The Catholic University of Korea. His research focuses on organizational theory, government innovation, and cultural policy. He served as the President of the Korean Association of Public Administration in 2013. He has served as the President of the Korea Environment Institute since 2014.

Preface

It was not long after the declaration of independence in 1948 that Korea experienced the Korean War in 1953 that laid the nation to waste. Korea's per capita income was below $100 at that time. The Korean government initiated a five-year economic development plan and achieved miraculous performance. American public administration played a critical role in this process by helping Korean scholars and practitioners identify strategies for national development. Koreans have benchmarked many dimensions of American public administration systems and internalized them so that those systems would best suit the context of Korean society.

Time flew so fast. Korea became one of the leading nations in the world with more than $30,000 in per capita income, becoming a country that developing countries want to benchmark in terms of its national development model. Korea is now facing new challenges in designing cooperative relationships between the private and public sectors as well as in balancing democratic values with efficiency to upgrade the quality of life for citizens.

We are confident that the whole story, starting from the government-driven, efficiency-based national development model for rapid economic growth to new governance practices where citizen values and societal values are balanced with efficiency, will provide tremendous insights to developing countries that want to become prosperous and growing nations.

From such a point of view, the Seoul Association of Public Administration decided to publish an English textbook that could introduce the whole story of Korea's government and national development. The contributing authors in this book are the top experts who have studied each area in the field of public administration for a long time. We hope that this book will serve as an important channel to developing countries as well as to domestic scholars and practitioners for research and reference or government operations.

This book project is the product of considerable labor. The authors who contributed chapters to this book are obvious contributors, but many other people provided tremendous efforts to complete this volume. These people include Lam Yong Ling from Routledge, who patiently waited for our manuscripts and arranged all the schedules for the whole publication process in a timely manner as well as Younghwan Jeon, research assistant from Kookmin University, who helped construct the index.

Finally we would like to appreciate our family members for their patience with our compulsive attention to this effort.

Kwang-Kook Park, Wonhee Lee,
and Seok-Hwan Lee

1 Understanding public administration in Korea

The need for sharing models in government reforms

Kwang-Kook Park, Wonhee Lee, and Seok-Hwan Lee

Every country in the world is struggling to enhance its level of productivity in an era of limited resources. Regardless of what type of political and economic system each country has, government at all levels is pressured to produce more output with fewer input. Both the public and private sectors should equally contribute to the welfare of society in order for a nation to be prosperous. It should be noted, however, that a productive public sector leads to a productive society.

The Korean government has provided an important model of development, especially for nations around the world in the process of developing. Because Korea's rapid economic growth in such a short period has astounded the world, many countries have shown interest in learning the forces driving economic development. Among others, the role of the public sector was critical, and it is necessary to share Korea's experience for nations in similar situations that want to avoid errors as well as to benchmark success stories. Many books dealing with the Korean economic development model and the New Village Movement have come out, and many issues have been discussed. However, little has been discussed dealing with specific government reforms, practices, and operations in specific areas such as performance management, administrative control, human resources management, and e-government initiatives.

This book is a response to those demands. Scholars in the public sector came to agree on publishing a book that would introduce the real practices and lessons from Korean government reforms and innovations so that other countries can benchmark real cases. In doing so, the authors have tried, not only to focus on success stories, but also share some failures with the same attention. Initiated and sponsored by the Seoul Association of Public Administration, the contributing authors tried to identify lessons learned from practices in the Korean government at all levels.

Part I of this book discusses a variety of roles of government in Korea. Part I mainly focuses on Korean government initiatives for economic development along with efforts for overcoming challenges to planning in addition to organizing issues.

The first chapter by M. Jae Moon, "The Evolution of the Developmental State and Government Capacity in Korea: Achievements and Challenges," points out that Korea is a peculiar example that demonstrates compressed developmental successes in both politics and economics. Many scholars and practitioners have attributed Korea's successes to an effective developmental state through which the Korean government played a critical and leading role in designing economic development plans, mobilizing national resources, coordinating economic actors, and implementing proactive interventionist economic policies. Positing two contrasting developmental paths – the dictatorial (authoritarian) regime-based D_1 Path and democratic regime-based D_2 Path –, it is argued Korea is an exemplary model of the D_1 Path and demonstrates the significance of state (administrative) capacities. The D_1 Path requires effective management of corruption while the D_2 Path requires effective consensus-building mechanisms to ensure economic development. The Korean experience offers a set of implications for developing countries, including the significance of clean and capable bureaucratic systems, planning and coordinating capacity, political stability, leadership, legitimacy, and effective adaptation to environmental changes. With the increasing complexity of the administrative environment and the growth of the business sector and civil society, however, Korea has shifted from the D_1 Path to the D_2 Path where state and bureaucracy work, not as leaders, but as facilitators and enablers. Notably, the D_2 Path has been promoted in the name of good governance by many international institutions such as the World Bank and the United Nations.

In his chapter, "The Role of Planning and Government in Economic Development," Jin Park emphasizes that the roles played by economic planning during the 1960s and 1970s include focusing, coordinating, motivating, and capacity-building. Government intervention replacing the market could potentially be detrimental to the national economy if wrong choices are made.[1] Since the Korean government has been reasonably competent and relatively untainted by corruption, its intervention was a positive factor in economic development. Park concludes that the role of government is crucial at earlier stages of economic development but less so in mature stages of the economy. Therefore, the government should attempt to reduce market intervention as the economy grows. When the economy is at an early stage of development, input factors such as labor and capital determine most of a nation's income growth. As per capita income grows, however, total factor productivity (TFP) becomes a much more important source of growth. The government is a good mobilizer of resources, but not a good innovator, and this is why government should refrain from further interference with the market in the developed stage.

Keunsei Kim and Hyunshin Park's chapter, "Korean Government Organization: The Developmental State and Its Transformation," examines changes in the developmental state in South Korea in terms of state administrative structures. From a review of previous theoretical discussions, they identify some key characteristics of the developmental state: executive-centered public administration, strong central agencies, extensive economic functions and exclusive social functions, and directive policy tools. The analysis showed both consistency and change in the Korean developmental state. First, in spite of the recent growth of the legislature and the courts, the executive-centered public administration system still remains strong. Second, the top priority of the state still lies in economic functions, but its importance has been challenged by the demands of social integration. Third, the central management agency has strongly maintained its organizational arrangements, although its staff and budgetary resources have decreased. Fourth, state intervention has changed from direct to indirect means. In sum, this study argues that the basic structure of the Korean developmental state system has not been reduced, but rather, it has transformed into new functional configurations and new means of social and economic intervention.

Part II of this book sharpens the focus on public-sector management issues in terms of both micro and macro points of views. This not only includes personnel, financial management, and performance management issues within an organization but also highlights local government, urban administration, and state-owned enterprises in a broader framework.

Kyung-Ho Cho's chapter, "Korean Public Personnel Management," highlights how the importance of personnel administration is becoming stronger in the Korean civil service day by day. Until recently, the Korean civil service effectively utilized position classification, based on the rank-in-person system, and efforts have been made in the last ten years to institutionalize social equity in personnel systems to fulfill the democratization of the administration. The Korean civil service has also been striving to understand social issues and administrative demands from a customer perspective in order to deal effectively with rapidly changing administrative demands. In addition, the civil service has been putting efforts into dealing with administrative demands that prioritize the public interest rather than private interests.

In his chapter, "Budget and Financial Management," Wonhee Lee argues that since Korea established the First Republic, the development of budgetary functions can be understood in three stages: industrialization (1948–1987), democratization (1988–1997), and globalization (1998–the present). During the industrialization period, the role of the budget was to support economic development. Under authoritarian regimes from 1961 until the late 1980s, the budget was considered an instrument supporting economic development by presidential will. Many meaningful fiscal reforms have been tried since the democratization movement of 1987. The trend was to strengthen transparency, participation, and accountability. The whole system was challenged by civil society after the financial crisis of 1997. The Korean government began to implement significant budgetary reforms in 2004 called the "Three Plus One reforms," and the National Finance Act of 2006 was enacted to reflect the new system. The new system included the introduction of the National Fiscal Management Plan, top-down budgeting, performance management, and digital accounting. Simultaneous implementation of the interrelated reforms proved to be very effective. Through this kind of development, the budget in Korea contributed to the industrialization, democratization, and globalization of Korea society.

Seok-Hwan Lee's chapter, "Performance Management in Korea: Challenges and Prospects," argues that performance management in the Korean public sector was initiated by the launch of the so-called innovation management initiative in

2003 when the Roh Moohyun Administration took the office. The Blue House believed that performance management should be done in a systematic way to have government focus on innovation in every aspect of delivering public services as a major driving force in making the initiative a success. After that, the Ministry of Government Administration and Home Affairs (MOGAHA) has had to spend a significant amount of time educating and training public officials in performance management as well as in the need for performance management in the public sector. He continues to argue that performance management is now taking place in government at all levels, and its focus is moving from government-driven to citizen-driven performance where citizen inputs and engagements matter in developing performance measures and evaluating the importance of performance measures to them. Public-sector employees are now required to work beyond the boundaries of organizational chart following the concept of Unreasonable Objectives-focused Organization (UOFO). This chapter emphasizes that top management support and commitment is a necessary first step to make performance management a success. Finally, he concludes that performance management is not a panacea for solving organizational problems. It is a problem-defining rather than a problem-solving procedure.

In his chapter, "Local Government," Young-Chool Choi highlights how local government in Korea has faced enormous changes in the past 20 years. The Local Autonomy Act of 1988 has brought about significant changes to the system of local government in Korea, expanding the powers of local authorities in a number of respects. The increase in the power of local authorities must be balanced against increasing practical constraints on freedom of action as a result of significant reductions in central government support and cuts in government spending. This chapter aims to offer an introduction to, and an account of, the local government system of Korea that may appeal to those seeking an overview of the area as well as a critical and contextual approach that will be of interest to those actively researching in the area of local government. The chapter reviews the historical background to local government in Korea and elaborates the rules governing the status and scope of the activities of local authorities. It also deals with the internal organization of the local authorities and their democratic dimensions. Then, it discusses the functions of local authorities; the coordination of the different levels of governance, supervision, and inspection of local authorities; and local finance. Finally, it presents future policy issues regarding local government in Korea including the role of local government, decentralization, and local government reorganization.

Sang Cheoul Lee's "Roles and Reforms of Public Enterprises" discusses how public enterprises are still playing an important role: their estimated expenditures today are almost twice as much as those of the different levels of government. On the other hand, public enterprises have been criticized severely due to excessive demands by labor unions and budgetary waste by management. The Korean government enacted the Act on the Management of Public Institutions based on the Organisation for Economic Co-operation and Development's (OECD) Guidelines on the Corporate Governance of State-Owned Enterprises. On the basis of the act, the government has established the Committee for Public Institution Management to exercise centralized ownership over public enterprises and to enforce management evaluation strictly. It has also put in place the Public Disclosure System to strengthen the transparency of public enterprises. However, the act has not considered minority shareholder rights or competitive neutrality in public enterprises. Blurred and duplicated lines of accountability among government departments have been a chronic problem in the management of Korean public enterprises. This chapter reviews the experience of governance reform in Korea's public enterprises as well as future tasks through relevant theoretical issues.

Jong Youl Lee and Chad Anderson's chapter, "Urban Development," details the historic and contemporary growth of cities in heavily urbanized Korea, beginning with basic terms related to urban development, so critical to national development in Korea. The government took an active role in urban development following the devastation of the Korean War. Urbanization initially followed a common pattern in Korea familiar to developing nations, moving from clearing informal settlements off of high-value land to make way for private development in the 1950s to gradually more participatory and inclusive methods through the twentieth century. However, conflict has continued in urban development right up to the present, and the new millennium has seen redevelopment and cultural and environmental development in Seoul counterpoised against a new welfare paradigm de-emphasizing physical development. Current Korean local governments use market-compatible development tools such as business subsidies through tax abatements, lower interest rates, cheap land, and enterprise zones as well as planning and public-private entrepreneurialism. Korea has used most development methods in its modern history, making it a good example for comparison. The chapter reviews some of the best-known development projects in Korea, including new town developments, Seoul's Cheonggye-cheon restoration, and New Songdo.

Seunghwan Myeong's chapter, "Electronic Government," argues that e-government is more than just deploying information technologies. It requires consideration of various configurations and types of e-government implementation. For example Korea has been driven towards building an Information and Communications Technologies (ICT) infrastructure since its government realized that building an information-oriented society is directly associated with national competence. The country has emphasized the development of ICT-related businesses and information-oriented public administration systems, and as a result, e-government has become more diverse and efficient. However, it is very difficult to provide a standardized model of e-government since each country has a different historical and political background as well as a different level of technical expertise. E-government study should not fall into the dichotomy between art and science in the era of governance. It should entail both consensus building and effective implementation, while selecting a good leader to orchestrate good governance for good performance. The bureaucratic and New Public Management (NPM)-oriented e-government model is declining in popularity because of the narrow and managerial perspective while ignoring differences in philosophy, history, culture, politics, and government among countries. People involved in e-government in the future will need the capability to predict and analyze in a timely manner, the ability to dialogue and moderate with local and global clients, and a philosophy for balancing democracy and efficiency.

Part III of this book deals mainly with accountability and innovation issues. The authors investigate a variety of issues ranging from anti-corruption and administrative control efforts for securing transparency to government reform and innovation for responding to the demands of citizens.

Sung-Jun Myung's chapter, "Administrative Control: Ensuring Accountable Bureaucracy," argues that the marked increase in citizen demands and specialization in society led to the rapid growth of the executive branch in its size and mandates. Announcing the advent of the administrative state, the dominance of the executive and its relative empowerment disrupted the balance of the three branches, allowing more discretionary power. As a way to ensure the responsibility of the executive, administrative control has continued to take an important place in the field of public administration. All three branches – the legislative, executive, and judicial – have taken more active approaches since the authoritative regimes have stepped down. The control system employed thus far is necessary for advancing democratic governance and preventing an oversized government bureaucracy from exercising discretionary power improperly. The National Assembly, Korea's legislative body, ensures administrative responsibility by exercising its power to investigate government affairs and to hold open hearings to confirm high-ranking government appointees in addition to its traditional law-making activities. The judiciary is another institution that calls for responsible behaviors by the executive through interpreting laws, correcting improper administrative actions, and relieving injuries to citizens. Internal measures taken by the executive branch have been an important tool to improve their own performance as well as securing responsible behavior by its members. Self-audits by their own respective agencies, evaluation by managing agencies within the executive and the Supreme Audit Institutions, and ombudsmen are all compelled by law.

Kilkon Ko's chapter, "Historical Review of Anticorruption Policy in Korea: Progress and Challenges," reviews the evolution of anti-corruption policy and examines their effectiveness at controlling corruption. The review suggests that the Korean government has targeted different types of corruption with different tools. For instance, while some types of corruption such as administrative and petty corruption were effectively controlled, citizens requested a higher level of integrity in government by calling for the control of different types of corruption. The main direction of Korea's anticorruption policies can be summarized as a shift in targets from petty to political corruption, a shift in tools from political campaigns to an institutional approach, and a shift in scope from the administrative sphere to the broader public sector and to civil society. The lesson that can be drawn from this experience is that anticorruption policy should be the result of successive and responsive efforts balancing political and institutional approaches.

The final chapter, "Government Innovation" by Kwang-Kook Park, deals with several hot issues related to government innovation. The first section investigates how government innovation has evolved from the Roh Administration to the Park Administration. The second section focuses on illuminating the diverse perspectives related to government innovation and on analyzing the key elements that individual theories of government innovation have tried to emphasize. The third section introduces two types of best practices that have been made by applying theories of government innovation to governmental agencies over the last two decades. One is the Corruption Impact Assessment developed by the Anti-Corruption and Civil Rights Commission. The other is e-government, including the Business Process System, E-People, the On-Line Civil Service Portal, and the Government Integrated Data Center. Finally, the chapter concludes that government innovation should be interpreted as an ongoing process, not a static phenomenon, because of the continual changes to the government environment. At the same time, it is necessary to understand that government innovation should be carried out in order to accomplish the values of democracy, efficiency, transparency, and equity without sacrificing other values in the name of enhancing the particular value.

Efficient, effective, and responsive government is the final destination of public administration. Reforms and innovations differ from individual country to country. The practices and lessons identified in this book may represent only a small part of government efforts to strengthen the competitiveness of the public sector. Those countries that want to learn lessons from the experience of Korean government should also understand the different contexts and cultural backgrounds that are unique to the Korean government. Nevertheless, the findings and lessons identified in this book will provide other developing countries with an important basis for searching out creative solutions for government reforms and innovations. Efficient, effective, and responsive government is the final destination. We will continue to improve government performance, while trials and errors are evaluated over and over again. In this sense, comparative perspectives will offer insights into how government is performing to meet the demands of citizens.

Note

1 One example of a wrong choice is Indonesia's aircraft industry whose chairman, a long-time Minister for Science and Technology, became president of Indonesia (Chang, 2013).

Part I
Role of government

2 The evolution of the developmental state and government capacity in Korea
Achievements and challenges[1]

M. Jae Moon

I. Introduction

South Korea has been known as a rare case demonstrating both compressed economic growth and political democratization. It has been even argued that it is the only country in the world that was relatively recently colonized and has become an official member of the Development Assistance Committee (DAC) of the Organisation for Economic Co-operation and Development (OECD). Considering various political, administrative, social, and cultural factors, many believe that the strength and nature of the developmental state in South Korea made compressed economic development possible (Haggard, 1990; Woo-Cummings, 1999).

In fact, South Korea was one of poorest countries in the world. Its GDP was only USD 2.1 billion in 1961 and heavily relied on official development assistance (ODA) for basic social needs. South Korea experienced rapid economic growth with an annual growth rate of about 10 percent in the 1970s and 1980s. Its GDP grew to USD 10.8 billion in 1972, USD 64.3 billion in 1980, USD 270.3 million in 1990, USD 533.35 billion in 2000, and USD 1.1 trillion in 2012 (Economic Statistics System of the Bank of Korea, 2014). The South Korean economy began to grow beginning in late 1960s, after the implementation of strong industrial policies by the authoritarian Park Chunghee regime, which has been contrastingly labeled an economic champion and political dictator. Economic growth was followed by political democratization, which gradually began with the demise of Park's regime. Political democratization was later accelerated by the birth of the civilian government of Kim Youngsam, which interestingly marks the gradual decline of the developmental state in South Korea.

Those who pay attention to the role of the developmental state tend to be interested in the autonomous role of the state and its interventionist approach in order to understand factors contributing to economic successes, particularly of the East Asian Newly Industrialized Countries (NICs) whose economies grew rapidly between the 1960s and 1980s. The compressed economic growth was not well explained or understood by classic liberals and neoliberals who emphasized the significance of the market in economic growth. Responding to the

limitations of neoliberal explanations of economic growth in NICs and following the new image of the state proposed in Theda Skocpol's *Bringing the State
Back In* published in 1985, many state theorists worked on developing models
of the developmental state and paid attention to the state and its institutional
capacities in resource mobilization, allocation, and policy coordination beyond
market power. The concept of the developmental state basically refers to the
understanding, justification, and acknowledgement of the somewhat positive
role of the state, which facilitates "the structural transition from a primitive/
agrarian to a modern/manufacturing society" (Kasahara, 2013: 3).

Revisiting the concept and typologies of the developmental state, this chapter
is designed to review the evolution of the developmental state in South Korea,
particularly focusing on two elements including core elements of administrative
capacity and the nature of interventionist policies. Based on an examination of
both the positive and negative sides of South Korea's experience of economic
development driven by its developmental state, this chapter offers policy implications for other developing countries.

II.   Debates on the developmental state

South Korea has been placed at the center of the developmental state debate
that primarily began in the mid-1980s. Some may trace developmental state
perspectives all the way back to the pre-modern mercantilist period and associate
its central themes with long-standing debates over imperfect markets, market
failures, and the role of the state as an intervener and corrector that fixes market
failures in societies (Kasahara, 2013). However, the development state model
was primarily proposed, debated, and structured in the 1980s in the course
of intensive discussions about the proactive and intervening roles of the state
in the market for transforming the economy and industrial structure for the
long-term economic gain of society. For example the developmental state, with
its "embedded autonomy," is a main institutional mechanism through which
a country is pushed and transformed into a higher-level productive structure
from a primitive and agrarian economy to a manufacturing economy so that the
country can be placed in a better and more advantageous position in the global
division of labor (Evans, 1995). The developmental state often picks winners
and losers in the course of implementing strong industrial policies and justifies
authoritarian regimes for their efficient and effective policy-making systems at
the price of democratic values and the equal distribution of economic gains
obtained from economic growth.

It is not clear whether the developmental state is defined simply based on the
nature (often proactive and intervening) of institutional arrangements of a state
and its industrial (economic) policies regardless of actual outcomes, particularly
the economic performance of the state. For example should a country that
has implemented structured and proactive industrial policies similar to other
developmental states but failed in attaining economic outcomes still be labeled
a developmental state? It is widely accepted that the developmental state not

only has such characteristics as autonomous state power, market intervention, and control over economic and social activities but is also equipped with the policy capacity that enables the state to mobilize resources for industrialization and make continued progress in economic growth (Minns, 2001).

This indicates that the developmental state was proposed as a conceptual tool for the explanation and justification of the proactive and interventionist role of the state in industrialization and economic growth rather than as an objective and value-free concept. It also assumes positive economic performance driven by a strong state that has competent administrative machinery with the capacity to mobilize, plan, coordinate, and implement. This indicates that the developmental state is basically bounded by the economic growth of a state and not simply defined by the intentions and characteristics of the state. Economic growth often cannot be achieved without appropriate autonomous state capacity and quality of government (effective administration) for policy planning and implementation. Government capacity particularly refers to a state's ability in strategic planning, mobilizing resources, coordinating, and implementing policies to obtain economic growth. This often requires a relatively stable polity, less corrupt and effective administrative apparatus, and strong leadership. These characteristics include such elements required for "state building" as stable, well-functioning, and durable institutions with administrative and political personnel for "a centralized and autonomous state" (Tilly, 1975; Fukuyama, 2004). Government capacity often needs to be understood in connection with the scope of the function of state (Fukuyama, 2014). Fukuyama (2004) suggests that different countries are placed in a different locus in the quadrant based on the scope of the functions (minimalist, intermediate, and activist functions)[2] and the strength of the state representing the institutional capacities of state including rule of law (law enforcement), effective government for policy planning and execution, and the transparent and accountable operation of government.

Based on the degree of government capacity and degree of interventionist policy orientation (scope of state function), a similar typology of states is proposed: 1) a closed, underdeveloped state; 2) an open, underdeveloped state; 3) a developmental state; and 4) a developed state. A closed, underdeveloped state (i.e. underdeveloped or developing socialist countries) refers to a state that is low in government capacity and market while an open, underdeveloped state is also low in government capacity but is market oriented. A developed state is characterized as a state with a high level of government capacity and a strong market-oriented policy while a developmental state is one with high government capacity and an interventionist policy orientation.

As indicated in Figure 2.1, Korea was an open, underdeveloped state when it was liberated from Japan because its government capacity was limited but geared toward a market economy. Entering the 1960s, South Korea became a developmental state when the Park regime began to initiate strong economic development plans and also expanded and strengthened the administrative apparatus for governance and economic functions. South Korea's developmental state further advanced in the 1970s as it implemented more interventionist economic policies.

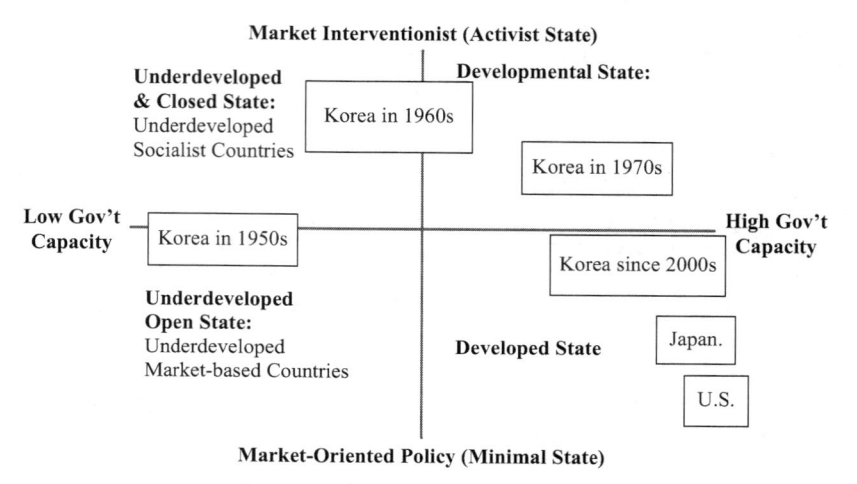

Figure 2.1 A typology of state by interventionist policy orientation and government capacity

South Korea was transformed from developmental state to developed state from the 2000s with continued economic growth and the demise of the Park regime, as it became increasingly engaged with the global economy and politically democratized.

Despite its success in Asian NICs in the 1970s and 1980s, the developmental state model has not been widely adopted by other developing countries. Not many developing countries have had sustained, successful economic achievements with high rates of economic growth. Some African countries such as Rwanda have recently followed the developmental state model that South Korea pursued in the 1970s and 1980s. The intellectual discussion regarding the developmental state has gradually declined since NICs such as South Korea and Taiwan changed their economic policy orientations to become less interventionist in the course of political democratization and economic globalization.

There are two potential development paths for developing countries. Each path refers to a distinctive combination of the nature of political regimes and government capacity as summarized in the following simple equation:

$$D_1 = D \text{ (Dictatorial/Authoritarian Regime)}$$
$$+ C \text{ (Capacity of State + Corruption Control)} \quad (1)$$
$$D_2 = D \text{ (Democratic Regime)} + C \text{ (Capacity of State}$$
$$+ \text{ Consensus Building)} \quad (2)$$

The first development path (D_1) is the development path for authoritarian (often somewhat dictatorial) regimes, and the other one (D_2) is for democratic regimes. Neither an authoritarian nor a democratic regime guarantees economic development for developing countries. Arguably there is a set of preconditions that facilitate economic development in different political regimes. For example

	Political Regime	Government capacity (Necessary Factors)		Examples
D1 Path	Authoritarian Regime	Institutional capacity for resource mobilization, policy formulation and implementation, Leadership, Bureaucratic machinery	Effective Control of Corruption	Korea
D2 Path	Democratic Regime	Institutional capacity for resource mobilization, policy formulation and implementation, Leadership, Bureaucratic machinery	Effective Consensus Building	U.S., Japan (?)

Figure 2.2 Two development paths

authoritarian regimes cannot effectively pursue economic development unless they are well equipped with government capacity such as institutional capacities[3] (i.e. resource mobilization, policy planning, coordination, and implementation) and effective control of corruption. This path is rarely found because authoritarian regimes (dictatorial regimes) are often doomed to corruption. The second development path (D_2 Path) is a developmental model for democratic regimes. Democratic regimes can pursue economic development effectively only when they have a high level of institutional capacity along with effective consensus-building mechanisms. Developing democratic regimes are likely to suffer from chaotic political situations where systematic consensus-building and decision-making processes are not well established. It is clear that South Korea followed the first development path in the 1960s and 1980s. However, the first development path is neither desirable nor appropriate for South Korea any longer because South Korea's economy has become too complex and too mature to be orchestrated simply by the state while its democratic political system has been greatly advanced. The next section will review the evolution of the developmental state in South Korea and discusses both the government capacity and interventionist economic policies that led to compressed economic growth. It should also be noted that external factors such as global economic conditions as well as the geopolitical situation are also significant parts of the development equation.

III.   The origin of South Korea's developmental state and economic growth

South Korea is a classic example of the developmental state in that it protected its market from global competition while it introduced interventionist economic and industrial policies with effective planning and implementation capacities mainly exercised by the bureaucracy. Taking advantage of the expanding global economy, South Korea pursued an export-oriented strategy rather than an import-substitution strategy, which enabled South Korea to build up manufacturing industries effectively and swiftly penetrate the global market based on its competitiveness in cost and quality of labor.

The origin of South Korea's developmental state is the Park Chunghee regime, which established itself after the military coup of 1961 and continued for 18 years until Park's assassination in 1979. Under the Park regime, South Korea experienced a rapid economic growth with strong and stable government capacity along with strong interventionist policies. Like many developing countries, South Korea was basically an authoritarian state under the Park regime, which repressed political demands for democracy for the sake of political stability and efficient and strategic management of economic growth. Park's regime often justified authoritarianism for the sake of protecting the country from the threat of communism and preparing for national unification in competition with the North Korean regime.

President Park put an emphasis on domestic political stability and economic prosperity from the beginning of his presidency. Content analysis of his inaugural speeches (Lee and Moon, 2011) shows that he began to stress economic development more in his second inaugural speech than the first one, which indicates a change in the national agenda. The frequency of selected words in his second inaugural speech in 1967 was economy (8), modernization (6), construction (6), industry (6), and development (2), which were mentioned less in his first inaugural speech: economy (6), construction (5), modernization (2), and growth (2). President Park used growth (6) and development (4) more frequently in his third inaugural speech in 1971. He first mentioned exports (2) in his third inaugural speech. President Park began to stress economic prosperity (17) in his fourth inaugural speech in 1972 as the nation entered the *Yushin* Era.

Unlike many other developing countries, luckily South Korea enjoyed a high degree of government capacity, which was required for effective implementation of complicated policies for industrialization. South Korea's state was basically autonomous in nature, which allowed the government to implement aggressive and proactive economic plans and to mobilize and allocate various resources in strategic ways. South Korea effectively maintained the quality of its administrative bureaucracy by recruiting capable civil servants through open-competition civil service examinations. This allowed South Korea to be free from the destructive nepotism and ascriptive recruitment problems often observed in many developing Asian countries. Administrative elites who had served the Japanese colonial administration remained after liberation, which was criticized by North Korea as well as those who wanted to root out the colonial legacy in South Korea. Despite the recruitment of administrative elites at the beginning of the independent state after the World War II, South Korea continued to depart from the traditional ascriptive recruitment system and strengthened its achievement- or merit-based recruitment, which became a firm foundation of a competent administrative apparatus (Paik, 1991). Despite the continued

Table 2.1 Content analysis of inaugural speeches of presidents and national agendas

	Governance	Economy	Society
Rhee Syngman (1948)	Communism (6), World (6),	Economy (1), Construction (1)	Welfare (1)
Rhee Syngman (1962)	Freedom (14), Military (11), War (9), Unification (9), Democracy (7)	Production (2), Construction (1)	
Rhee Syngman (1956)	Communism (4), Japan (4), War (4), US (3)	Economy (6), Production (6), Growth (4)	Welfare (3), Education (3)
Park Chunghee (1963)	Nation (13), Revolution (9), Order (4),	Economy (6), Construction (5), Prosperity (4),	Welfare (1), Equality (1)
Park Chunghee (1967)	Democracy (19), Nation (9), Unification (7),	Economy (8), Modernization, Construction, Industry (6)	Welfare (2)
Park Chunghee (1971)	Nation (7), Democracy (9), Unification (8)	Growth (6), Development (4), Economy (3), Export (2)	Welfare (1)
Park Chunghee (1972)	Nation (22), *Yushin* (16), Unification (11),	Prosperity (17), Development (7), Industry (2),	Welfare (3),
Park Chunghee (1978)	Nation (12), National power (6), Unification (6)	Development (8), Industry (5), Economy (4),	Welfare (3), Education (1)
Chun Doohwan (1980)	Democracy (32), Law (8), Constitution (7)	Growth (12), Economy (11), Corporate (7)	Welfare (12), Education (8)
Chun Doohwan (1981)	Law (20), North Korea (10), Constitution (7)	Growth (8), Development (5)	Poverty (7), Welfare (5), Quality of Life (5)
Roh Taewoo (1988)	Democracy (30), World (12), Peace (10)	Collaboration (7), Development (7), Growth (4), Economy (3)	Happiness (4), Welfare (3), Olympic (2)
Kim Youngsam (1993)	New Korea (12), World (9), Democracy (6), Reform (5), Corruption (4)	Economy (5), Corporate (3), New Economy (2), Competition (2)	Education (4)

(*Continued*)

Table 2.1 (Continued)

	Governance	Economy	Society
Kim Daejung (1998)	South-North (14), Democracy (11), Collaboration (10), World (9)	Economy (27), Corporate (20), Overcoming (10)	Welfare (3), Education (7)
Roh Moohyun (2003)	Northeast Asia (18), Peace (17), World (14),	Economy (8), Prosperity (7), Springboard (3)	Culture (5), Balance (3), Local (3)
Lee Myungbak (2008)	World (17), Advancement (15), Culture (15), Technology (9), Future (8)	Corporate (14), Economy (11), Industry (10), Development (10), Competition (9), Market (8)	Collaboration (9), Education (9), Environment (8), Welfare (7),

Source: Adapted from Lee and Moon (2011).

promotion of open-competition civil service examinations for apolitical recruitment, political appointees and high-ranking officials were geographically biased under the Park regime. For example 27.5 percent of cabinet members were from Kyonsang-do province, where President Park was also from (Paik, 1991). Competitive recruitment also resulted in increased numbers of administrative elites from graduates of particular elite universities such as Seoul National University, Yonsei University, and Korea University. For example the proportion of the Seoul National University graduates in administrative positions increased from 36.8 percent from 1948–1967 to 42.9 percent in 1980.

With an increasing number of administrative elites coming from elite universities, substantial numbers of administrative elites were also recruited from the military after the military coup of 1961. Many young military officers switched from military careers to civil service careers as middle-level managers (comparable to Grade 5 in the current civil service system) as *Yushinsamugwan* particularly after the coup-like *Yushin* constitutional change in 1972. Although this recruitment system and the emergence of military elites as political appointees and administrative elites militarized the administrative system and turned it into a despotic administrative instrument for policies introduced by the top leadership, it also helped to strengthen the managerial capacity of the state administrative apparatus as it was primarily based on open-competition civil service examinations.

President Park made efforts to reorganize government agencies 12 times after he assumed the presidency in 1963. He proposed 2 *Won* (Super Departments), 12 *Bu* (Departments), 1 *Cheo* (administration), 5 *Cheong* (agency) and separated planning functions from implementation functions in government operations by creating the Economic Planning Bureau (EPB), which replaced the Department of Economic Development. Among other things, the EPB concentrated authority by combining key economic functions previously found in various departments: planning functions from the Department of Construction, budgeting functions from the Ministry of Finance, and statistics functions from the Ministry of the Interior. With both budget and planning authority, the EPB became a highly capable and autonomous administrative unit for economic policy. In particular, the Agency of Foreign Aid under the Ministry of Economic Development was transferred to the Agency of Government Procurement, which was supervised by the EPB. The EBP was composed of capable and professional bureaucratic elites who were mainly trained as economists and policymakers. The EPB played a central role in coordinating economic policies working with all the related administrative units, including the Ministry of Finance, the Ministry of Commerce and Industry, and the Ministry of Agriculture and Fisheries. The EPB was in charge of establishing the five-year economic development plans, which specified all the details of economic development such as targets for GDP growth and trade, industrialization strategies (i.e. promotion of heavy and chemical industries in the early 1970s), and various economic policies like foreign direct investment and monetary policies.

Park's regime also established the Office of Planning and Coordination, which was headed by the deputy minister in the Prime Minister's Office. The Office of Planning and Coordination was in charge of managing and coordinating inter-ministerial conflicts and tension in policy positions and budget allocations. With the support and direction of the Presidential Office, South Korea effectively managed policy coordination and strategically mobilized resources particularly for industrialization. Many elites were trained by and emerged from the EPB and the Office of Planning and Coordination and later formed the South Korean administrative elite.

In pursuing strategic five-year economic development plans, South Korea used annual Economic Management Plans (EMPs) as instruments for monitoring annual targets as well as for making necessary adjustments reflecting the changing economic environment. The EPB played a critical role in drafting yearly EMPs and providing annual budgetary guidelines, which characterized the South Korean economy as guided capitalism under a mixed economy rather than as a free and open economy. The Economic Ministers Consultation Meeting (EMCM) and the Industrial Policy Deliberation Council (IPDC) headed by the deputy minister were also significant institutional mechanisms where economic policies were coordinated and arranged while inter-ministerial conflicts were managed (Choi, 1991).

It should also be noted that South Korea established various think-tanks to support economic planning and government coordination. Think-tanks were often matched with individual agencies and provided necessary policy information and economic data. For example the Korean Development Institute (KDI), the Korea Institute for Industrial Economics and Technology (KIET), the Korea Research Institute for Human Settlements (KRIHS), the Korea Rural Economics Institute (KREI), the Korea Institute of Population and Health (KIPH) were matched with the EPB, the Ministry of Trade and Industry, the Ministry of

Construction, the Ministry of Agriculture and Fisheries, and the Ministry of Health and Social Affairs, respectively (Whang, 1991)

Another important part of government capacity was control of corruption, which always increases transaction costs and is detrimental to development. Political corruption and administrative corruption are often particularly widely structured in developing countries. Authoritarian governments are often doomed to corruption because rent-seeking activities by politicians or bureaucrats are easily practiced because of the rigid nature of the political and administrative environment. Corruption was arguably controlled well in South Korea in the course of economic development compared to other countries at a similar development stage even though various forms of corrupt practices were still found.

The capable administrative apparatus was instrumental in the realization of "guided capitalism" and a "mixed economy" that aimed to promote the business activities of private enterprises and allow state intervention for the sake of efficiency and the national interest (Whang, 1991). The Office of National Tax Administration, established in 1966, became instrumental in the effective mobilization of resources necessary for economic growth and social development by avoiding political interruption in tax collection businesses. Minns (2001) highlights four fundamental pillars for South Korea's interventionist policies: 1) private ownership of industry, 2) state control of finance, 3) state planning, and 4) maintenance of a low-wage economy in the course of economic growth (p. 1031). Among other things, state control of finance was the most powerful policy tool for Korea's developmental state. South Korea held control over most financial assets and financial institutions, which was effective for its interventionist industrial policies. Interventionist policies included strategic resource allocation for investment, strong regulation of capital movement and financial institutions, and intention of market pricing (Minns, 2001).

One typical example of South Korea's interventionist policy was the 8.3 Emergency Action for Private Loan Payment, which was taken by the Park regime in 1972. The action basically froze firms' private loans to relieve their financial stress by permitting firms to delay their loan payments for three years and by enacting a favorable monthly interest rate of 1.35 percent. The government even provided 200 billion won to relieve short-term bank loans for businesses. The emergency action was indeed an extraordinary interventionist measure that disrupted financial markets for the sake of business interests (Kang, 1976). This action helped drop the ratio of interest expense to net sales from 9.9 percent in 1971 and 7.1 percent in 1972 to 4.6 percent in 1973 while improving the ratio of net profits to net sales from 1.2 percent in 1971 and 3.9 percent in 1972 to 4.6 percent in 1973. This action later further tightened the business–government relationship and helped to stimulate economic activities and the export performance of private companies.

Many interventionist policies were effectively handled by the South Korean state because the banking system was largely nationalized and most financial assets were controlled by the state. The nationalization of the banking system and financial control enabled the state to allocate financial resources strategically for targeted

Table 2.2 Financial indicators in manufacturing industries[4] (unit: %)

	Debt/Equity Ratio*	Interest Expenses to Net Sales ratio	Net Profit to Net Sales Ratio
1963	92.2	3.0	9.1
1964	100.5	4.9	8.6
1965	92.7	3.9	7.9
1966	117.7	5.7	7.7
1967	151.2	5.2	6.7
1968	201.3	5.9	6.0
1969	270.0	7.8	4.3
1970	328.4	9.2	3.3
1971	394.2	9.9	1.2
1972	313.4	7.1	3.9
1973	272.7	4.6	7.5
1974	316.0	4.5	4.8
1975	339.5	4.9	3.4
1976	364.6	4.9	3.9
1977	350.7	4.9	3.5
1978	366.8	4.9	4.0

Source: Bank of Korea Financial Statements Analysis 1981, quoted in W.S. Kim (1991).

Note: Total liabilities/net worth

industries, which facilitated and accelerated industrialization in Korea (Minns, 2001). This was characterized as *Kwanchi-Geumyung* (government-controlled financing), which became a powerful policy instrument of the developmental state and strengthened state–business ties. This was a primary instrument in the emergence and growth of *chaebol* by allowing them to expand their businesses with state-guaranteed financing. While state–business ties were instrumental in the formulation and implementation of strategic industrial policies, they often disrupted financial markets and became a channel for potential corruption.

It should be noted that the Korean government took a proactive and strategic role in taking advantage of foreign financial sources such as foreign aid and loans for industrialization. The International Loan Repayment Guarantee Act of 1962 is an excellent example. The South Korean government guaranteed the repayment of any loan approved by the Ministry of Finance, the Bank of Korea, or the Reconstruction Bank, which enabled Korean companies to borrow foreign loans despite their low credit in the international financial market. The inflow of foreign capital to the Korean economy was primarily handled and managed by the Korean government.

The Park Administration also had a strong stance in limiting foreign direct investment in order to protect domestic companies. For example foreign direct

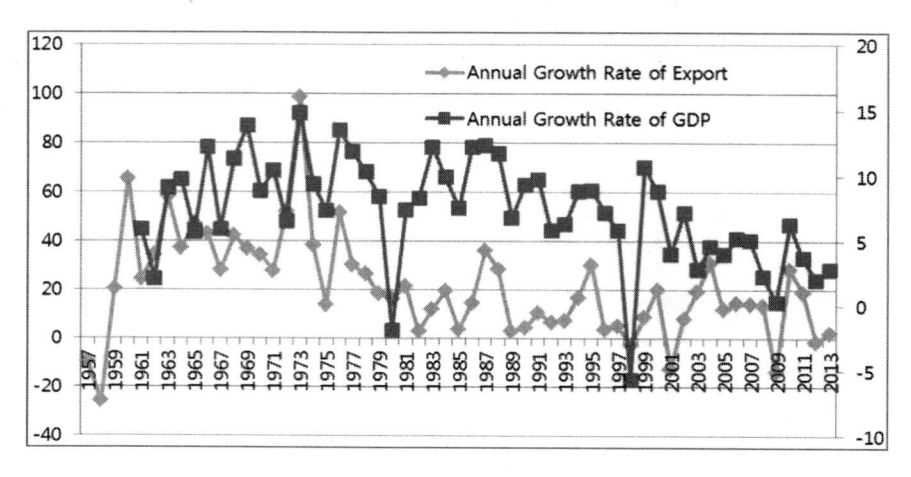

Figure 2.3 Annual growth rates for exports and GDP

Source: Global Trade Statistics System and Economic Statistics System of Bank of Korea http://stat.kita.net/stat/kts/sum/SumImpExpTotalList.screen.

investment was allowed in limited, targeted sectors such as heavy industry, the chemical industry, or industries for strategic export promotion. The government also strongly regulated the maximum ownership of foreign equity at 50 percent with an exception for foreign direct investment in the Masan Free Export Zone where full foreign ownership was allowed (Minns, 2001). Despite this exceptional clause for foreign ownership in the Free Export Zones, overall foreign ownership was very limited and accounted for less than 10 percent of total investment.

In addition to South Korea's interventionist policies in banking and finance, South Korea took advantage of public corporations in order to carry out capital-intensive infrastructure projects and deal with market failures with economic development strategies. Public corporations were often kept at arm's length because public corporations were under the full control of ministries and the Blue House. South Korea's public corporations grew rapidly in the course of the economic growth in the 1960s. While the number of corporations jumped from 52 in 1963 to 108 in 1973, they constituted about 9 percent of the Korean economy in 1972 from 7 percent in 1963 (Whang, 1991).

The South Korean government also had explicit and instructive policies for protecting the domestic market and promoting exports. The South Korean government's export promotion policy was very explicit, specific, and targeted. The government proposed and managed specific export targets for industries and firms. President Park convened regular meetings for monitoring monthly export performance and making policy decisions to ensure specific export targets were met. The government introduced various policy tools to drive exports. For example it offered export businesses various monetary incentives such as a 50-percent tax cut on export earnings as well as providing them access to loans and subsidies.

Thanks to the strong export drive in the 1970s, South Korea's exports jumped from USD 40 million in 1961 to USD 15 billion in 1979. South Korea celebrated the grand achievement of USD 10 billion of exports in 1977. As indicated in Figure 2.3 of annual growth rates, exports grew between 20 percent and 98.6 percent in the 1960s and 1970s. The annual export growth rate began to slow at the beginning of the 1980s but still remained relatively high until the end of the 1980s, particularly when the Seoul Olympics were held in 1988. Export growth began to slow down dramatically during the mid-1990s. Export growth rates were 3.7 percent, 5 percent, and –2.8 percent in 1996, 1997, and 1998, respectively.

With a continued increase in exports, South Korea reached unprecedented economic growth rates in the 1970s. As indicated Figure 2.3, annual GDP growth largely synchronized with export growth. South Korea's annual growth rate of GDP jumped from 2.1 percent in 1962 to 9.1 percent in 1962 then to 12.2 percent in 1966. In general, the annual growth rate of the economy stayed high in the 1960s and 1970s: 10.4 percent, 13.5 percent, and 8.4 percent in 1971, 1976, and 1979, respectively. In fact, the growth rate continued to remain high in the 1980s and 1990s until South Korea was hit by financial crisis in 1998. Since then, the annual growth rate of GDP has dropped below 5 percent (Economic Statistics System of the Bank of Korea, 2014).

VI. Demise or reconfiguration of South Korea's developmental state

With the assassination of President Park, South Korea quickly shifted from a centralized authoritarian state to a less centralized and more democratic state. Responding to citizen demands for democracy and to global pressure for adhering to global business standards for trade, foreign direct investment, and capital market regulation, South Korea transformed itself not only economically but also politically. While the domestic demand for democracy put increasing pressure on South Korea to shift its authoritarian regime to a more democratic political regime, global economic pressure led its economy to a more liberalized and open economic system where its conventional interventionist approach was often denounced by the global economic community. This section will discuss how South Korea's developmental state declined from the perspectives of changes in both political (changes in political regimes) and economic (changes in economic policies) dimensions.

As mentioned earlier, South Korea changed after President Park was assassinated in 1979, though the authoritarian regime largely continued until Kim Youngsam was elected in 1993 as the first civilian president after the Park regime. Despite the long-standing authoritarian regime between the 1960s and 1980s, South Korea experienced several peaks of political change that gradually moved its political wheels toward a more democratic system. The peaks included 1) the first divided government in 1978 during the Park regime, 2) changes to presidential terms and direct presidential election, 3) the appearance of a civilian president, 4) local autonomy and local elections, 5) peaceful transition of power from the ruling party to the opposition party, and 6) weakened policy planning and coordinating power.

First of all, President Park experienced a divided government for the first time during his administration in 1978, the year before he was assassinated. The opposition party obtained more seats than the ruling party in the 1978 general election. This was a strong indication that people really wanted to see democratic political change. Second, the people's demand for democracy began to spread and escalated in terms of the number of protests and labor disputes beyond college student protests on campus. Third, though the demise of the Park's regime did not ensure the establishment of democracy, the South Korean Constitution stipulated a presidential term limit, which was applied to President Chun Doohwan who served his single-term, seven-year presidency between 1981 and 1988. The continued demand for democracy in the middle of the 1980s later led to a reduction of the presidential term to five years and a change from indirect election to the direct election of the president in 1988, with Roh Taewoo succeeding Chun. Fourth, the authoritarian regime almost disappeared when civilian Kim Youngsam was elected as the 14th president of Korea in 1993. President Kim Youngsam initiated various political and administrative reforms to terminate the legacies of past military regimes. For example he abolished a long-standing core elite military group called the "Hanahwe," which Presidents Chun and Roh had created. President Kim also introduced "Real Name Accounts" to make financial transactions transparent, which was a critical step toward the eradication of corruption. The peaceful transition of power symbolized the complete transformation of the authoritarian government to democracy. Fourth, then centralized authoritarian government further faded when South Korea introduced local autonomy through local elections for local council members in 1991 and then for mayors and governors as well as in 1995. Fifth, South Korea experienced its first peaceful power transition from the ruling party to an opposition party when President Kim Daejung was elected the 15th president of Korea in 1998. Finally, the decline of South Korea's central policy planning and coordinating power caused the demise of the developmental state. For example the EPB, created in 1963 as a core agency headed by the deputy prime minister, began to weaken as the South Korean economy was further engaged in the global market particularly from the 1980s. The EPB was eventually dissolved and merged into the Ministry of Finance and Planning in 1994 and lost its legal status as an independent planning authority.

The size, scope, and strength of the administrative apparatus have also changed as South Korea pursues social development and democracy beyond the economic growth that the developmental state pursued. The South Korean government in general has more civil servants for intermediate functions than for core governing functions or economic functions (Moon and Joo, 1997) while the proportions have changed over time. South Korea is now more geared toward social functions than the governing and economic functions that used to be larger and more influential. The proportion of civil servants in economic functions was greatly reduced as South Korea shifted from a developmental state to a democratic, market-based state. As Table 2.3 indicates, the proportion of civil

Table 2.3 Changes in government officials by function

Year		1963	1965	1970	1979	1985	2000	2004	2013
Governing function		57,903	62,917	80,632	96,966	123,228	155,947	162,300	187,381
	%	25.56	25.07	23.65	24.36	26.95	28.40	27.55	30.43
Intermediate function		135,299	159,550	213,929	238,736	274,755	352.861	386,676	386,531
	%	62.07	63.59	62.74	59.98	64.46	64.26	65.63	62.78
Economic function		27,84	28,451	46,408	62,328	39,296	40,290	40,172	41,814
	%	11.37	11.34	13.61	15.66	8.59	7.34	6.82	6.79
Total		217,990	250,918	340,969	398,030	457,279	549,098	589,148	

Source: Data compiled from the Ministry of Security and Public Administration, https://org.mogaha.go.kr.

The categorization of state functions is primarily based on World Bank classifications.

servants in the area of economic functions was reduced from 18.57 percent in 1979 to 9.40 percent, 7.34 percent, and 6.79 percent in 1985, 2004, and 2013, respectively. In contrast, intermediate (social) functions of the state increased from 59.98 percent in 1979 to 64.46 percent in 1985.

In addition to the political change from an authoritarian regime to a democratic one and administrative changes in the size and scope of state functions, South Korea also responded to global economic pressures and began to liberalize its economy by loosening up long-held regulations and control over financial institutions and industries.

A decrease in the state's economic function appeared in changes in the direction of economic policies. One of the significant changes in the state–*chaebol* relationship, which was the core foundation for South Korea's interventionist policies, was the privatization of banks and non-bank financial institutions, which started in 1981 under the Chun Administration. The Korean government gave up its ownership in five major commercial banks in 1983 though it still held a great deal of influence over key financial decisions such as interest rates and policy loans (Minns, 2001) until the early 1990s. South Korea's control over interest rates began to weaken substantially when it introduced a policy liberalizing interest rates in 1988.

As *chaebol* continued to grow under the state's auspices, ironically, state autonomy was gradually limited and constrained because of *chaebol* engagement in the global economy and international financial system. The South Korean economy gradually began to open to the global economy and changed its stance on foreign capital and domestic market protection. For example South Korea allowed foreign security companies to open offices in 1981 as a gesture of economic opening to foreign capital.

Entering the 1980s when the global export market became more restrictive because of increasing protectionism and natural resource nationalism, the government–business relationship began to change in order to maintain and improve national economic competitiveness. For example South Korea gradually put more emphasis on technological innovation and promoted R&D funding rather than preferential loan packages for businesses (Whang, 1991). With increasing pressure from global economic norms and institutions to open and liberalize the economy as well as a growing private sector in the national economy, South Korea could not help but gradually move away from conventional interventionist policies and gear itself towards a more open and liberalized economy in order to effectively adapt to its increasingly complex and changing internal and external economic environment. In particular, South Korea removed import barriers such as non-tariff barriers as well as liberalized its economy for foreign capital. As a result, Korea's import liberalization ratio jumped from about 68 percent in 1979 to 84.4 percent and 95 percent in 1984 and 1988, respectively, while adopting a negative list system in 1984 to further liberalize foreign direct investment policies (Kim, 1991). South Korea also enacted the Anti-Monopoly Act in 1981 to promote competition and strengthen market mechanisms in the economy. South Korea has become a more open, competitive, and liberalized economy while also a more complex, diverse, complicated, and democratic society that experienced new sets of challenges such as economic and regional disparities, an aging population and low fertility, and other social conflicts and issues.

With these changes, the South Korean government has changed its policy position by shifting its role from controller to facilitator or often coordinator in order to meet new social demands for quality of life, social development, and citizen participation beyond economic growth. The conventional developmental state model does not fit any longer because the economy has become too big and complex to be managed and directed by the government. In particular, the central government continues to give away its leading position to local governments, citizens, and civic organizations.

Despite the gradual demise and transformation of the developmental state in South Korea since 1980s, the South Korean government arguably still maintains some key features of the developmental state in various ways (Chu, 2009). For example the state played a key role in developing information technology infrastructure and promoting information technology industries based on the National Informatization Plan, which was strategically prepared and has been executed since the 1990s. The South Korean government introduced various policy tools such as subsidies, tax incentives, and regulatory frameworks to promote information technology industries and develop information infrastructure. Based on the National Informatization Framework Act of 1995, the Korean government established the National Informatization Promotion Fund to support a set of activities for the establishment of an information and communications technology (ICT) infrastructure, e-government, the ICT industry, and ICT R&D projects. The fund was established with contributions from the government (about 40 percent), private telecommunication companies (45 percent), and other miscellaneous sources (14 percent). The government spent US$5.33 billion between 1994 and 2003 on ICT research and development (38 percent), informatization promotion (20 percent), ICT human resource development (18 percent), broadband infrastructure and promotion (15.1 percent), and infrastructure (7 percent) and standardization (3 percent) for the ICT industry. Using the fund, the Korean government was able to establish broadband infrastructure such as the Internet Super Highway (155M–5Gbps) and the education internet connection project for 10,400 primary and secondary schools (Suh and Chen, 2007). Chu (2009) also argues that South Korea continues to hold a developmental vision, continues to exercise the state's coordination and strategic planning roles, and utilizes public resources to achieve particular national goals, which often intervene in and structure the market in subtle ways. The top-down and preemptive roles of the state are arguably rooted deeply in South Korean society where the state has often been regarded as a paternalistic figure throughout its long history.

It should be also noted that the Ministry of Strategy and Finance is still influential as a budgetary agency in reviewing the annual budget plans of various ministries and plays a critical role in setting basic policy tones and coordinating basic economic policies though its centralized role has continued falling because of the complexities of the economy and the increasing autonomy of private economic actors such as the *chaebol*, labor unions, and consumers as well as increasing pressure from global economic institutions, trading partners, and other international economic actors.

V.   Conclusions and global implications for developing countries

The developmental state is not an objective and value-free term but a value-laden term. It implies compressed economic growth driven by an autonomous state that is equipped with the institutional capacity to effectively mobilize resources and administer complex economic policies for industrialization. This section will draw a set of implications from the experience of South Korea's developmental state and its contribution to economic development for developing countries. South Korea represents the D_1 path model, which indicates that the pursuit of economic development by an authoritarian state (often dictatorial state) is effectively done only when control of corruption is appropriately managed and government capacity is well equipped with effective institutional arrangements and civil service.

There is no single best development model that fits all countries because the domestic context and global geo-economic-political environment vary across time and countries. However, the development policy community believes that "institutions matter" to economic development (World Bank, 1997). Institutions basically represent various structural, behavioral, and cultural components that constitute the nature of the state and governance.

Some lessons can be drawn for developing countries based on the experience of the developmental state of South Korea, particularly focusing on state capacity in terms of the supply of institutional capacity (organizational design and management, political system design, legitimacy, and cultural and structural factors).

First of all, developing countries need to find their own developmental model by considering historical, political, economic, and cultural factors. As suggested, there are two major development paths. Though South Korea followed the D_1 path, the World Bank basically recommends the D_2 path under the name of "Good Governance." As the governance indicators (voices and accountability, political stability, government effectiveness, rule of law, control of corruption, and regulatory quality) imply, good governance basically assumes accountable, effective, and transparent governance. As the governance indicators suggest, the gap in political regime represented by "voice and accountability" among countries of different income levels is smaller than those of other administrative institutional factors such as government effectiveness, rule of law, and control of corruption. This arguably suggests that administrative institutional factors are more significant than political factors (voice and accountability), which become more significant in high-income countries.

Second, developing countries should design and manage their governing institutions to effectively administer complex economic policies for industrialization.

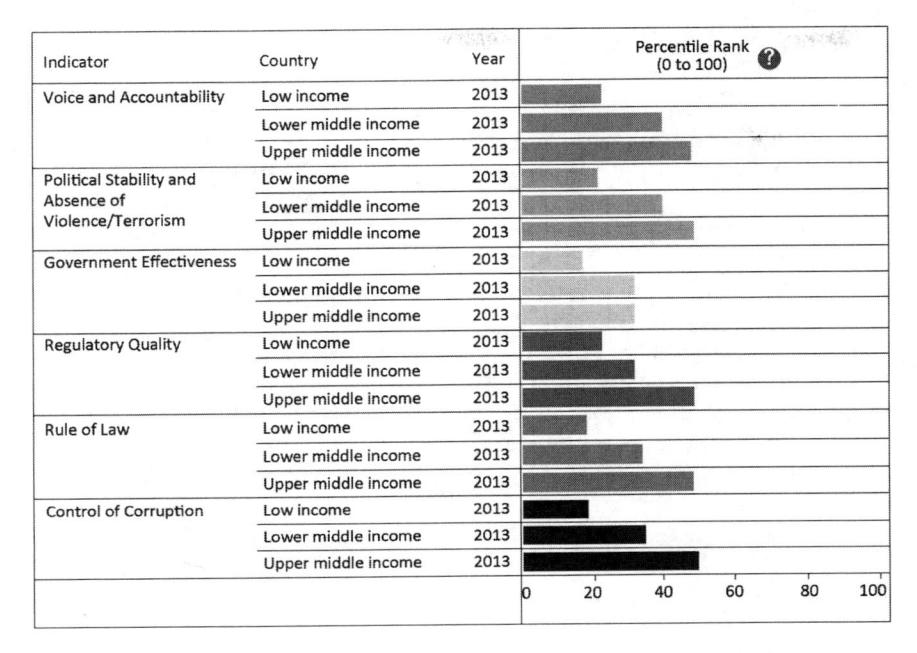

Figure 2.4 Comparison of governance indicators by income levels

Source: World Bank Governance Indicators, http://info.worldbank.org/governance/wgi/index. aspx#reports.

Many believe that the establishment of the EPB and its capacity and authority for planning and coordinating economic policies were the most significant factors that contributed to stable and compressed economic growth in South Korea. It is also worth paying attention to the separation of planning from implementation, making the head of the planning unit superior to other implementation units. The head of the EPB was deputy prime minister who had the authority to coordinate economic policies and manage the different policy positions of various department and agencies.

Third, a competent and reliable bureaucratic system appears to be critical. In the 1960s and 1970s, civil servants were highly respected in South Korea. The recruitment exam was extremely competitive, and its procedure was transparent, which helped to make the civil service an elite group enjoying public respect and support. Developing countries need to recruit capable civil servants based on merit and need to avoid nepotism in recruitment through open-competition exams. Elite civil servants were often highly proud of their position and social status, which made them committed to their service.

Fourth, political stability appears a significant factor. Those countries with a low level of political stability because of violence or terrorism cannot effectively mobilize and allocate resources for industrialization. It is important to maintain strong but desirable democratic governing institutions in order to maintain political stability.

Fifth, the legitimacy of the state is also critical. Lack of state legitimacy is certainly an institutional cost. Long-standing authoritarian regimes often suffer from lack of legitimacy. It is important to note that developing countries should try to minimize the institutional costs of legitimacy problems with respect to creating, operating, maintaining, and transitioning regimes. Despite unprecedented economic achievements, the Park regime had continued legitimacy problems particularly with the beginning of the regime and the creation of the *Yushin* regime.

Sixth, it is important to shift a country from a nation-building stage to a state-building stage (Fukuyama, 2004). The commitment of leadership is always essential in shifting and upgrading institutional capacity. Strong leadership and the capacity of technocrats under the Park regime were critical to the transition to state-building in South Korea. Seventh, developing countries should carefully scan their political and economic environment to make any necessary adjustments in economic and political regimes. South Korea has made positive political and economic adjustments in responding to pressures for political democracy and economic liberalization. Despite positive adjustments to a changing environment, South Korea has not yet successfully transformed from the developmental state and continues to evolve. The legacy of the developmental state still shadows the state, which is asked to deal with various problems rooted in the origin of the developmental state.

Appendix
Governance indicators by region

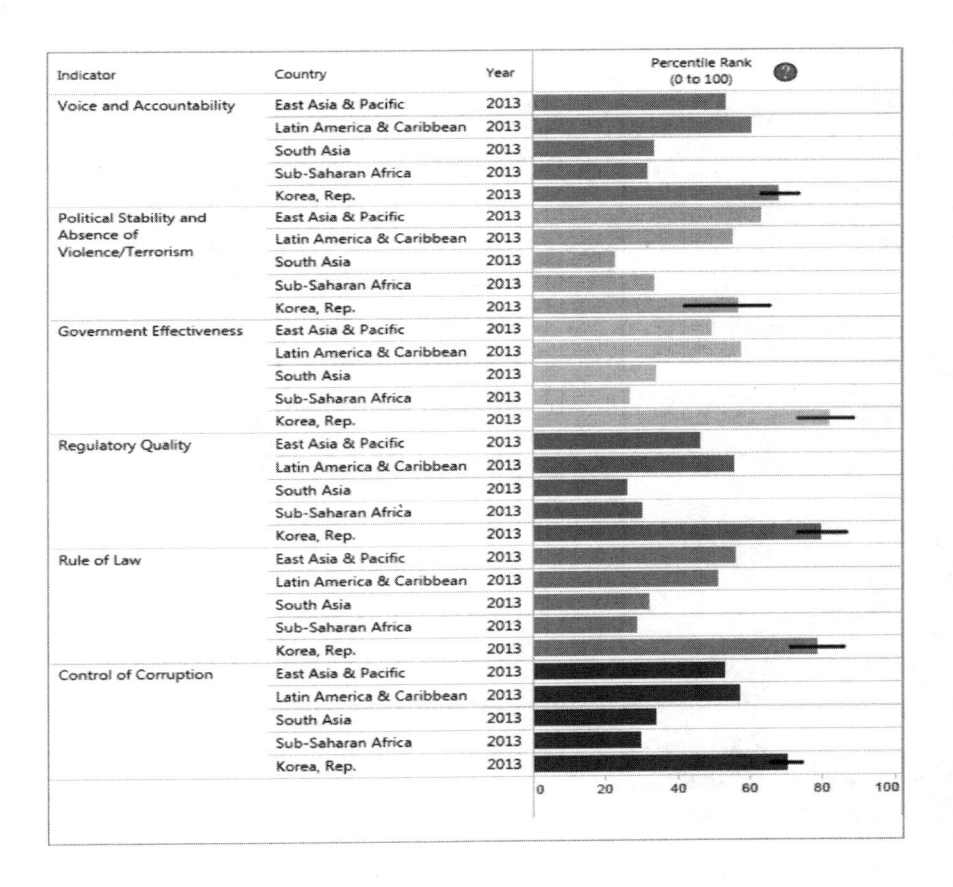

Notes

1 This chapter is written based on a paper presented at the international conference to celebrate the second anniversary of the National Museum of Korean Contemporary History that was held on December 5, 2014. A previous version of this chapter appeared in *Korea and the World* published by the National Museum of Korean Contemporary History in 2014.
2 The World Bank classification is as follows: minimal functions include defense, law and order, property rights, macro-economic management, and public health. Intermediate functions include protecting the poor, antipoverty programs, and disaster relief. Intermediate functions include education, environmental protection, utility regulation, anti-trust, financial regulation, consumer protection, redistributive pension, family allowance, unemployment insurance, etc. Activist functions are fostering market, cluster initiative, asset redistribution, etc.
3 Fukuyama (2004) understands it in the context of "the supply of institutions," which includes organizational design and management, political system design, basis of legitimacy, cultural and structural factors, etc.
4 http://joohyeon.com/169.

References

Choi, B. 1991. The structure of the economic policy-making institution in Korea and the strategic role of the Economic Planning Board (EPB). In *A Dragon's process: Development administration in Korea*. Edited by Caiden, G. and Kim, B. West Hartford, CT: Kumarian Press, Inc.

Chu, Y. 2009. Eclipse or reconfigured? South Korea's developmental state and challenges of the global knowledge economy. *Economy and Society*. 38(2). 278–303.

Economics Statistics System of the Bank of Korea. http://ecos.bok.or.kr (Accessed on November 15, 2014).

Evans, P. 1995. *Embedded autonomy: States and industrial transformation*. Princeton: Princeton University Press.

Fukuyama, F. 2004. *State building: Governance and world order in the twenty-first century*. Ithaca, NY: Cornell University Press.

Global Trade Statistics System. http://stat.kita.net/stat/kts/sum/SumImpExp TotalList.screen (Accessed on November 15, 2014).

Haggard, S. 1990. *Pathways from the periphery*. Ithaca, NY: Cornell University Press.

Kasahara, S. 2013. The Asian developmental sate and the flying geese paradigm. Discussion paper. UNCTAD, United Nations.

Kim, B. 1991. An assessment of government intervention in Korean economic development. In *A Dragon's process: Development administration in Korea*. Edited by Caiden, G. and Kim, B. West Hartford, CT: Kumarian Press, Inc.

Lee, E. and Moon, M. 2011. National agenda change and reorganization of government. *Korean Organization Studies*. 59–106.

Migdal, J.S. 2001. *State in society: Studying how states and societies transform and constitute one another*. Cambridge: Cambridge University Press.

Ministry of Security and Public Administration. https://org.mogaha.go.kr

Minns, J. 2001. Of miracles and models: The rise and decline of the developmental state in South Korea. *Third World Quarterly*. 22(6). 1025–1043.

Moon, M. and Joo, K. 2007. A comparative study on government size, scope of function, and strength of government in three administrations. *Korean Journal of Public Administration*. 45(3). 51–80. (in Korean)

Paik, W. 1991. The formation of the governing elites in Korean society. In *A Dragon's process: Development administration in Korea*. Edited by Caiden, G. and Kim, B. West Hartford, CT: Kumarian Press, Inc.

Skocpol, T. 1982. Bringing the state back in. *Items (Social Science Research)*. 36 (June 1–8).

Suh, J., and D.H.C. Chen. 2007. *Korea as a knowledge economy: Evolutionary process and lessons learned*. Washington, DC: The World Bank.

Tilly, C. 1975. Western-state making and theories of political transformation. In *The formation of national states in Western Europe*. Edited by Tilly, C. Princeton: Princeton University Press.

Whang, J. 1991. Government direction of the Korean economy. In *A Dragon's process: development administration in Korea*. Edited by Caiden, G. and Kim, B. West Hartford, CT: Kumarian Press, Inc.

Woo-Cummings, M. 1999. *The developmental state*. Ithaca, NY: Cornell University Press.

3 The role of planning and government in economic development

Jin Park

I. Historical overview

Just 50 years ago, Korea was not very different from many countries in Africa in terms of per capita GDP. It was one of the most economically and socially despondent countries in the world in 1960. In just one generation, however, Korea became a member of the Organisation for Economic Co-operation and Development (OECD) in 1996 and now has the 11th largest economy as of 2015 according to the International Monetary Fund (IMF). Samsung, Hyundai, Kia, and LG have become well-known world brands. A brief look at the social indicators yields equally impressive results: Korea's high-speed Internet is one of the fastest in the world, and life expectancy has now reached over 81. All of these certainly could not have been achieved without the help of government – the help of planning by government, to be more exact. What was the role played by the government and planning in Korea?

Phase 1: era of direct market intervention (1960s–1970s)

The First Economic Development Plan (1962–1966) was formulated with an emphasis on poverty reduction and tried to prioritize investment projects not only by the government but also by private companies. Foreign aid and loans were an integral part of resources as domestic capital mobilization was insignificant to the point of being negligible. The Korean government started with an import-substitution policy, but the investment and the growth targets set by the government were not properly fulfilled due to a lack of capital. The plan was formulated based on scanty information and statistics; hence, a lofty and unfeasible goal was set. The government had to re-adjust its targets and changed the policy to an export-orientation through devaluation of the currency. The government secured a considerable sum of foreign capital through diplomatic normalization with Japan and dispatching the military to the Vietnam War.[1] The export-oriented policy was universally applied to all firms without exception in Korea. Thus, the role of the government was not to pick the winners in the market. The main focus of the plan was concentrated on agricultural development; the expansion of energy and infrastructure; and the development

Table 3.1 Average annual growth rate of five-year plans of South Korea (1st–7th)

Economic Development Plan	Period	Target Rate	Actual Rate
1	1962–1966	7.1%	8.5%
2	1967–1971	7%	10.5%
3	1972–1976	8.6%	11%
4	1977–1981	9.2%	7.1%
5	1982–1986	7.6%	10.3%
6	1987–1991	7.5%	10%
7	1992–1996	6.9%	7.4%

Source: National Archives of Korea (2014), http://archives.go.kr/next/search/listSubjectDescription.do?id=006119&pageFlag=.

of industries such as fertilizing, oil refining, and chemicals. The average growth rate during this period was 8.5 percent, surpassing the set goal of 7.1 percent.

The Korean economy saw a surge in growth based on the sustained export-oriented policy during the Second Economic Development Plan (1967–1971). As in the Lewis model (1954), massive migration from rural areas supplied a highly motivated, low-cost labor force sufficient for the urban industrial sector. This plan was the first to be fully fleshed out, with three subcategories (gross target, target for industries, and investment priorities) and used more rigorous methods and more accurate data. The emphasis was put on industrial development such as steel, chemical, machinery including automobiles and shipbuilding. The seeds of the proactive Heavy and Chemical Industries (HCI) drive after 1973 were planted in this second plan. Even though the plan targeted self-sufficient agriculture products, grain imports increased dramatically during this period. Social issues such as population control and human resource development were also included in the plan. The average growth rate was 10.5 percent, way above the targeted 7 percent, but it was at the cost of foreign debt and trade deficit.

The Economic Planning Board (EPB) began to utilize more economic policies than resource mobilization in formulating a plan based on the growth of the private sector from the Third Economic Development Plan (1972–1976). As a result, the line ministries most pertinent to the economic development plan rose as active agents in economic planning. The Korea Development Institute (KDI), established in 1971, played an important role in providing analytical models and tools. However, the HCI drive after 1973 was more aggressive than the third plan initially projected. The Presidential Office selected the priority investment projects, which were promptly assigned to private companies to carry out with government support and protection, a stark divergence from the previous economic development plans. The government, in the end, ended up selecting the winning firms in the market. In this respect, the level of the HCI drive from 1973–1979 was much more intense and prone to distorting the market than the universal export promotion of the 1960s. Focusing on the selected HCI was a good idea, but the selection of private companies is somewhat questionable, and prioritizing investment projects in the private sector was obviously much more than just an adequate level of state intervention. Naturally, there were more disadvantages than benefits to this excessive intervention by the government.[2] However, the growth of the HCI was exceptional, as the Table 3.2 shows. Exogenous variables in this period were not all that favorable to South Korea: the first oil shock and the partial withdrawal of US troops from Korea. What put an end to these miseries wrought by the adverse environment was a surge in construction in the Middle East. Regionally balanced growth was first mentioned in this third plan, as most of the resources were concentrated around the urban areas and southeast part of Korean Peninsula during the 1960s.

The Fourth Economic Development Plan (1977–1981) was put forth by a pool of experts drawn from various fields. In order to speed up the HCI drive, the plan included issues such as structural transformation in manufacturing and a shift of comparative advantage. However, the consequences of overinvestment in HCI began to reverberate throughout the peninsula in the form of insolvent enterprises. The South Korean economy was already precarious due to serious inflationary pressures placed by the second oil shock in 1979. After the assassination of President Park in October 1979, the plan adjusted itself toward stabilization from the downright expansion of HCI. For the first time after the Korean War, Korea's annual growth rate became negative in 1980. Although it was the only five-year plan that did not meet

Table 3.2 Annual output growth by sector (unit: %)

	1953–1960	1960–1970	1970–1980	1980–1990	1990–2000	2000–2009
Agriculture, forestry & fishing	2.3	4.0	1.6	3.5	1.9	1.8
Mining			4.7	–0.2	–1.3	–0.3
Manufacturing	12.7	16.8	15.8	12.2	8.4	5.4
• Light industries			12.7	7.0	1.1	–0.6
• Heavy and chemical industries			*17.2*	*14.4*	9.8	6.6
Public utilities and construction	9.3	19.2	10.3	10.3	2.7	3.3
• Public utilities			15.8	17.6	10.3	5.8
• Construction			10.1	9.7	1.4	2.6
Services	3.8	8.6	6.8	8.4	6.1	3.6
Gross domestic product	3.8	8.4	9.0	9.7	6.5	3.9

Source: Bank of Korea (http://ecos.bok.or.kr), cited in Sakong and Koh (2010).

Table 3.3 Share of the top ten exports out of total exports from 1960s–1980s (unit: %)

Rank	1961		1970		1980	
1	Iron ore	13.0	Textile	40.8	Garments	16.0
2	Tungsten	2.6	Plywood	11.0	*Steel plate-rolled products*	5.4
3	Raw yarn	6.7	Wigs	10.8	Footwear	5.2
4	Coal	5.8	Iron ore	5.9	*Ships*	3.6
5	Cuttlefish	5.6	*Electronic goods*	3.5	*Audio equipment*	3.4
6	Live fish	4.5	Confectionery	2.3	Man-made filament fabrics	3.2
7	Graphite	4.2	Footwear	2.1	*Rubber products*	2.9
8	Plywood	3.3	Tobaccos	1.6	Woods and wood items	2.8
9	Rice	3.3	Iron products	1.5	*Video equipment*	2.6
10	Swine bristle	3.0	*Metal products*	1.5	*Semiconductors*	2.5

Source: Institute for International Trade (http://www.kita.net), cited in Sakong and Koh (2010).

Note: The italicized items are in the HCI category.

the target of 9.2 percent annual growth rate, the achieved rate of 7.1 percent was surprisingly less devastating.

From the 1960s to the 1980s, the industrial structure of Korea was dramatically transformed as can be seen in major exports. Only two items – plywood and iron ore – in the top ten export items of 1961 survived in the list of 1970, and only three items of 1970 list – plywood, electronic goods, footwear – remained in the 1980. The number of top ten products categorized as HCI was six in 1980, raising from only two in 1970.

Phase 2: era of intervention through financial markets (1980s–1997)

The Fifth Economic and Social Development Plan (1982–1986), the first development plan under the new President Chun, was geared toward stabilizing the economy against the tide of impending inflation and insolvent companies caused by years of rapid economic growth and over-investment in HCI. In order to curb the inflation, the budget of 1984 was frozen to the level of 1983, the one and only instance of doing so in Korean history. Balanced or shared growth across income classes and geographical regions highlighted as well. Other major drives were opening up the domestic market to imported goods and driving the major conglomerates to compete against one another by implementing a policy of competition. The process of opening up the market weakened the role of the state in general, but the regulation of the conglomerates reinforced the discretionary intervention of government.

Korea experienced a boom during the sixth plan (1987–1991) thanks to both the stability and restructuring process of the early 1980s and the strong Japanese yen caused by the Plaza Accord in 1985. The trade balance turned into a surplus in 1986, which lasted for four years until 1989. The Seoul Olympics in 1988 and globalization after the fall of the Soviet Union were also contributing factors in this thriving period. Meanwhile, an economic bubble was slowly taking shape. The labor movement became active and even militant, causing labor costs to surge with so much celerity as to impede industrial competitiveness after 1987, which was the first year of full-fledged democracy in Korea. Many of the social welfare systems such as the national health and national pension systems were adopted or expanded to accommodate more demand from citizens. The plan, however, lost its effectiveness due to the expansion of the private sector and the degree to which the economy was open. Nonetheless, the government managed to maintain intervention in the market through the financial sector and regulations.

The Seventh Economic and Social Development Plan (1992–1996) was the last formal development plan in Korea. Despite its claim to be a five-year plan, it was not respected much by the new president Kim Youngsam (1993–1998) who formulated his own "New" Five-Year Economic Plan (1993–1998) to match his presidential term. The new plan focused on market reforms but, in reality, put emphasis on expansionary measures since Korea was in a recession in 1993.[3] To meet the stipulated conditions for OECD membership, the Korean government opened up its capital and commodity markets and overvalued the Korean currency to maintain a high GDP per capita in USD. As a result, the trade surplus of 1986–1989 instantly became a deficit from 1990–1997.[4] The number of merchant banks,[5] whose non-performing short-term loans became the direct cause of the economic crisis in 1997, increased from 6 to 30 during this period. Despite the expansion of the global business and the financial sector,

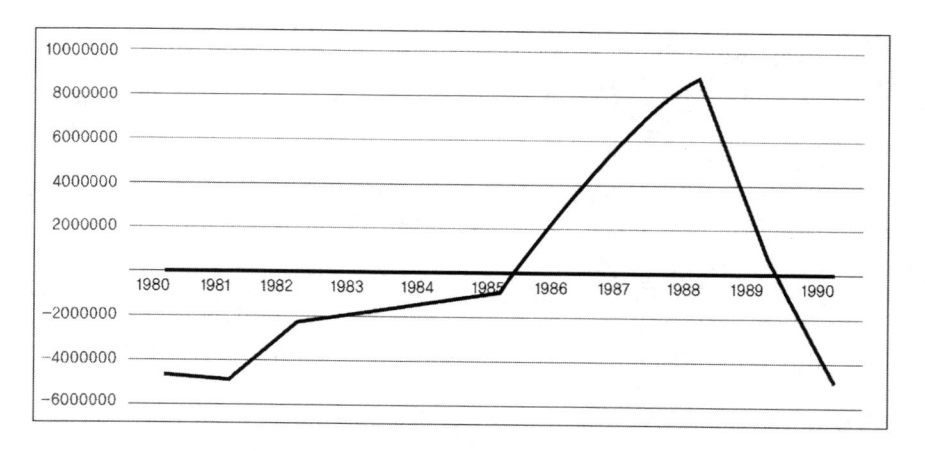

Figure 3.1 Trade balance during the 1980s

Source: Bank of Korea (2014).

the government still held fast to its grip on the market, using its influence on the banking sector. Continued government intervention eventually caused private companies to lapse into moral hazard and even led them into a false belief of "being too big to fail," which was the root cause of the financial crisis of 1997.

Phase 3: era of intervention through government spending and regulation (1998–now)

President Kim Daejung (1998–2003) conducted reforms to the following four sectors: corporate, financial, public, and labor. He tried to reduce the role of government by the active privatization of state-owned enterprises, massive deregulation, and reduction of public employees, which were by and large successful. Since the financial crisis was believed to have come mostly from failure on government's part, "more market and less public" was a widely accepted tenet in directing the reforms. Public funds amounting to 155 trillion won[6] (around USD 160 billion) were spent during 1998–2001 to rescue banks ridden with huge non-performing loans. Korea was finally able to overcome the crisis in 1999 through sound fiscal balance, the reform efforts, and strong export performance.

In a desperate attempt to ameliorate the flailing economy, however, the government was feeling perhaps a bit too philanthropic with the budget spending; venture companies were assigned excessive budgets, the repercussion of which later exhibited itself in the form of a venture bubble burst in 2000–2001. As another initiative for beefing up total demand, the government encouraged the use of credit cards, which again led to the bursting of yet another bubble, this time, credit cards in 2003. Government and the private sector learned two lessons: (1) too much market intervention by the government can create a moral hazard on the part of the private sector, and (2) too much demand promoted

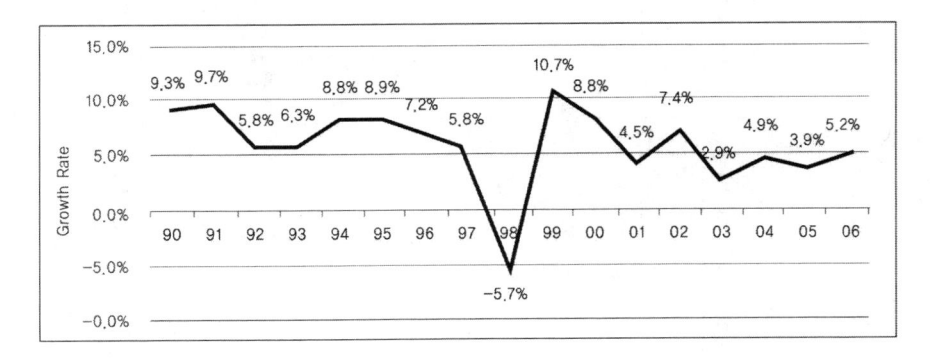

Figure 3.2 GDP growth rate before and after the 1997 crisis

Source: Korea National Statistical Office (2014), http://www.index.go.kr/potal/stts/idxMain/selectPoSttsIdxSearch.do?idx_cd=2736&clas_div=&idx_sys_cd=526&idx_clas_cd=1.

by the government can create bubbles. Government intervention in the financial market was significantly reduced, but the role of government continued to provide a presiding presence with expanded fiscal expenditures, while economic planning was replaced with the five-year, mid-term fiscal planning.

What President Roh Moohyun (2003–2008) had in mind was not reducing costs but enhancing the performance of the public sector. Consequently, spending and employment in the public sector dramatically increased. In order to reduce the burden of expenditures on the fiscal balance, the government utilized corporate bonds from State-Owned Enterprises (SOEs), thereby increasing their deficits, mostly in construction-related fields. President Lee Myungbak (2008–2013) put forward "small government," but in a misaligned attempt. He ended up decreasing only the number of ministries and government-affiliated organizations but did not in any way reduce the role of the public sector. In order to accomplish his national agenda, including the Four Rivers Project and overseas resource development, the Lee Administration let SOEs risk dangerous encounters with their huge accumulated debts, which have been larger than that of the central government since 2010. President Park Geunhye (2013–2018) faces an aging population, a slowdown in growth and employment, a widening income gap, and the challenge of increasing social welfare expenditures. The government has reacted to these problems by increasing government expenditures including a very generous subsidy to Small and Medium-sized Enterprises (SMEs).

After President Kim's reform at the end of twentieth century, there was a steady increase in the role of government in terms of expenditure and regulation

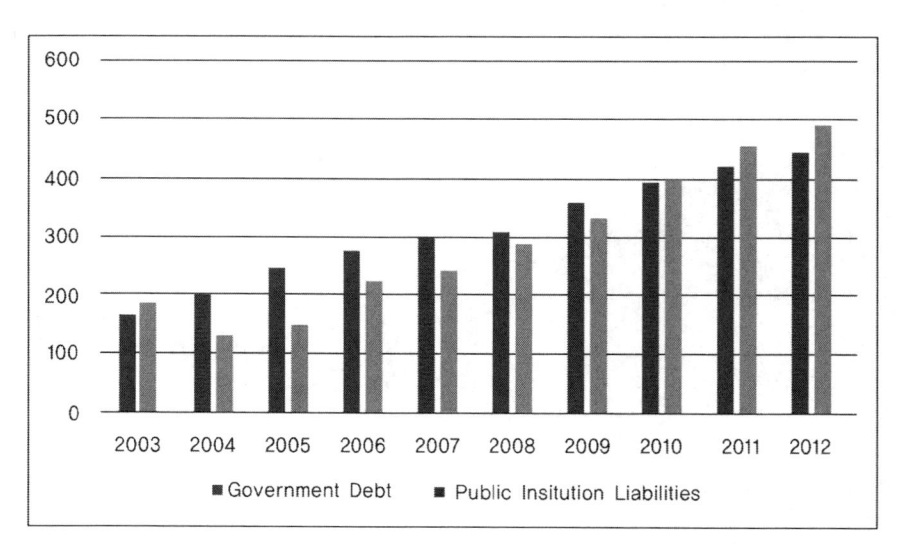

Figure 3.3 Debt trends of government and public entities

Source: Ministry of Strategy and Finance (2014), http://www.index.go.kr/potal/main/Each DtlPageDetail.do?idx_cd=1106.

Table 3.4 Major sector resource allocation and total expenditure trends (unit: trillion won)

	2007	2008	2009	2010	2011	2012	2013	2014
R&D	9.8	11.1	12.7	13.7	14.9	16.0	17.1	17.7
Industry, SMEs, energy	12.6	14.7	20.8	15.1	15.2	15.1	16.7	15.4
Social Overhead Capital (SOC)	18.4	20.5	25.5	25.1	24.4	23.1	25.0	23.7
Food, agriculture, forestry, and fisheries	15.9	16.8	17.4	17.3	17.6	18.1	18.9	18.7
Health, welfare, and labor	61.4	68.8	80.4	81.2	86.4	92.6	99.3	106.4
Education	30.7	36.1	39.2	38.3	41.2	45.5	49.9	50.7
Culture, sports, and tourism	2.9	3.3	3.6	3.9	4.2	4.6	5.1	5.4
Environment	4.0	4.5	5.7	5.4	5.8	6.0	6.5	6.5
National defense	24.5	26.6	29.0	29.6	31.4	33.0	34.5	35.7
Diplomacy, unification	2.4	2.8	3.0	3.3	3.7	3.9	4.1	4.2
Public order, security	10.9	11.7	12.4	12.9	13.7	14.5	15.2	15.8
General public administration	42.3	45.9	51.6	48.7	52.4	55.1	56.2	57.2
Total expenditures	237.1	262.8	301.8	292.8	309.1	325.4	349.0	355.8

Source: National Assembly Budget Office (2014), http://www.nabo.go.kr/Sub/Finance_2014/fn01–11.jsp#.

since 2000. Deregulation was a national agenda during this period, but without any visible accomplishment. Total government expenditures have risen rapidly in recent years following rising demand for health, welfare, and labor expenditures. However, the proportion of Social Overhead Capital (SOC) and support for industry continue to manifest themselves at a high rate despite their dubious efficacy.

It can be said that the overriding feature of Korean government, as reflected in its heavy involvement with subsidizing SMEs, does little good for the market. Korea's ratio of low interest rate loans to SMEs out of GDP is the highest among OECD countries (Kim, 2014) and is producing many so-called zombie SMEs whose operational profits are lower than their interest payments.[7] These "zombie" companies are injurious to others and do no justice to the market because they reduce the profits of other, perfectly stable, firms by below-cost tendering. Too lenient a support system is a problem not only when firms exit the market but also when they enter it. The Korean government's support for start-up businesses was 3.8 percent of the GDP in 2011, which is significantly higher than that of the other OECD countries.[8] Such government intervention replaces or distorts the outcomes of the market. It is time for Korea to forget the successful government intervention of the 1960s and 1970s and to start reducing its intervention in the market.

II.   The role of government and planning in the economic development

1.   *The role of the government during 1960s–1970s*

The government in Korea played a more active role in the market than governments of more developed countries. First, market failures present opportunities for the government to start industries through SOEs because the private sector is usually reluctant to initiate a certain business when it lacks capital. A private company would not venture to make a huge investment even when it has the necessary capital due to the years full of risk and uncertainty ahead. The state-owned steel company established in 1968 is such an example of a government attempt to penetrate the market with an SOE. Infrastructure such as harbors, highways, dams, and electricity were also supplied and/or operated by SOEs.

Another role for the government is protecting infant industries. The government may choose to protect and endorse industries predicted to have a promising future. Such measures should only be enacted for a brief period of time during which the industry is still in its nascent stage and only target those with high potential. The HCI drive and protection during 1970s is such an example.

Some offer different, contrasting views on the role of government in Korea's economic development. The neoclassical point of view by Wolf (1988) argues that the Korean government tried to promote competition as in the case of export promotion policy and thus faithfully complied with market principles. Revisionists such as Amsden (1989), however, have pointed out that many of Korea's interventions were employed with complete disregard to market principles as in the case of HCI drive. The World Bank (1991, 1993) tried to mitigate these two conflicting views by asserting that the government intervention was made in a market-conforming way – HCIs were selected based on their track records and the latent potential of the industries. Thus, it could be said that the prospective outcome of the market was not wholly decided by the government. The World Bank went further to argue that a contest is different from the market in that, in a selective intervention such as HCI promotion, it was not the market but a contest from which a winner emerges. A contest has a preliminary screening process, referees, and interaction between referees and contestants, all of which are conspicuously absent in the market.

A contest produces a similar result to the market when its referees are neutral and competent. Although the Korean government cannot be fully credited with such a description, the economic development that has been reaped so far indicates that it was reasonably neutral and competent. At least, its corruption and incompetence did not have an adverse effect on major economic decisions. What could have contributed to the neutrality and the competence of the Korean government?

2.   *Factors for a good referee*

Neutral government

One of the initial conditions of Park Administration (1961–1979) was the dissociation of political power from economic power. It had only been recently that Korea started to operate under the system of capitalism. Businesses were in their fledgling states under Japanese colonial rule. The land reform in the late 1940s was especially devastating for large landowners, but they could not immediately become capitalists precisely because the restitution they received became useless during the Korea War (1950–1953). A covert network between business and the government was formed during the Lee Administration (1948–1960), which was promptly eliminated by the student uprising of April 19, 1960, forcing President Lee to resign the presidency. Thus, the Park Administration (1961–1979) commenced without any understanding or connection between government and business. The fact that CEOs of major corporations were arrested for tax evasion just two weeks after the coup d'état of May 16, 1961, illustrates that the Korean government was not in clandestine collusion with the business.

The government officials were also relatively neutral for other reasons. The Economic Planning Board (EPB), a ministry newly established in 1961 to act as a control tower for economic planning, was able to remain impartial since it did not have any direct stakeholders in the private sector. Another factor was the ambition with which government officials vied for the post of minister, which is very common in Korea's presidential system. Civil servants had no choice but to maintain their reputation for objectivity if they had even the slightest intention of becoming political appointees in the future. Members of the EPB were often appointed as (vice) ministers of line ministries. The pension system for civil servants[9] introduced in 1960 and reinforced under President Park guaranteed post-retirement security for many civil servants, which proved useful in maintaining their neutrality.

Competent government

The competence of government is judged by its recruitment system – whether it screens for competent and intellectual talent. Korea has historically maintained an entrance examination for civil servants since the tenth century. The first modern form of the exam was introduced during the Japanese colonial era, subsequently went through a revision process in 1963, and has remained mostly unaltered since then.[10] The exam was conducted in a transparent and an extremely evenhanded fashion that did not allow for any possibility of corruption. The smartest of the top tier joined the government through this fair screening process because of a relatively inadequate number of jobs offered in the private sector. The exam was beneficial as well in its influence to society as it enabled social mobility, for it did not require any schooling or family background. It allowed, as they say, many "dragons to emerge from the creek."[11] These new civil servants, as well as those already working in the civil service, honed their skills and capacity in the Central Officials Training Institute (COTI) refurbished in 1961 from its original form in 1949.

As the hub of economic planning and policy, one of the EPB's mandates was basically to negotiate with other ministries. Since the EPB needed a sound and logical basis to gain the upper hand in haggling with other ministries, its organizational culture became open, free, and encouraging toward discussion among themselves. The frequency and openness with which they conversed among themselves gave employers a visibility through which to assess the competence of their peers. Thus, employees of the EPB, in order to secure themselves a good reputation, worked exceptionally hard, which was considered essential for their future career goal of becoming political appointees.

Government-funded think-tanks also sustained the competence of the government. Specialists were ever more in need since Korean government agencies do not carry out in-house research with their staff most often on rotation. Universities in the 1960s and 1970s were not equipped with the capacity to supply the necessary expertise. Thus, the government established the Korea Institute for Science and Technology (KIST) and the Korea Development Institute (KDI) in 1966 and 1971, respectively, as well as many other research institutes in engineering or social sciences in the 1970s. In order to attract top-notch researchers who mainly received their PhD in the United States, the government offered huge compensation for them to return home. This is why those institutes were not part of the government but private-sector entities sponsored by the government. Nonetheless, they played an important role as advisors nudging the government toward the right decisions.

3.   *The role of planning*

Priority and focus in industries

Economic planning sets priorities not only in projects but also in industries. It has long been a subject of dispute whether balanced or unbalanced growth is more effective for economic development. In a small economy, however, unbalanced growth seems inevitable. Certain investment projects should be given priority and more emphasis than others since there are different rates of return among investment projects. This is equally valid at an industry level. When the capital is limited, investments evenly distributed across too many industries will result in no economies of scale for any industry. Reorganizing the industrial structure can only be in concurrence with unbalanced growth. The industries in which developing countries now have comparative advantage are generally primary sectors such as agriculture and mining. Developing countries will not be able to join the league of advanced countries as long as they cling to the current structure of industry.[12]

Korea's selection of HCIs was a typical example of putting an emphasis on future, not current, comparative advantage. The Korean government selected six

HCIs in 1973: steel, ship-building, chemical, machinery (automobiles), electronics, and non-ferrous metals. Out of the six, the first five now make up 70 percent of Korea's exports. The government, in selecting HCIs, used a selective screening process that stimulated competition among industries and firms. In this respect, government intervention and planning did not discourage market competition much.

The following questions were asked in selecting the industries to focus on. First, will the industry be successful in the future? Initial conditions such as geo-economic characteristics, natural resources, and the level of skill and technology were taken into consideration for the answer. Second, does the industry create a sufficient linkage effect – that is will the focus industry also benefit other industries? Lastly, is it a big enough industry now, and will it continue to be so in the future? Both short-run and long-run domestic and international demand was considered as well.

Coordination

Economic planning is useful in coordinating industries with infrastructure, research, and training. Lack of such coordination impedes and even precludes economic development. When the private sector lacked of capital and information, it was the role of government to ensure that industries of national focus were equipped with a source of inputs,[13] target markets, and infrastructure. The first coordination was between industries. The selected HCIs had visible linkages amongst themselves. The steel industry uses electricity generated by refined oil and is in turn used in manufacturing ships. Therefore, the steel industry has a forward linkage effect for ship-building and a backward effect for the chemical industry such as in oil refining.

The second coordination was between industry and location. In order to maximize linkage effects, all the HCIs were located in cities such as Ulsan, Pohang, and Gumi, which are all in the southeastern part of the Korean Peninsula.[14] The government is responsible in carefully and strategically selecting these industries and their locations. However, after the 1980s, the Korean government shifted its policy to encourage balanced regional growth.

Third, coordination was made between industries and infrastructure such as electricity, the water supply, and transportation. Power plants and harbors were built around industrial complexes to support the HCI. These industrial complexes were linked to the Seoul metropolitan area with railways and highways. It was the government that supplied industry with the necessary infrastructure.

Oil and Chemical → electricity → steel, non-ferrous metal → ship-building, automobile ← electronics

Figure 3.4 Linkage effects among selected industries

* A → B ← A: Industry A offers inputs or intermediate goods to Industry B. Then Industry A has a forward linkage effect on Industry B, and Industry B has a backward linkage effect on A.

Fourth, the government also provided industry with research and training. Many government-funded research institutes[15] were established during the 1970s to support the selected HCIs. Vocational high schools were also set up to provide human resources for the HCIs.

Motivation

Economic planning also inspired motivation among Koreans. Contrary to the current stereotypical portrayal of Koreans as hardworking, Koreans tended to be less than committed and without much motivation in the first half of the century. What could have motivated Koreans? President Park (1961–1979) proclaimed that the government would only support those who helped themselves, expunging the sense of dependency and encouraging a rigorous work ethic. The Saemaul (New Village) Movement was one example. All villages in Korea were grouped into three categories, elementary, self-help, and self-reliant, according to the level of their motivation and cooperation in economic development. The higher the level a village was accorded, the bigger its government subsidy would be. The government made it clear that it would only provide support for those who improved themselves, not those who needed improvement.

Korean companies during the 1950s enjoyed easy profits through import quotas, but by this time, they were also permeated the resolution to expand themselves and yield more exports. The more exports a company recorded, the lower the interest rate was on loans provided by the government. There was no customs tax for imports of the raw material needed for manufacturing export goods, and the corporate tax was lowered for those who intended to export. The president showed his commitment by overseeing policy implementation himself, by attending the Monthly Trade and Export Promotion Meeting, for example.

Capacity building

A compulsory six-year primary education had already been in effect during the 1950s to cultivate citizens capable of fulfilling their civic duties and social roles, but it was only with a 1962 act that the law became more strictly enforced. In order to supply primary school teachers, a teachers' college was established in 1962. The center of attention shifted from secondary education to vocational high schools in the mid-1960s along with the reform of public license certification through the Occupation Training Act of 1967. Government scholarships for PhDs in advanced countries were introduced in 1977. As can be seen, economic planning placed different emphases on education depending on the developmental phase: compulsory primary education in the early 1960s, vocational high schools from the mid-1960s to 1970s, and tertiary education after the late-1970s.

The capacity of the government and its employees was very important because they had to make many important decisions in the course of economic development.[16] The Central Official's Training Institute was established in 1961, along with many government-funded think-tanks for devising more logically consistent policies.[17] Competent government was rendered possible by reforming recruitment, evaluation and compensation, training, bureaucracy, and the working environment.

The government shared the research outputs of government think-tanks with the private sector to maximize technology transfer. Many Korean companies acquired their manufacturing skill through Original Equipment Manufacturing (OEM) and Original Development or Design Manufacturing (ODM), all encouraged by government policy. In this respect, the government played a very important role in building capacity of individuals and firms, not to mention of the government itself.

III.   The role of government agencies in economic policy

1.   The different roles of the president and the EPB during 1960s–1970s

The main players in economic planning were the Presidential Office and the administration, notably the EPB from 1960s to 1970s. The National Assembly was not an active contributor to the process.

The president and the Presidential Office

President Park (1961–1979) not only gave a vision for the future but also collected necessary information, monitored the process, served as a mediator between different views, and provided the impetus for those involved by presiding over various official meetings. The Monthly Economic Trend Report Meeting for example included all the important decision makers in economic policy such as the ministers, the governor of the Bank of Korea, the presidents of government-run banks, major posts in the National Assembly, and members of the Presidential Committee for Economy and Science. Major economic trends and issues were discussed in this arena, and decisions over controversial issues were made by the president himself and shared not only among all participants but also among citizens through the news media.

Established in 1964, the Presidential Committee for Economy and Science was also chaired by the president. This advisory committee was composed of standing members, mostly former high-ranking government officials, and non-standing members, mostly from economics or science and technology in academia, and their status was deemed to be equal to that of a minister. Since the Committee had a separate secretariat and its members could maintain a certain level of neutrality, it served as a fresh voice that assisted the president with perspectives different from those of the government on many occasions. More often than not, their propositions would be readily received by the president.

The prime example of the president's strong commitment to his national agenda is the Monthly Trade and Export Promotion Meeting, which broke off from the Monthly Economic Trend Report Meeting in 1965. The previous month's exports were reported to the president every month, and the means to promote and tackle obstacles for exports were discussed, not only among major ministers but also among businessmen. The president was more than enthusiastic in assisting the private sector. He was, in a way, regarded as the CEO of all CEOs and certainly acted as one. This is a typical example of how a president can deliver a national agenda to both the administration and the business.

The Senior Economic Secretary to the president was a powerful position that served as a liaison between the ministry and the president. President Park had two Senior Economic Secretaries, one for economic policy and one for the HCI, which manifested his resolution and emphasis on economic development.[18] Since President Park ascribed more power to the EPB, senior economic secretaries were relatively inactive during the 1960s. After 1972, however, they became equally influential when the Presidential Office initiated the HCI drive, to which the EPB was rather circumspect in its approach.

The Committee for the HCI Drive established in 1973 with the prime minister as chair, was in fact controlled by the Presidential Office since the Senior Economic Secretary to the President for the HCI was the head of the Secretariat of the Committee. The HCI drive was the president's number one national agenda. With the staunch support of the president, then Senior Economic Secretary Oh remained in power for eight years (1971–1979) and led the HCI drive, ambivalent toward the policy direction of the EPB, which preferred more private-sector–driven HCI development. The president wanted to build up the HCI as fast as possible because he wanted a strong defense industry based on the HCI and because he wanted to set a new national vision after he changed the constitution in 1972, which enabled him to serve unlimited terms of six years. The conclusion of the Presidential Office was, therefore, more massive government-initiated promotion of the HCI, but this caused many side effects such as over-investment, inflation, early deterioration of light industries, and a network of collusion between government and business.

The Economic Planning Bureau (EPB) and line ministries

The EPB was established in 1961 with four main bureaus for economic planning, national budget formulation, foreign aid and capital, and economic and social statistics. The Minister of the EPB was accorded with the prestige and power of a deputy prime minister, enabling him to preside over the line ministries. The Planning Bureau of the EPB had an overarching and powerful influence over all public agencies. Thus, it was not only an intermediary coordinator but also a reformer of all other line ministries.

There are certain conditions that must be met for an organization to effect reform. First, it should be strongly empowered by the president. Second, the organization should focus on working with other agencies. Reform would be relegated to secondary importance as reform does not have urgency in most cases if it has any other preordained assignments. Third, it should have an open

Economic Vice-Ministers Meeting → Informal Economic Ministers Meeting

→ Official Economic Ministers Meeting → Meeting Chaired by the President (Cabinet Meeting, and others)

Figure 3.5 Economic policy decision-making process

and competitive culture that motivates its members to venture into reform initiatives, which inevitably entails resistance and therefore adversity. The EPB met all three criteria.

The process of planning had five stages: (1) The EPB identified the major directions of the plan and formulated detailed guidelines for each line ministry. This initial stage was of course conducted in close consultation with the Presidential Office. (2) Each line ministry formulated its draft plan for its respective sector, which was reviewed or, in many cases, rejected by the EPB, which demanded that certain corrections or additions be made. This process often spurred heated debates and sometimes negotiations between a line ministry and the EPB. However, during the first and second economic plans, the proposal was drafted predominantly by the EPB with marginal help from line ministries. (3) The plan was forwarded to the Presidential Committee for Economy and Science and then was finalized at the cabinet meeting. (4) Each ministry set a detailed plan of action to meet the target and deadline and regularly submitted progress reports to the EPB. (5) The EPB monitored and evaluated progress, which was subsequently briefed to the president through the Monthly Economic Report Meeting.

Although planning and economic policy was driven mostly by the EPB, there had to be a consensus among ministries as well. The Economic Ministers Meeting was an instance where a consensus-building process often transpired. This meeting was chaired by the Minister of the EPB with the participation of major ministers particularly pertinent to economic issues such as the Ministry of Finance, Ministry of Commerce and Industry, Ministry of Agriculture, Ministry of Construction, Ministry of Transportation, and so on. All economy-related agendas had to be approved in the meeting before they were forwarded to the cabinet meeting. Informal economic ministers meetings would often be held prior to the official one in order to form a consensus among key ministries in a casual manner. As a preliminary step before the Economic Ministers Meeting, an Economic Vice-Ministers Meeting was conducted by the EPB's vice-minister. Together, these meetings worked toward building a consensus; the EPB worked as a secretariat and consequently as a gate-keeper that checked all economic agendas before they were submitted to meetings.

2. *Evolution of the EPB and the Ministry of Finance (MOF)*

The EPB has been in a constant rivalry with the MOF since its establishment in 1961 when the budget office was relayed to the EPB from the MOF. The conflict between the planning ministry and the MOF is commonly observed in many other countries. There are four major roles of an economics ministry: planning, budgeting, tax and financial policy, and economic policy coordination. Among the four, in many countries including Korea, the planning and budgeting functions are jointly assigned to one agency. However, controversy arose in deciding where the role of economic policy coordination should be entrusted, either to planning and budgeting, or to tax and financial policy? South Korea came up with different organizational arrangements, depending on the economic environment of the time.

Rivalry between the EPB and the MOF from 1961–1994

The budgetary function was wrenched away from the MOF and subsumed under the EPB on its establishment with the rationale that planning should be in alignment with budgeting. The EPB was able to work as a superior policy coordinator precisely because its minister held a bureaucratic position equivalent to that of deputy prime minister above the line ministries and also because it was strongly endorsed by the president. The EPB also had the power to allocate resources through budget expenditures and mobilization of foreign capital. As the secretariat of many formal processes such as the Economic Ministers Meeting, the EPB was able to influence economic broad issues. Since the EPB was a central agency unencumbered by any stakeholders in the private sector, it was able to allow its members to remain neutral.

The MOF was in charge of treasury functions, taxation, the stock market, and domestic and international financial policies on banking and insurance.[19] Since the MOF was not able to control companies through banks and tax offices, it had a more direct influence on the private sector than the EPB, which had only a diluted and indirect influence on firms through government expenditures. As a result of this difference, the MOF had more stakeholders in the private sector and tended to be more conservative and reserved in economic reform.

The EPB's two major pillars, planning and budgeting, were not necessarily in harmony at all times. Wherever the annual budget sought to realize the five-year plan, there was a possibility that the Budget Office might reject the plan formulated by the Planning Bureau. During the 1960s–1970s, however, such discrepancies did not occur for two reasons: the president's clear emphasis on the importance of the plan over the annual budget and government revenue exceeding the predictions in the plan thanks to economic growth turning out higher than initially expected. The conflict between the plan and the budget did not manifest itself until the 1970s, but it became visible when economic growth slowed down in the early 1980s.

The Planning Bureau's relative attenuation to the MOF was caused in 1980s by the change in government intervention from direct to indirect measures through state-run or commercial banks. The MOF had much more diverse macroeconomic policy tools such as taxes and interest rates. Policy coordination among line ministries became increasingly difficult as they gained more autonomy after the democratization of 1987. The role of economic planning declined as a trend after the 1980s.

The era of experiments (from 1994 on)

President Kim Youngsam (1993–1998) merged the EPB with the MOF in 1994 to form the Board of Finance and Economy (BOFE) to streamline economic policy coordination. Internal communications within the BOFE were in disarray because of its colossal size as a ministry created out of two large and extremely disparate organizations. The Minister of BOFE was burdened with so much responsibility that some responsibilities were left unattended, which is one of the main reasons why the government could not properly sense the upcoming economic crisis in 1997.

Right after the crisis, the BOFE was bifurcated into the Ministry of Planning and Budget (MPB) and the Ministry of Finance and Economy (MOFE). The MPB was a return to the EPB without the economic coordination and international cooperation functions. Although the MPB was only given the planning and budgeting functions, it had a new role of public-sector reform. This fragmentation was generally accepted as a rebuke to the BOFE, which had failed to detect the crisis in advance, let alone preempt it.

The resurfacing of the rivalry between the MPB and the MOFE lasted only a decade before the Lee Administration (2008–2013) merged the two again to form the Ministry of Strategy and Finance (MOSF). All the problems of the BOFE continue to plague the MOSF with an added problem: the lack of a neutral mediator. The MOSF could not maintain the impartiality on which

Table 3.5 The changing roles of the planning ministries

	EPB (1961–1994)	BOFE (1994–1998)	MPB (1998–2008)	MOSF (2008–)
(Fiscal) Planning	Yes	Yes	Yes	Yes
Public-sector reform	Partially	Partially	Yes	Partially
Budgeting	Yes	Yes	Yes	Yes
Policy coordination	Yes	Yes	MOFE	Yes
Treasury	MOF	Yes	MOFE	Yes
Tax	MOF	Yes	MOFE	Yes
International cooperation	MOF	Yes	MOFE	Yes
International finance	MOF	Yes	MOFE	Yes
Finance and supervision	MOF	Yes	MOFE FSC (supervision)	FSC
Evaluation of ministries	Yes	PM	PM	PM
Competition policy	Yes	FTC	FTC	FTC

FSC: Financial Service Commission, PM: Prime Minister's Office, FTC: Fair Trade Commission the EPB and the MPB had prided themselves, for the MOSF is only an economic ministry, not a ministry in charge of all areas. The minister of the MOSF tends to focus on revitalizing the economy, an urgent issue of now, paying less attention on fiscal balance, which is an issue of the distant future. The primary strategic goal of the Budget Office in the MOSF around 2010 was not "fiscal balance" but "revitalization of the economy," which is a clear example of the Budget Office being under the influence of short-term economic policy goals.

Another problem with the emergence of the MOSF is that the Korean government lost its neutral reformer of the public sector, the MPB. Since the MOSF has many policy tools for market intervention, it will not take any reform measures to diminish its power over the market. There is a Korean saying, "A Buddhist monk cannot have his hair cut by his own hands," meaning that you cannot easily solve your own problems. The role of the government is the hair of the MOSF. In this respect, integration and separation of the two ministries after 1994 have been experiments on the way to Korea finding the best model of organizational division.

VI. Lessons learned

The role played by the Korean government in economic development went through a series of changes in range and direction over time. Whereas the 1960s were characterized by the overall promotion of industries and exports, direct intervention in the market reached its peak in the HCI drive of 1970s. Although direct measures were replaced by indirect intervention via banks, the government's active role in the economy persisted through the 1980s and 1990s, which was one of the root causes of the economic crisis in 1997. The government's grip on the market was loosened temporarily by market-oriented reform under the leadership of President Kim Daejung (1998–2003), but the government wasted no time in reinstating its power and continues to exhibit itself even to this day.

The roles played by economic planning during the 1960s and 1970s were focusing, coordination, motivation, and capacity-building. Government intervention replacing the market could potentially be detrimental to the national economy if wrong choices are made.[20] Since the Korean government has been reasonably competent and relatively less tainted by corruption, its intervention was a positive factor in economic development.

In general, the role of government is crucial in earlier stages of economic development, but less so in the mature stages of the economy. Therefore, the government should attempt to reduce market intervention as the economy grows. When the economy is in an early stage of development, factor inputs such as labor and capital determine most of a country's income growth. As per capita income grows, however, total factor productivity (TFP) becomes a much more important source of growth. The government is a good mobilizer of resources but not a good innovator, and this is why government should refrain from further interfering with the market in the developed stage of the

Table 3.6 Potential growth rate and contributions (unit: %)

Period	GDP (%)	Capital Stock	Labor Inputs	TFP
1971–1980	8.6	4.9	2.3	1.7
1981–1990	9.3	3.6	1.8	5.4
1991–2000	6.3	3.1	1.0	2.1
2001–2010	4.3	1.6	0.8	2.5
2011–2020	3.5	1.4	0.6	2.3
2021–2030	3.1	1.3	0.0	1.6

Source: Kim (2014).

economy. In order to enhance the potential growth rate of Korea, we need to reduce regulations and subsidies, which weaken market competition.

However, withdrawal from the market is exceedingly difficult for a government that has enjoyed decades of steering the market toward wherever it wished. Since such intervention was successful during the early development period of Korea, the government thinks that it will be still successful now. It takes a great reform effort to reduce government intervention, and only a strong and neutral reformer without any intention of market intervention can make this reform happen.

Notes

1 Korea contributed troops to the Vietnam War from 1965 to 1973.
2 These included over-investment and subsequent restructuring, inflation, and collusion between government and business. Light industry did not become a high value-add industry since it had been relatively neglected after 1973.
3 However, the government should have restructured and reformed the supply side rather than boosted the demand side as the recession was driven by oversupply and the loss of industrial competitiveness, not by the lack of demand.
4 The year 1993 was the only exception, recording a USD 800 million surplus.
5 Conglomerates owned these banks, many of which used to be in the informal sector until the 1980s.
6 Compare this number with the national budget and GDP of 2000, which were 291.8 trillion won and 635.2 trillion won, respectively.
7 The ratio of zombie companies in terms of asset value reached 15.6 percent as of 2013 compared to 13 percent in 2010 (Jeong, 2014).
8 United States (0.1 percent), Canada (0.8 percent), France (0.5 percent), Chile (1.0 percent) according to NABO (2014).
9 Although the general pension system was introduced in 1986, three occupation-based pension systems for civil servants (1960), the military (1960), and teachers (1975) were introduced earlier. Due to the generous payment scheme relative to contributions, they have been subsidized by the general account, which resulted in huge accumulated debt. The Korean government is trying to reform these pension systems.
10 Before 1963, it was a qualifying exam, but it became an appointment exam. In a qualifying exam, those who passed the cut-off points were given only a

qualification to become a civil servant. But in an appointment exam, the government selects a necessary number of applicants and appoints them.

11 This is a South Korean expression, meaning a person becoming successful despite their humble background.

12 Only a country with a small population and fertile land can enjoy high income specifically within the agricultural sector as is seen in New Zealand with a population of 4.5 million.

13 This includes human resources, technology, and intermediate goods.

14 As an industrial site, the southeast coastal region had advantages in that the sea is deeper with less tidal effects than the southwest side of the peninsula. Major trading partners, Japan and the United States, were also closer to the east coast. However, this geographical concentration touched off political backlash from the other regions especially from the southwest part of Korea.

15 Research institutes for chemicals, electronics, telecommunication, and machinery, for instance.

16 Economic development is measured by labor, capital, and productivity, which are determined by fundamental factors such as market efficiency, property rights, transparency, social capital, and openness, which are all influenced by the government.

17 The Korea Development Institute (KDI) was established in 1971 to support economic planning by the Economic Planning Board.

18 He even had a third Senior Economic Secretary from 1969–1970 and 1972–1974.

19 The MOF heavily intervened even in monetary policy during the 1960s–1990s without much respect for the independence of the Bank of Korea. After 2000, the central bank's autonomy has been significantly enhanced.

20 One example of a wrong choice is Indonesia's aircraft industry whose chairman, a long-time Minister for Science and Technology, became president of Indonesia (Chang, 2010).

References and Further Readings

Amsden, Alice H. *Asia's Next Giant: South Korea and Late Industrialization*. New York: Oxford University Press, 1989.

Bank of Korea, *Current Account and Trade Balance*, Accessed Nov 14th, 2014, http://www.index.go.kr/potal/main/EachDtlPageDetail.do?idx_cd=2735#quick_02 (In Korean)

———, *Gross Domestic Product*, Accessed Nov 13th, 2014, http://www.index.go.kr/potal/stts/idxMain/selectPoSttsIdxSearch.do?idx_cd=2736&clas_div=&idx_sys_cd=526&idx_clas_cd=1 (In Korean)

Chang, Ha-Joon. *23 Things They Don't Tell You about Capitalism*. New York: Bloomsbury Press, 2012.

Choi, Kwang, and Chung, Chin-Seung. *Economic Development and Economic Policy in Korea*. Seoul: Korea Development Institute, 2006.

Eichengreen, Barry J., Perkins, Dwight H., and Kwanho, Shin. *From Miracle to Maturity: The Growth of the Korean Economy*. Cambridge, MA: Harvard University Asia Center, and Distributed by Harvard University Press, 2012. (In Korean)

Hyun, Oh-Seok. Role of Government in Economic Development. In *Economic Development and Economic Policy in Korea*. Seoul: KDI School, 2006.

Jeong, Daehee. *Negative Effects of Delay in Restructuring Zombie Companies*. Seoul: Korea Development Institute, 2014. (In Korean)

Kim, Chung-yum. *From Despair to Hope: Economic Policymaking in Korea*. Seoul: Korea Development Institute, 2011.

Kim, Sung-Tae. Ch.2 Evaluation on the Fiscal Sustainability. In *Assessment and Policy Recommendation for Fiscal Soundness.* KDI, 2014. (in Korean)

Korea Industrial Complex Corp, *Status of Industrial Clusters,* Accessed Nov 9th 2014, http://www.e-cluster.net/en/index.jsp (In Korean)

Lewis, W. Arthur. Economic Development with Unlimited Supplies of Labor. *The Manchester School* 22: 139–91, 1954.

Ministry of Strategy and Finance, *Asset Sizes of State-Owned Enterprise and Quasi-Government Agencies,* Accessed Nov 12th 2014, http://www.index.go.kr/potal/main/EachDtlPageDetail.do?idx_cd=1100#quick_02 (In Korean)

Ministry of Strategy and Finance, *Government Debt,* Accessed Nov 12th, http://www.index.go.kr/potal/main/EachDtlPageDetail.do?idx_cd=1106 (In Korean)

National Archives of Korea, *A 5-year Economic Development Plan,* Accessed Nov 13th, 2014 http://archives.go.kr/next/search/listSubjectDescription.do?id=006080&pageFlag (In Korean)

National Assembly Budget Office (NABO), *Allocation of Finance by Field,* Accessed Nov 11th, 2014, http://www.nabo.go.kr/Sub/Finance_2014/fn01–11.jsp# (In Korean)

National Assembly Budget Office, *Major Issues and Problems in the Government Policy Supporting Venture/Start-up Business,* 2014. (In Korean)

Oh, Won-chul. *Korean Economic Construction Model Vo. 7.* Seoul: CEOI, 1999. (In Korean)

Sakong, Il, and Koh, Youngsun. *The Korean Economy: Six Decades of Growth and Development.* Seoul: Korea Development Institute, 2010.

Wolf, Charles. *Markets or Governments: Choosing between Imperfect Alternatives.* New York, NY: Oxford University Press. 1988

World Bank. *World Development Report: The Challenge of the Development.* New York: Oxford University Press. 1991

———. *The East Asian Miracle.* New York: Oxford University Press. 1993

4 Korean government organization

The developmental state and its transformation

Keunsei Kim and Hyunshin Park

I. Introduction

The paradigm of governance in democratic capitalist societies since the late 1970s has been changed to rolling back the state. The old paradigm – the Keynesian welfare state, nationalization of public enterprises, the classical style of business regulation, progressive income tax structures, and traditional public management styles – became extinct in advanced countries during the 1980–1990s (Hood, 1994: 1–2). The new paradigm was characterized by deregulation, privatization, monetarism, supply-side economics, flatter taxes, and new public management. The conservative experiments were guided by three principles, the "virtuous three Es": economy, efficiency, and effectiveness (Thomson, 1992; Pollitt, 1993: 59). One of their key agenda items was to attack the public service.

Under this context, the reform of government bureaucracy has been one of the common goals of contemporary governments. The Thatcher government in Britain in 1979–1989, the Fraser government in Australia in 1975–1983, and the Reagan government in the United States 1981–1989 tried to cut government bureaucracy in terms of spending, staffing, and organizational configuration. Through policy diffusion in international society, some other countries followed the trend. Asian countries have also been influenced by this megatrend. Public-sector reform in Japan has been an important issue since the 1980s. President Roh Taewoo in South Korea began to attempt cutback administrative reforms in 1988–1993. Subsequent presidents have repeatedly taken this trajectory.

The Korean state was cited as an exemplar of state-directed economic growth in the 1970s. Korean society has undergone both political and social democratization since the downfall of the authoritarian regime around 1987. Political democracy ensures successive ruling party changes: conservative from 1987–1997, liberal from 1998–2007, and again conservative after 2008. Every corner of society has also encountered the decline of the traditional hierarchal system. In particular, the Korean government has driven several administrative reforms under the slogan of "small government." The Kim Daejung Administration introduced a series of reforms based on market governance after the monetary crisis and International Monetary Fund (IMF) regulations in 1997. One of the key aims of the reforms was to transform the developmental state with more democratic and market governance (Peters, 1996). The ideas of New Public Management and New Governance have been familiar buzzwords of administrative reform in the Korean government in recent decades.

However, there have been many examples of the limitations of more participatory and market governance. Historically strong central agencies of the developmental state have once again become the pilot agencies of small government reform and distorted the state for their interests.

This issue is not confined to the case of the Korean developmental state. It is a key debate among statists after the New Right reforms of 1980–2000 (Levy, 2006). Has the state been reduced along the lines of neoliberalism or just reconfigured with the new global environment? The debate might apply to the case of the developmental state. Has the Korean developmental state transformed fundamentally or just been reconfigured? This chapter tries to examine this issue from the perspective of state administrative structure.

The prototype of the Korean developmental state was firmly established by the Park Chunghee government in the 1970s. Beginning in 1980, successive administrations have tried to change the developmental state system in one way or another through a series of administrative reforms. This chapter collects administrative structural data of the Korean central government from 1980–2007. The span of data collection covers the period from 1980 to 2007: President Chun Doohwan (1980–1988), Roh Taewoo (1988–1993), Kim Youngsam (1993–1998), Kim Daejung (1998–2003), and Roh Moohyun (2003–2008).

The data about organization, staff, and budget comes mostly from government publications and internal documents published by the Korean government. The budget is usually considered a major measurement of state size and function by the statists (Castles, 2007). Staff is a basic resource of government and an indicator of the changing nature of government activities because it provides and produces the major goods and services of government as the principal agent of central social and economic processes (Peters, 1980). Organizations (bureaus and divisions) are basic building blocks of state apparatus and a good indicator of the changing nature of government activities (Peters, 1988).

This chapter uses three typological studies of state apparatus and government agencies. First, each central ministry is classified into Clark and Dear's (1984) categories of state function and apparatus by main job contents. Second, the budget of the ministries is analyzed according to the budget types of Dunleavy (1991). The ratio of the core budget indicates the degree of the direct production of public services, and the ratio of bureaus and program budgets indicates the degree of the indirect provision of public services. Finally, there are three types of government agencies from the political institution perspective: presidential agency, congressional agency, and central agency. Wilson (1986: 376) identified two broad types of government agencies: presidential agencies and congressional agencies.[1] Wilson notes that there are many agencies that have neither a presidential nor a congressional orientation and that can act somewhat independently of either institution. This study adds the central management agency to represent this third type.

II.   Developmental state and administrative structure

1.   *State administrative structure*

State administrative structure refers here to the mechanism transforming administrative inputs into outputs (see Figure 4.1). The input side of the structure consists of administrative resources for producing public policy and public services, which means organization, personnel, and funds. The throughput side of the structure means how to make public services, i.e. whether government provides the services in direct or indirect ways. The output side is what state functions public administration produces.

Figure 4.1 classifies state functions and their apparatus using Clark and Dear's (1984) typology. They present a more systematic framework for the analysis of the state apparatus; their form–function–apparatus logic[2] imposes a fairly rigid framework for analysis. Here, the state apparatus refers to the set of institutions and organizations through which state power is exercised. The goal of the capitalist state is the protection, maintenance, and reproduction of capitalist social formation.

The first function, the consensus state apparatus, consists of the agencies that ensure that all social groups have access to the process of the social contract as well as simultaneously defining the conduct of proceedings. This function includes the sub-functions of politics, law, and repression. Second, the production state apparatus includes the agencies that secure the conditions of capitalist accumulation by regulating social investment and social consumption. This function includes public production, public provision, and the treasury. Third, the integration state apparatus is made up of the agencies that promote the physical and social well-being of all groups in society, as well as their ability and willingness to participate in the social contract. Health, education, welfare, information, communication, and media belong to this as sub-functions. Fourth, the executive state apparatus includes the agencies that ensure the operation and overall compatibility of the various state sub-apparatuses and monitors the reproduction of the state apparatus itself. Administrative and regulatory agencies belong to this category.

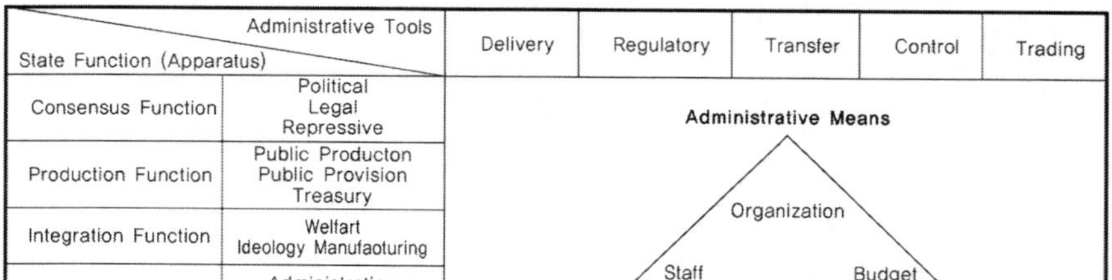

State Function (Apparatus) \ Administrative Tools		Delivery	Regulatory	Transfer	Control	Trading
Consensus Function	Political Legal Repressive					
Production Function	Public Producton Public Provision Treasury					
Integration Function	Welfart Ideology Manufacturing					
Execution Function	Administration Regulation					

Figure 4.1 The framework for state administrative structure

Source: Kim (2005: 125).

In developing an analytical framework of government agency, Dunleavy (1991) presents five basic agency types.[3] These are delivery, regulatory, transfer, contract, and control agencies.

First, delivery agencies are the classic line bureaucracies that directly produce outputs or deliver services to citizens or enterprises, using their own personnel to carry out most policy implementation. This function is usually labor-intensive, so it tends to have a large core budget in relation to the function.

Second, regulatory agencies limit or control the behavior of individuals and enterprises or other bodies, using licensing systems, reporting controls, performance standards, or similar systems. Since they primarily inspect and move paper, their core budget absorbs a high proportion of their bureau or program budget. Regulatory agencies appear cheap in budgetary terms because they externalize many of their costs onto the regulated.

Third, transfer agencies handle the payment of subsidies and entitlements from the government to private individuals or firms. They are mainly money-moving organizations, so their core budget absorbs only a fraction of the bureau budget. The bureau budget usually absorbs most of a transfer agency's program budget.

Fourth, contract agencies are concerned with developing service specifications or capital projects for tendering, and then they contract with private-sector firms or not-for-profit organizations. Contract agencies' core budgets typically absorb only a modest share of their bureau budgets, although more than would be the case for transfer agencies. Bureau budgets of course make up almost all of a contract agency's program budget.

Fifth, control agencies channel funding to other public-sector bureaus in the form of grants or intergovernmental transfers and supervise how these other local organizations spend money and implement policy. The core budgets of control agencies typically comprise only a fraction of sums transferred, and the bureau budget is also a small part of the program budget.

In addition to these basic agencies, Dunleavy adds three additional agencies to create an exhaustive typology for analysis: taxing agencies, trading agencies, and servicing agencies. They are ignored here because these additional agency types are not completely distinct from the basic five types.

2. Structure and change of the developmental state

The concept of the developmental state was developed by Johnson's (1982) case study of Japan. To explain the success of Japanese economic growth, he pointed out the planned rationality that is the basic idea of the developmental state, an alternative way of government intervention in contrast with both the US's market rationality and the USSR's ideological planning (Johnson, 1982: 18–26).

The Korean state was cited as an exemplar of state-directed economic growth. The Korean case definitely belongs to the category of the developmental state coined by Chalmers Johnson (1982). There were many studies explaining Korea's rapid economic growth from the perspective of the developmental state, although these discussions declined during the democratization of the 1980s and the economic crisis of 1997–1998. The background of this trend reflects the position that neither the authoritarian nature of the Korean developmental state nor the cozy government–industry complex were suitable for the globalization era and were fundamental reasons for the 1997 economic crisis (Cotton, 2000; Park, 2000).

In contrast, the reason for the crisis cannot be found in the developmental state itself but in the weakness of state capacity as a precondition of the developmental state (Weiss, 1998; Yang, 2005; Kuk, 2008). This position pointed out that the direct reason could be traced from the fast and poorly-prepared deregulation and liberalization policies under the Kim Youngsam Administration. It maintains the state bureaucracy still needs to play an important role even in a globalization environment. Rapid economy recovery and the IT policy of the Kim Daejung Administration, strong pursuit of a Free Trade Agreement under the Roh Moohyun Administration, and "green" growth under the Lee Myungbak Administration are examples (Kim, 2008).

In this context, there is some discussion whether the developmental state was dismantled or transformed into another form. Weiss (2000) maintains that the Korean developmental state changed into neoliberalism by nature under government-initiated economic liberalization in the 1980s. The abolition of the Economic Planning Board, which was the main agency guiding economic development, symbolized the dismantling Korean developmental state. Minns (2001) also notes that the decline of the Korean developmental state started in the 1980s, mainly due to the growth of social classes that could challenge the state's relative autonomy.

However, some studies point out the complicated development of the Korean state, and there is no conclusive alternative to the developmental state (Jo, Jung, and Lee, 2006). Lee, Lim, and Chung (2002) examined the government–big business and government–IT–venture relations and found that, since the economic liberalization and stabilization policies of the 1980s, the Korean state has changed from the developmental state into a regulatory state, especially around the 1997 monetary crisis, but still maintains the nature of a developmental state. Lim (2006) studied policies on the IT industry and noted that government still intervenes in business in a vertically coordinated mode of governance, which is a legacy of the developmental state. In a similar vein, Yang (2005) and Kim (2008) maintained that the authoritarian developmental state of the past has not ended but that the present state is an accumulation of the nature of the regulatory state and the neoliberal state built on the base of the developmental state.

Previous research on the Korean developmental state can be classified into two groups. The first focuses on the historical origin and change of the Korean developmental state (Kim, 2000; Yang, 2005).[4] Second, many previous studies have focused on the nature and change of the Korean developmental state in terms of industrial policy (Sonn, 1998; Park, 2000; Kim, 2008).

The developmental state posits that state autonomy and state capacity guides the market economy (Skocpol, 1985: 9–16).[5] The relative autonomy of the state means that the state is relatively independent from the demands of specific interests and pursues putative national interests ahead of social class interests

(Leftwich, 1995: 408). However, this this does not mean isolation but for strong central coordination and implementation of national goals in a close relationship with diverse stakeholders (Onis, 1991: 123–124). Therefore, there is intimacy or partnership in government–industry relations (Johnson, 1982; Evans, 1995),

There are two necessary conditions regarding state capacity: cohesiveness of the bureaucracy and administrative means (Chibber, 2002). Internally, cohesiveness of the bureaucracy enhances administrative efficiency. At the micro-level, school ties and the bureaucratic culture of state bureaucrats are cited as the main factors for cohesiveness (Johnson, 1982). At the meso-level, the state needs a strong pilot agency or "nodal agency" to coordinate and lead diverse government agencies in order to achieve an effective development strategy (Chibber, 2002). Externally, administrative means provide the material foundation for the state's capacity to control elements of the external environment.[6] For example the state controls key resources such as the money supply. The state had public ownership of the banks and used the central bank to guide business toward national industrial policy goals (Chang, 2004).

The literature on the developmental state identifies several key characteristics of its government organization and structure.[7] First, the developmental state heavily depends on executive-centered public administration rather than legislative-centered public administration. The Japanese political system was heavily dominated by the bureaucracy, and the Diet was a sort of rubber-stamp "puppet-Diet" (Johnson, 1982: 50). The Japanese legislature did not work as in Western countries. The pattern of policy making is that Cabinet bills originated and were drafted exclusively within ministries then were passed to the Liberal Democratic Party (LDP) for approval and introduction into the Diet.

This nature of executive-centered public administration is contrary to legislative-centered public administration (Rosenbloom, 2000). The state considers the political process of the legislature as wasteful from the perspective of administrative efficiency for achieving the national goals of economic development. The ideal of rational planning managed by a technocratic bureaucracy has prevailed in the Korean developmental state.

Second, economic growth was planned and implemented by a pilot agency, such as the Economic Planning Agency (EPA) and Ministry of International Trade and Industry (MITI) in Japan. The developmental state has stronger central management agencies than line ministries.

Third, the priority of the developmental state lies in economic development in that it strongly emphasizes economic functions and strongly ignores the social functions of the capitalist state. The state gave top priority to economic development for more than 50 years with the Japanese consensus for a high-growth system (Johnson, 1982: 305–307). This priority on economic development says that the production function will be the top priority of the developmental state. This chapter will look at the relative proportion and change of production functions from 1980–2007.

Fourth, the developmental state intervenes in the economy's growth through a policy mix that includes fiscal, monetary, and industrial policies. In particular, the state guides the business sector in direct ways, such as by establishing public enterprises to support and guarantee export companies. The state created government-owned banks such as the Japan Development Bank to guide industrial policy via the power to make or to refuse "policy" loans to the business sector (Johnson, 1982: 200).

In general, the Korean case is very similar to the Japanese developmental state. One difference is that economic development during the 1970s and early 1980s was guided by authoritarian regimes. This reinforces the state-centered direction of economic planning and development.

III. Historical review of the Korean developmental state organization

1. *Executive-centered public administration*

The Korean governing system has been characterized as a sort of "imperial" presidency. It implies that the president wields overwhelming power over the legislature and the courts. This system still persists.

However, it is also true that there have been some changes that have increased the power and function of the legislature and the courts. There is a trend toward legislative-centered public administration. The number of legislative bills proposed by the National Assembly has increased dramatically since 2000. The National Assembly's supporting agencies were also recently set up with the creation of the National Assembly Budget Office (NABO) in 2003 and the National Assembly Research Service (NARS) in 2007.

Figure 4.2 shows the substantial increase in Korean National Assembly support staff. Around the period of the restoration of political democracy in

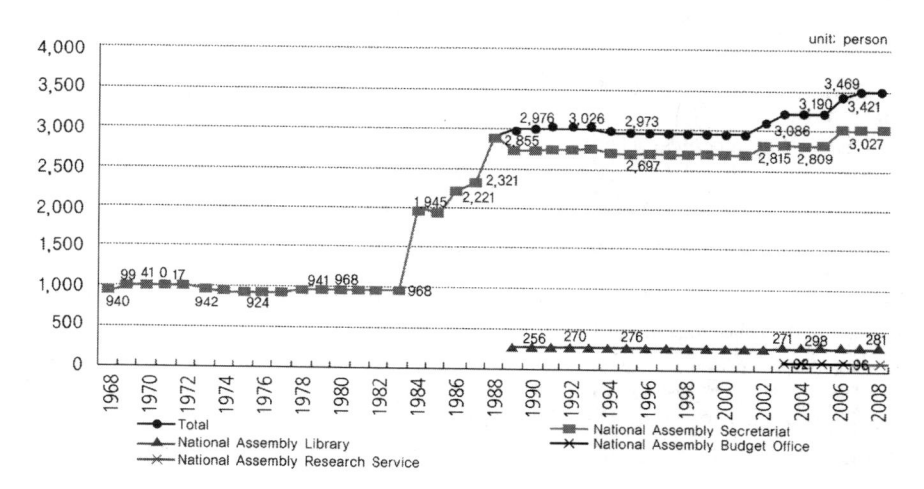

Figure 4.2 Legislative support organization staff

Source: Korea Law Service Center (Ministry of Government Legislation).

the 1980s (1984–1988), the total number of staff (staff members of standing committees, personal aides of the legislator, and the staff of the legislative supporting agency) had increased about three times over. The establishment of the NABO and the NARS also saw another big jump in legislative staff from 2003–2007.

One of the capacities of the executive versus the legislative branch can be measured by the ratio of staff and budget among the branches. In spite of the recent increase in the proportions of the legislature and the courts, Table 4.1 shows that the executive branch is still dominant, taking more than 95 percent of the central government manpower.[8] Therefore, it is premature to say that that the Korean governing system has changed from an executive-centered administration to a legislative-centered public one.

2. The change of central ministry state functions

The developmental state put priority on the state function of economic development. To examine the transformation of the Korean developmental state the proportion and change of the state functions are examined according to Clark and Dear's classification.

2.1. Overall trends

It might be helpful to understand state change by sketching the overall changes and by delving into analyses of state functions. The organizational size of the central government incrementally increased from 1,353 to 2,263 organizational units, increasing 1.9 percent annually and 67.3 percent in total from 1980–2007. Similarly, central government manpower grew from about 400,000 to above 600,000, increasing 1.5 percent annually and 50.2 percent in total. The budget expanded from about 10 trillion won to above 200 trillion won, increasing 11.8 percent annually and 1,916.0 percent in total during the period. The figures in Table 4.2 show that the Korean state has grown by a great measure in recent decades.

2.2. State function and apparatus

Figures 4.3 through 4.5 indicate the proportion of the state functions in terms of administrative means, including organization, staff, and budget. The proportion of organizational units (total size of bureaus and divisions) in the economic production function in the Korea state has decreased consistently, from 42.0 percent in 1980 to 26.5 percent in 2007 (Figure 4.3). On the contrary, the execution function increased its organizational units from 13.5 percent to 23.0 percent in this period, especially after 1997. The integration function fluctuated administration by administration, but overall it expanded from 18.6 percent to 25.5 percent in the period. Unlike the other functions, the organizational size of the consensus function was very stable at about 25 percent.

Table 4.1 Manpower by government branch

(Units: Person, %)

Classification	1980	1988	1989	1993	1998	2003	2007	Average Change Rate	Total Change Rate
Total	445,267	503,997	528,026	581,539	569,345	596,741	624,041	1.26	40.23
Legislative branch	1,176 (0.26)	2,879 (0.57)	3,000 (0.57)	3,046 (0.52)	3,346 (0.59)	3,086 (0.52)	3,469 (0.56)	4.09	205.10
Judicial branch	5,637 (1.27)	8,652 (1.72)	9,018 (1.71)	10,080 (1.73)	12,438 (2.18)	14,207 (2.38)	15,858 (2.54)	3.91	181.32
Executive branch	437,646 (98.29)	491,592 (97.54)	515,131 (97.56)	567,422 (97.57)	553,561 (97.23)	578,308 (96.91)	603,563 (96.72)	1.20	37.91
Office of the President	808 (0.18)	874 (0.17)	877 (0.17)	991 (0.17)	– –	1,140 (0.19)	1,151 (0.18)	1.32	42.45

Source: Ministry of Public Administration and Security, *Statistical Year Book.*

Table 4.2 The overall change of administrative means (average values)

Unit: Number, Person, Billion Won

Classification	Chun Doohwan (1980–1987)	Roh Taewoo (1988–1992)	Kim Youngsam (1993–1997)	Kim Daejung (1998–2002)	Roh Moohyun (2003–2007)	Average Change Rate	Total Change Rate
Organization	1443.8	1661.6	1739.0	1658.0	1958.4	1.9	67.3
Staff	442,548.0	509,806.4	557,693.8	551,629.8	586,258.2	1.5	50.2
Budget	16,619.9	35,425.7	90,496.3	153,994.6	193,120.8	11.8	1,916.0

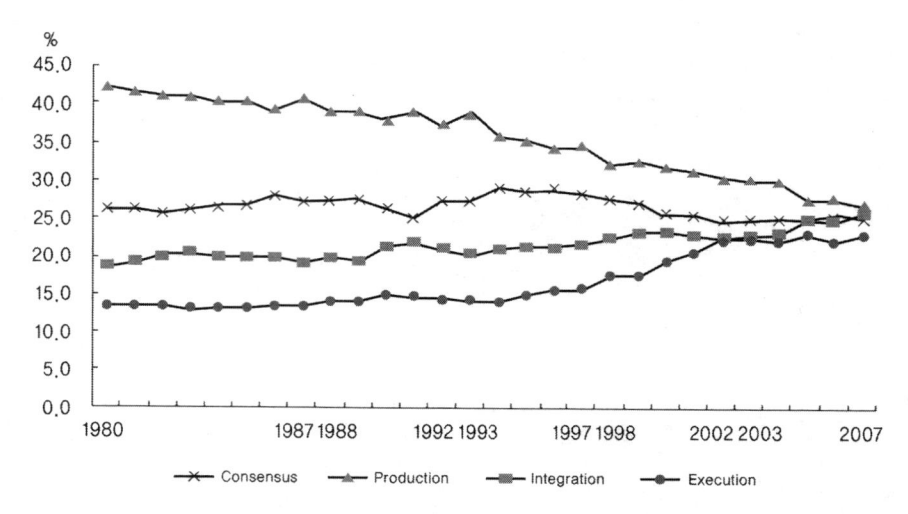

Figure 4.3 Changes in organization size among state functions, 1980–2007

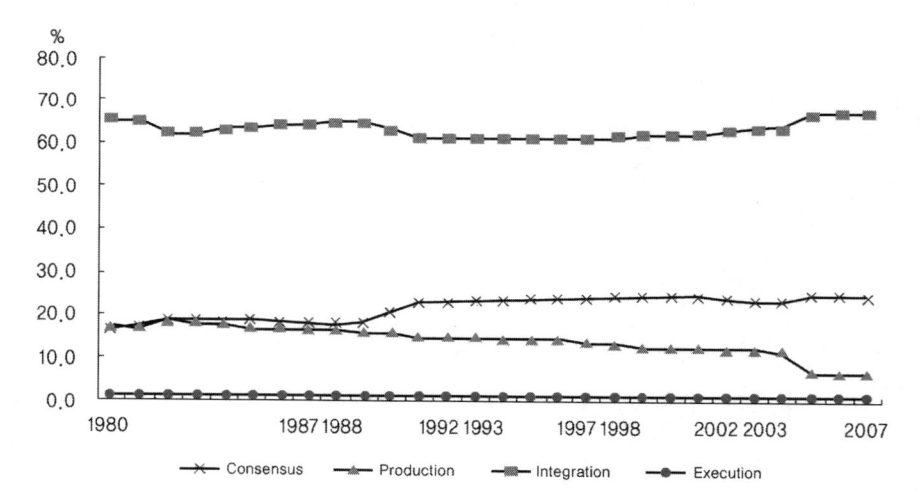

Figure 4.4 Changes in manpower among state functions, 1980–2007

The staff side shows similar trends. The proportion of staff in the production function decreased the most among the state functions, from 17.2 percent to 7.1 percent in the period. The proportion of consensus and the execution were relatively stable.[9] The integration function also showed some fluctuations but was roughly a stable 65 percent during the period. The large measure of the integration function implies its labor-intensive nature.

However, the budget side shows a somewhat different aspect. The basic priorities and composition of the budget among state functions were close to

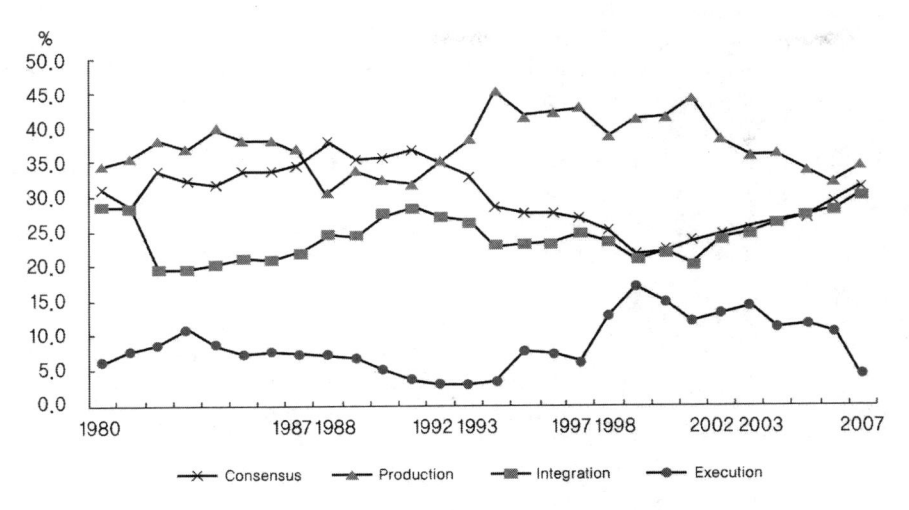

Figure 4.5 Changes in budget among state functions, 1980–2007

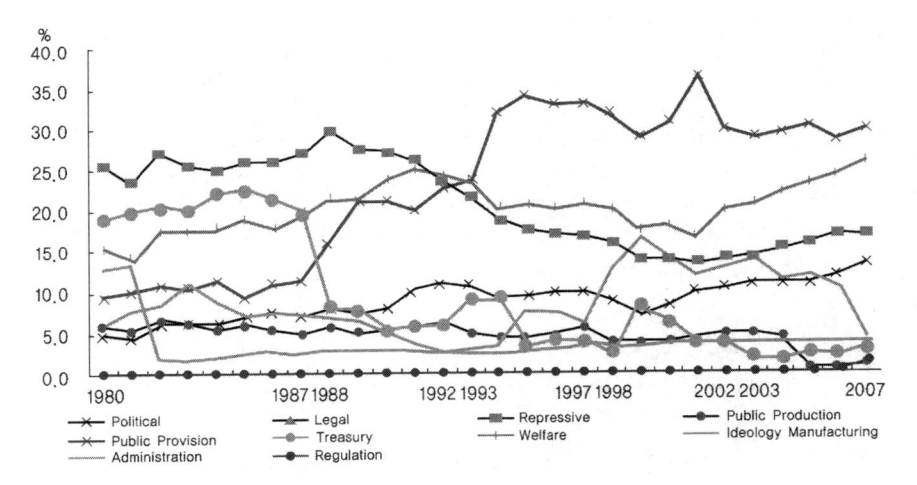

Figure 4.6 Changes in budget in the state apparatus, 1980–2007

the same at the end of the period as at the beginning although there were some fluctuations under different political regimes with the production function at 35 percent, the consensus function at 31 percent, the integration function at 29 percent, and the executive function at 6 percent. One interesting point is that there is some covariance of the production function and the execution function, which are the key state functions of the developmental state.

In terms of the state apparatus, in Figure 4.6, the winners were public provision, welfare, and political apparatus, and the losers were treasury, ideology, manufacturing, repression, and public production. The biggest budget gainer was the public provision apparatus. Its portion of the budget expanded from 10 percent to 30 percent. This fact implies growth and change in the nature of the Korean developmental state. The second biggest gainer was the welfare apparatus. It started at about 15 percent of the central government budget in 1980 and expanded to 26 percent in 2007. This social integration demand seems to limit the growth of the Korean developmental state. The political apparatus also gained significantly in the budget. It grew from 5 percent to 13.6 percent of the central government budget, which reflects the democratic transformation of the Korean state since the 1980s.

In sum, the Korean developmental state put top priority on economic production. However, the priority has been challenged by the emerging importance of the social integration function. The absolute size of the administrative means of the production function is still big, but the proportion of the state functions has moved from the production functions toward the integration functions under the more liberal governing parties in 1997–2007. Therefore, it is fair to say that there has been a functional transformation in the Korean developmental state.

3. *Strong central management agencies*

An important aspect of the developmental state is the role of pilot agencies that lead and coordinate economic development. Changes in the central management agencies are examined here according to Wilson's types of government agencies.

Figure 4.7 shows that the proportion of organizational units (total number of bureaus and divisions) in the central agencies was maintained in the early 1980s and increased incrementally later. The proportion started from 7.9 percent in 1980, reached 10.5 percent in 1990, then slightly decreased in the later 1990s, and again rebounded after 2000.

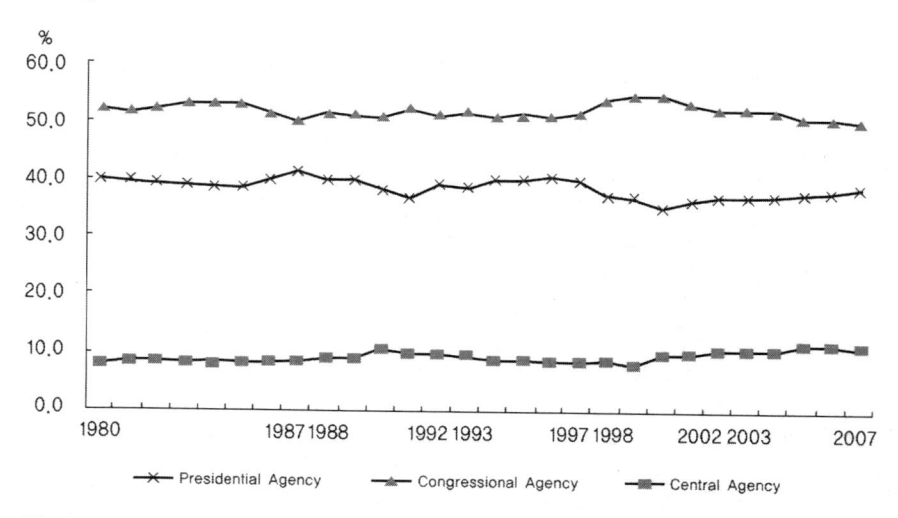

Figure 4.7 Changes in the organizations in the central government, 1980–2007

However, the staff and budget sides of central agencies dropped slightly but consistently. Figures 4.8 and 4.9 show these trends. Contrary to the staff increases in the presidential agencies and the congressional agencies, that of the central agencies decreased 3.8 percent in the period. On the budget side, the central agencies lost a big portion in the government reorganization under the Kim Youngsam Administration with the dismantling of the Economic Planning Board, which had been the headquarters of the Korean developmental state. After this critical reduction, the central agencies again steadily regained budget funds.

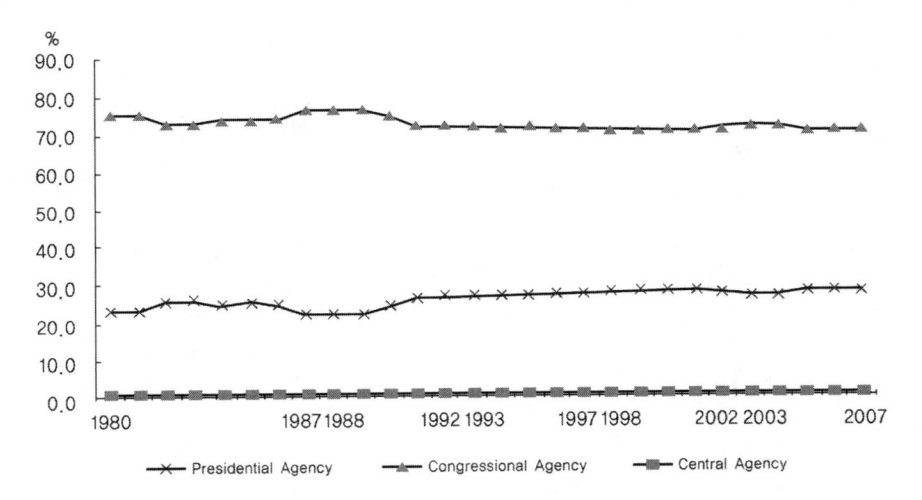

Figure 4.8 Changes in manpower in the central government, 1980–2007

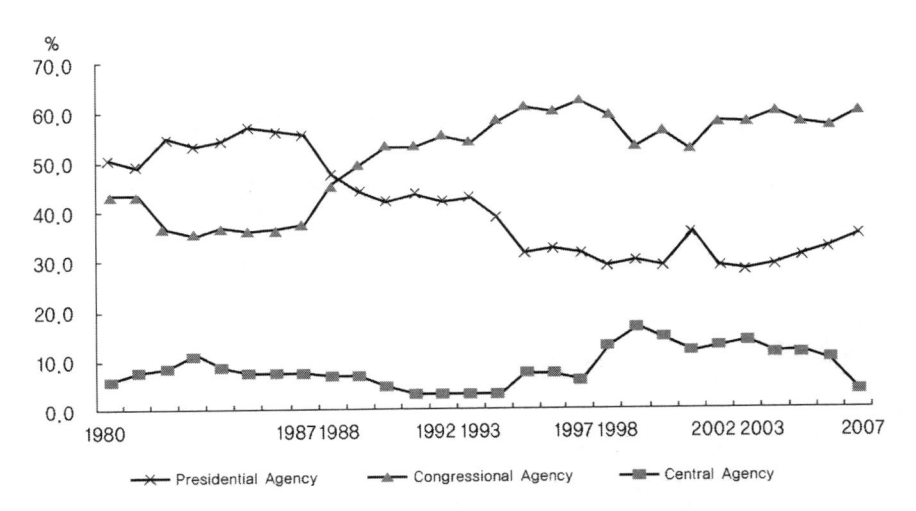

Figure 4.9 Changes in budget in the central government, 1980–2007

These facts show that the institutional foundation of the developmental state is still persistent and even stronger in organizational means. The current conservative government maintained the Ministry of Strategy and Finance, which seems to be a revival of the Ministry of Planning and Budget in the heyday of the economic development era, in the reorganization of the ministries in 2008 under the principle of mega-departments.

4. Heavy directive service intervention

Finally, the means of Korean developmental state government intervention are examined. Figure 4.10 shows the relative composition of Dunleavy's budget types in the central government.

The proportion of the core budget that is the indicator of direct intervention decreased from 25.2 percent to 16.5 percent in this period. The major component of the budget is the bureau budget using the private sector to intervene. This took up about half of the central government budget, and its portion declined from 53.6 percent in 1980 to 48 percent in 2007. The prominent characteristic of the budget change is the increase of the program and super-program budget in this period. The program budget increased from 16.7 percent to 31.1 percent. The super-program budget was also actively used during the late 1990s and early 2000s.

This data indicates that the central government relied less on direct service production and depended more on indirect service provision in performing its duties. This change in the means of state intervention can be found in the increase in the super-program budget after 1988 and the program budget after 2000. The former was closely related to the introduction of Local Government Transfer Funds in 1991, and the latter was with the reform of agencies around

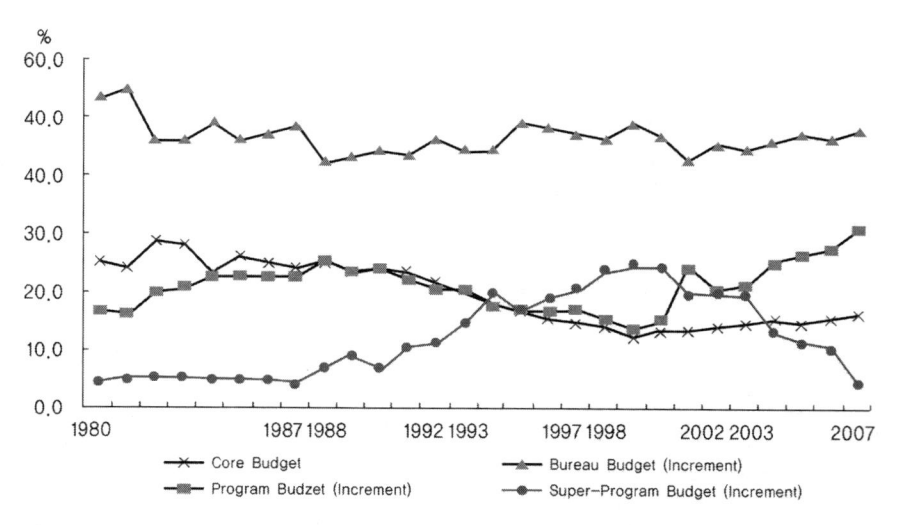

Figure 4.10 Changes in the budget type in central government, 1980–2007

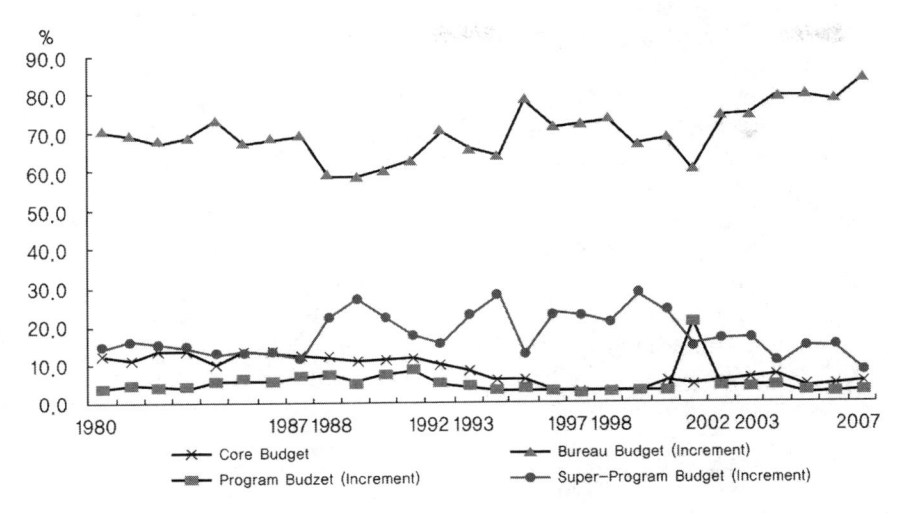

Figure 4.11 Changes in the production function budget type in the central government, 1980–2007

2000. Therefore, the nature of state bureaucracy changed from delivery agencies toward control agencies, which implies a small but strong state.

In particular, the production function as the core function of the developmental state is a relatively dominant component of the bureau budget, 70.3 percent in 1980 to 84.3 percent in 2007, as shown in Figure 4.11. The relatively high proportion of the super-program budget indicates the high propensity for using public bodies in intervening in the economy. However, the portion of the core budget consistently decreased from 11.8 percent in 1980 to 5.3 percent in 2007. These facts say that the production function was carried on more by the public provision apparatus and less by the public production apparatus.

In sum, this reveals the upward trend of indirect intervention using the bureau and program and super-program budget and the downward trend of direct intervention consuming the core budget. This analysis shows that Korean developmental state intervention became more indirect.

IV. Conclusion

This chapter aimed at examining the change of the developmental state in South Korea in terms of central government organization. From a review of theoretical discussions, it determined some key characteristics of the developmental state: executive-centered public administration, strong central agencies, the extensive economic function and exclusive social function of the ministries, and direct state intervention through extensive public agencies.

The analytical finding of this chapter showed the consistency of and changes in the Korean developmental state and its organization. First, in spite of recent growth to the legislature and the courts, the executive-centered public admin-istration system has remained strong. Second, the top priority of state functions still lies in the economic function, but its importance and proportion has been challenged by the demands of the social integration function. The means of state intervention changed from direct public production to indirect public provision. Third, the central management agencies have strongly established their organizational arrangements, although their staff and budget resources have decreased. After a severe reduction in the 1987 government reorganization, the central budget agency has regained its powerful resources. The change of the execution function also generally supports this trend. Fourth, the means of state intervention changed from direct delivery to indirect control.

In sum, this study argues that the basic structure of the Korean developmental state and organization system have not been reduced, rather it has transformed into new functional priorities and new means of social and economic interven-tion. These changes to administrative structure indicate the restoration of state autonomy and state capacities after the reduction of state capacities in the 1980s.

Appendix

Korean central government: organization chart (2015)

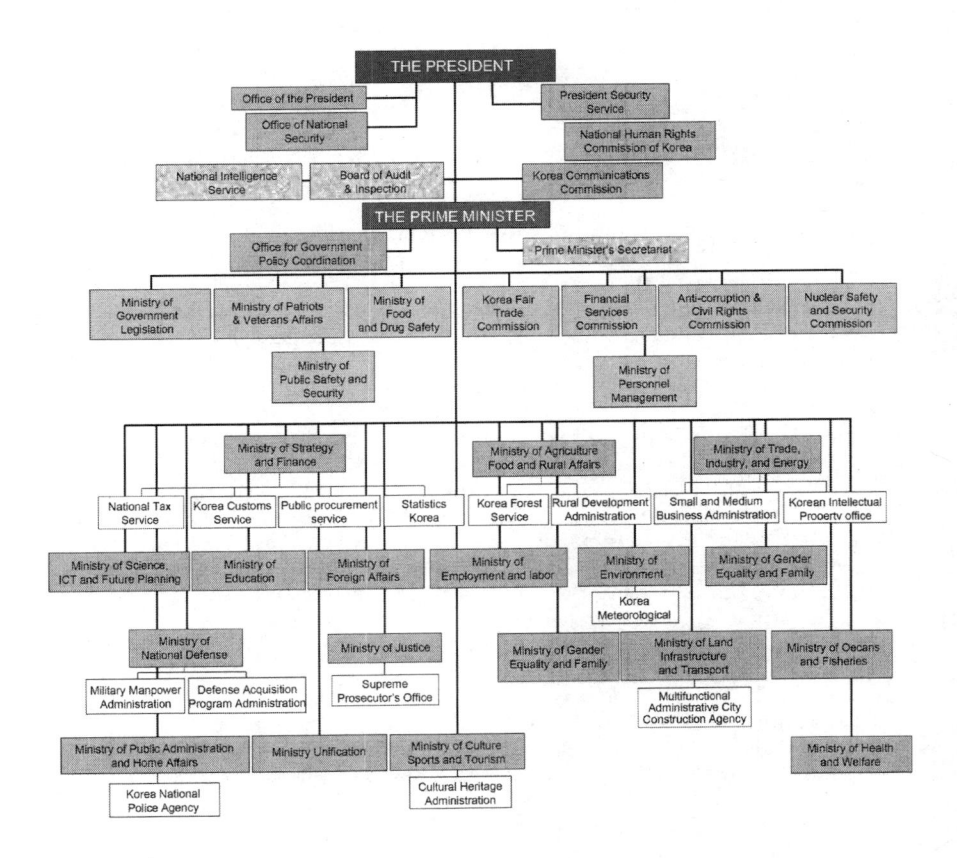

Notes

1 "Presidential agencies" include those that carry out policies that do not distribute benefits among significant groups, regions, or localities. Thus, they do not (usually) affect important congressional constituencies or at least do not affect them differently in different places. Examples of "presidential agencies" are the State Department, the Treasury Department, the Justice Department, the Defense Department, the Central Intelligence Agency, and the Arms Control and Disarmament Agency in the US case. "Congressional agencies" are those whose actions have a more pronounced distributional effect within the country. Examples of these are the Department of Agriculture, the Interior Department, the Department of Housing and Urban Development, the Army Corps of Engineers, the Small Business Administration, and the Veteran's Administration.

2 Clark and Dear (1984: 36–49) maintain that a proper analysis of a state *apparatus* requires an understanding of state *functions*, which in turn must be derived from the analysis of state *form*. Here, the question of state *form* is derived from an understanding of how and why a particular state structure arrives from a given social formation. State *function* refers to those activities undertaken in the name of the state, that is what the state actually does in a capitalist society. State *apparatus* refers to the mechanisms through which these functions are executed.

3 Dunleavy's agency types stem from an understanding of budget types (Dunleavy, 1991). First, the core budget consists of running costs for personnel and goods directly consumed by its operations, plus any capital expenditures on equipment or buildings directly needed for basic functions. Second, the bureau budget includes the core budget plus any money the agency directly pays out to the private sector. Third, the program budget includes the bureau budget, plus any money the agency passes on to other public-sector bureaus for them to spend. Finally, the super-program budget consists of an agency's program budget, plus any spending by other bureaus from their own resources over which the agency either exercises some policy responsibility, or that it can limit or expand in planning terms, or for which it can wholly or partially claim political credit.

4 There are two positions on the origin of the Korean developmental state. One notes the Japanese colonial period that built up a modern bureaucracy, a strong repressive apparatus (like the police), and a strong governing headquarters in the colony (Kim, 2001; Jun, 1992). The other maintains that the Korean developmental state formed around the 1950s (Park and Ko, 2005).

5 The developmental state also has other natures, including development-oriented political leadership and embedded autonomy based on the partnership between the government and a special class (Haggard and Moon, 1983; Park, 2000).

6 The Park Chunghee Administration is generally judged to be the prototype of the Korean developmental state. According to Kim (2000), troops dispatched to Vietnam and the diplomatic normalization with Japan in the mid-1960s became the material foundation while the landslide victory in the parliamentary elections of 1963 contributed the political basis required to drive the developmental state.

7 Leftwich (1995) notes the main factors of the developmental state: a determined developmental elite, relative autonomy, a powerful, competent, and insulated economic bureaucracy, a weak and subordinate civil society, effective management of non-state economic interests, and repression, legitimacy and performance.

8 In comparison, the United States Congress took about 1.2 percent of the manpower of the federal government (about 30,000) in 2003, twice the portion and ten times the number of its Korean counterpart (Kim and Kwon, 2005).

9 The personnel classification of the Special Service (policemen, teachers) makes up a substantial proportion of the consensus and integration functions in the central government of Korea.

References

Castles, F. ed. (2007). *The Disappearing State?: Retrenchment Realities in an Age of Globalisation.* Cheltenham: Edward Elgar.

Chang, H. (2004). *Globalization, Economic Development and the Role of the State.* London: Zed Books.

Chibber, V. (2002). "Bureaucratic Rationality and the Developmental State," *American Journal of Sociology*, 107(4): 951–989.

Clark, G. and M. Dear. (1984). *State Apparatus: Structures and Language of Legitimacy.* Boston: Allen & Unwin.

Cotton, J. (2000). "The Asian Crisis and the Perils of Enterprise Association: Explaining the Different Outcomes in Singapore, Taiwan and Korea." In R. Robinson, M. Beeson, K. Jayasuriya, and Hyukrae Kim, eds. *Politics and Markets in the Wake of the Asian Crisis*, pp. 151–168. London: Routledge.

Dunleavy, P. (1991). *Democracy, Bureaucracy, and Public Choice: Economic Explanation in Political Sciences.* New York: Harvester Wheatsheaf.

Evans, P. (1995). *Embedded Autonomy: States & Industrial Transformation.* Princeton: Princeton University Press.

Haggard, S. and C. Moon. (1983). "The South Korean State in the International Economy: Liberal, Dependent, or Mercantile?" In J. Ruggie, ed. *The Antinomies of Interdependence: National Welfare and International Division of Labour*, pp. 131–189. New York: Columbia University Press.

Hood, C. (1994). *Explaining Economic Policy Reversals.* Buckingham: Open University Press.

Jo, Hyungje, Keun-hwa Jung, and Jeonghyop Lee. (2006). "A New Model of Progressive Development in Korea," *Trend & View*, 67: 58–92. (in Korean)

Johnson, C. (1982). *MITI and the Japanese Miracle: The Growth of Industrial Policy, 1925–1975.* Stanford: Stanford University Press.

Jun, Sang-in. (1992). "The Origins of the Developmental State in South Korea," *Asian Perspective*, 16(2): 181–204.

Kim, Keunsei. (2005). "Restructuring of State Administrative Structure in the UK," *The Korea Public Administration Journal*, 14(1): 120–156. (in Korean)

Kim, Keunsei and Soonjung Kwon. (2005). "Restructuring of State Administrative Structure in the US," *Korea Public Administration Journal*, 14(3). (in Korean)

Kim, Il-young. (2001). "Origin, Building, Development, and Prospect of State in Korea," *Korean Journal of Political and Diplomatic History*, 23(1): 87–126. (in Korean)

Kim, Il-young. (2000). "Building a Developmental State in Korea," *Korean Political Science Review*, 33(4): 121–143. (in Korean)

Kim, In-young. (2008). "Rethinking the Capitalist Developmental State (CDS): The Transformation and Features of the CDS after 1997 Economic Crisis in South Korea," *Korean Journal of Northeast Asia*, 47: 183–204. (in Korean)

Kuk, Minho. (2008). "Korean Economic Crisis and Developmental State Mode," *Society and Theory*, 13: 213–249. (in Korean)

Lee, Yeonho, Yoojin Lim, and Sukkyu Chung. (2002). "The Rise of the Regulatory State and Government-Business Relations in South Korea," *Korean Political Science Review*, 36(3): 199–222. (in Korean)

Leftwich, A. (1995). "Bringing Politics Back In: Towards a Model of the Developmental State," *Journal of Development Studies*, 31(3): 400–427.

Levy, J. ed. (2006). *The State after Statism: New State Activities in the Age of Liberalization.* Cambridge, MA: Harvard University Press.

Lim, Haeran. (2006). "East Asian Developmental State and Governance: With a Focus on the Industrial Policy of Korea and Taiwan in Information Period," *New Asia*, 13(1): 162–189. (in Korean)

Minns, J. (2001). "Of Miracles and Models: The Rise and Decline of the Developmental State in South Korea," *Third World Quarterly*, 22(6): 1025–1043.

Onis, Ziya. (1991). "The Logic of the Developmental State," *Comparative Politics*, 24(1): 109–126.

Park, Eunhong. (2000). "Developmental State Thesis: Rethinking its Origins, Structures, and Defects," *The Korean Journal of International Studies*, 39(3): 117–134. (in Korean)

Park, Sungjin and Kyungmin Ko. (2005). "The Origin of the Korean Developmental State," *Social Science Research Review* (Institute of Social Science of Sogang University), 13(1): 96–128. (in Korean)

Peters, B. Guy. (1980). *Public Employment in the United States: Growth and Change.* Center for the Study of Public Policy, University of Strathclyde.

Peters, B. Guy. (1988). *Comparing Public Bureaucracies: Problems of the Theory and Method.* Tuscaloosa: The University of Alabama Press.

Pollitt, C. (1993). *Managerialism and the Public Service,* 2nd ed. Oxford: Blackwell.

Rosenbloom, D. (2000). *Building a Legislative-Centered Public Administration: Congress and the Administrative State, 1946–1999.* Alabama: Alabama University Press.

Sonn, Ho-chul. (1998). "An Analysis of Kim Dae-Jung Government's Chaebol Reform: From the Perspective of State Theory," *Korea and World Politics*, 14(1): 45–71. (in Korean)

Skocpol, T. (1985). "Bringing the State Back In: Strategies of Analysis in Current Research." In P. Evans D. Rueschemeyer, and T. Skocpol, eds. *Bringing the State Back In,* pp. 3–37. Cambridge: Cambridge University Press.

Thomson, P. (1992). "Public Sector Management in a Period of Radical Change: 1979–1992," *Public Money & Management*, 12(3): 33–41.

Weiss, L. (1998). *The Myth of the Powerless State.* Ithaca: Cornell University Press.

Weiss, L. (2000). "Developmental States in Transition: Adapting, Dismantling, Innovating, not 'Normalizing,'" *The Pacific Review*, 13(1): 21–55.

Wilson, J. (1986). *American Government: Institutions and Policies,* 3rd ed. Lexington, MA: DC Heath and Company.

Yang, Jae-jin. (2005). "Developmentalism after Development: The Growth, Crisis, and Future of the Korean Developmental State," *Korean Public Administration Review*, 39(1): 1–18. (in Korean)

Part II
Public-sector management

5 Korean public personnel management

Kyung-Ho Cho

I. Development of the public personnel system in Korea

The development of modern nations is in fact centered on public officials who are the practical principals of the public administration system. Public officials are considered a vital variable that has significant influence on people's lives and national development via affecting the success or failure of policies and administration. Public personnel administration is known as a set of functions or an operational system that administers public officials who play a vital role during policy procedures.

The public personnel system in general can be divided into the procurement of human resources, development, administration, and regulation. The immediate objective of the public personnel system is to improve decision-making and implementation abilities through making the best use of public officials. The public personnel system in any country pursues such objectives and contributes to the ultimate realization of administration through productive or democratic government.

The modern Korean public personnel system was solidly established in the 32 years between the 1961 launch of the Park Chunghee government in which military administrators exerted a great influence on administration until Kim Youngsam took over the government in 1993. These were the years when the ex-military presidents Park Chunghee, Chun Doohwan, and Roh Taewoo ruled. The military was the most significant administrative influence. and military personnel systems from foreign countries were introduced to Korea during these years.

However, Korea's administrative system started to experience rapid changes as it underwent peaceful citizen protests culminating in the June Democracy Movement in 1987. In the meantime, increasing the number of civil servants would be considered naturally in line with the expansion of administrative functions and the hypertrophy of government organizations during that time. As doubts upon the productivity of the public sector started to arise, civil society voices demanding "efficient personnel but smaller in scale" continued to get stronger. Different areas within society such as politics, economics, society, and culture also started to influence administration more equally.

Many developed countries have put a lot of effort into pushing administrative reforms during the early 1990s, and such efforts left Korean administration with the task of surviving in a borderless age of endless competition. Some of the major examples that show the international scene working as an important influence on Korean administration include open personnel, senior executive services, annual salaries, diffusion of family-friendly personnel policies, work–life balance, customer-focused administration, and improvement of administrative statistics. Korea officially implemented local government once again as the country went through the election of local government heads in 1995. This decentralized as well as liberalized Korean personnel administration. The Roh Moohyun Administration launched forward-looking policies in 2003 based on commission decisions and on collective action by civil servants. The Government Employee Union Act came into place in 2006 along with a new emphasis on intrinsic democratic values in the personnel administration.

Korean personnel administration has recently been moving towards a human resource management direction. In other words, the Korean public personnel system is developing a strong awareness that its performance is influenced by government employees' knowledge, skills, and capacity, while also considering them to be valuable assets essential when achieving organizational goals.

In addition, personnel administration has begun to take a strategic approach when managing civil servants, trying to satisfy each and every worker's desires and expectations rather than simply meeting those of the organization. This explains how the recognition of the public personnel system not only profiting the organization but also providing personal benefit and development for civil servants has been getting stronger. The public personnel system has been trying to bring about better outcomes from organizations through starting more active and various personnel policies and programs in order to motivate civil servants to focus on the government and to increase organizational flexibility and is continuing to expand as well. Flexible work shifts and part-time work for civil servants, which have been emphasized since the Lee Myungbak Administration, are examples of the efforts to improve the administration's diversity and flexibility through the public personnel system.

II.   Characteristics of Korean public personnel system

1.   General characteristics

The public personnel system is often explained based on systems theory. This is not only because the organic connectivity among various activities implementing the personnel system becomes clearer if an open system model is applied but also because it is possible to get a grasp of the functions and roles of the personnel system in relation with its external environments (Nigro and Nigro, 1994: 49; Park et al., 2014: 17). The Korean public personnel system will be explained based on systems theory in this chapter. Figure 5.1 explains the Korean public personnel system at a glance. The public personnel system is composed of different subcomponents as a system and close mutual relationships exist among these components. As such, it possesses the general characteristics of a system,

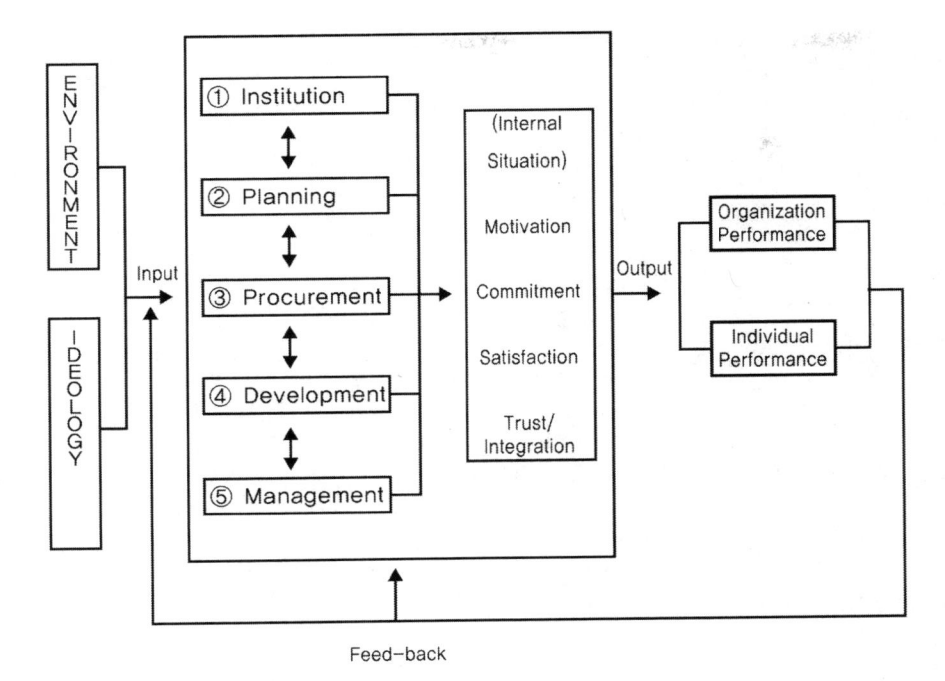

Figure 5.1 Personnel administration system

such as having a boundary separating itself from the external environment. The public personnel system maintains and develops itself by having functional links among its components and receives recognition by working out with inputs from the environment.

The environment of the Korean public personnel system can largely be divided into the political environment, the financial environment, the social environment, and the legal environment. Figure 5.2 shows the development of the Korean public personnel system in chronological order. If the era prior to the 1990s is called the passive personnel administration period, the current era, where an emphasis on human capital management (HCM) stands out, can be explained with the increased recognition of human resources from around the 1997–1998 foreign exchange crisis.

Personnel administration receives various demands and expectations from the political environment comprised of the president, the National Assembly, mass media, the public, NGOs, and the private sector. Korea had to go through a depressing political state from its founding through the Fifth Republic (1948–1987). However, different personnel policies started being put in place as the nation went through the 1995 local government elections and administration changes in 1998 and 2003. For instance, the issue associated with the quality of civil servant life was carried forward during the Kim Daejung administration,

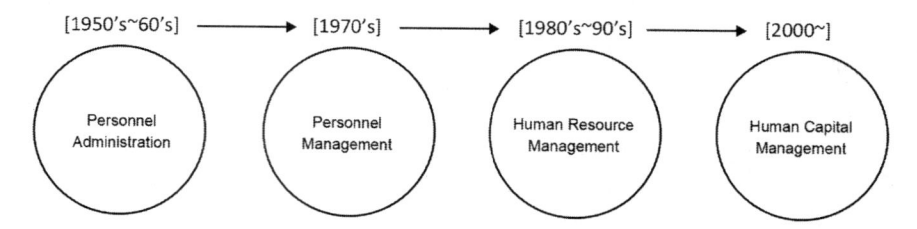

Figure 5.2 Korean personnel administration by era

and the efforts to strengthen the independence of the central personnel agency were implemented during the Roh Moohyun Administration.

Economic health is another environmental factor that heavily influences personnel administration. This is because personnel administration activities are highly influenced by the national budget. Personnel administration had to carry the burden of reductions when Korea experienced economic crisis in 1997. Economic growth has recently become stable, and the government has started actively seeking personnel policies in order to secure talented individuals. The five-day work week in particular was implemented in July 2004, and since then, Korean personnel administration has been making a transition from the old structure of a developing country to a new developed-country structure that focuses on capital, techniques, and productivity. In addition, civil servants are rapidly becoming more high-end and diversified in their leisure activities as their life patterns as well as the meaning of weekends change.

There are many social factors that can influence personnel administration. Social demographic changes such as the increase of women in the job market have brought a significant change to personnel administration employment and operations. A complex society generates complicated social problems and therefore makes it difficult to solve such problems. In this case, talented individuals that specialize in each field are needed as civil servants, and improvements to the standard of living and level of popular consciousness demand corresponding reforms of every civil servant's consciousness.

Personnel administration works on the basis of related laws, and these laws normally contain contents covering the rationality and justice of the personnel administration. Personnel law could cause the personnel administration to become ossified though it may reduce the arbitrariness of personnel administration. This is due to legal restrictions that make personnel administration deal inflexibly with changing situations.

Korean public personnel administration is affected by the administration of public law. Laws directly regulate administration and differ from the political, economic, and social environments that have an indirect effect on administration. Laws make it possible to predict administration, and they also decide procedures and founding principles. Likewise, administration and law seem to be in a hierarchical relationship from a normative perspective, but they are in fact in a complementary relationship or even in tension. The principles of the administration of public law are not thoroughly followed in today's complex society. It is the opposite of reality. In other words, administration forms laws in most cases rather than laws ruling administration.

2. *Career civil service system*

The career civil service system refers to a personnel system operated as young and talented individuals choose the civil service as a worthy career and work sincerely and with devotion. The career civil service system was established on systems and principles meant to induce long service and the sincere performance of duties. The institutional bases of Korean public personnel administration such as hierarchical tradition, closed recruiting, appointments focused on those with general capacity, and strict protection of job security all seem to follow the prototype of the career civil service system truthfully.

Career servants have the following attributes. First of all, they are committed to long service with the premise of working for a lifetime. Therefore, it is critical to recruit young and talented people. Next, possessing potential across a long term of service is more important than current capacity. Third, career civil servants start working up from the very bottom of the organization as they are committed to working for their lifetimes. Lastly, current civil servants are required to become "servants for all citizens" so patriotism and service are particularly emphasized, compared to other careers.

A guarantee of job security for career civil servants along with their political neutrality have made a huge contribution to maintaining stable administration during dark periods of party politics. Despite regime changes and political upheavals, Korea was able to develop as a nation largely due to the career civil service system (Yoo, 1997: 81).

On the other hand, the guaranteed job security and closed recruiting could give civil servants privileges that can cause concern about possibly lowering their responsiveness to the external environment. This could also hinder the recruitment of specialists for different government fields at the right times. The need of the people for services has recently been increasing in Korea along with demands for the increased utility of public-sector outcomes and expenses. In response, reform of the career civil service system is being pushed forward from various angles. Such reforms mostly include American personnel policies like position classification systems, open recruitment, and a focus on specialists. Reforms are also progressing in a way that incorporates aspects of private-sector human resource management methods and operating systems.

The following discussion summarize the plan for recent reforms of the Korean career civil service system. To start off, re-education or termination is being reviewed as a plan for dealing with incapable or insincere workers in order to manage human resources more effectively. However, the termination of incapable civil servants, which has already been put into place in some departments and agencies, has some room for improvement in terms of fairness. Second, open

Table 5.1 Comparison of the open position system and the job posting system

Classification	Open Position System	Job Posting System
System overview	Appoint the best person via competition with other people	Appoint the best person via competition with civil servants from other departments
Appointment range	Up to 20% of the total number of the senior executive service or management-level positions	Up to 30% of the total number of experienced members of the senior executive service
Job fields considered	General service, special service, officials in special government service (the senior executive service or management-level positions)	General service, special members of the senior executive service
Appointment criteria	Professionalism, significance, democracy, necessity for change, adjustment	Job commonality, policy integrity, necessity for change

recruitment is being reinforced. Open recruitment is recruiting qualified people through an open competition for particular positions. Korea has been running an open position system since 1999, while an open system for high office as well as a job posting system has been operating since 2006 when the Senior Executive Service (SES) was created. Table 5.1 shows a comparison between the open position system and the job posting system (MOSPA, 2013: 71).

Third, efforts are being made to secure the efficiency of the merit system. The career civil service can firmly root itself as a personnel policy when the system is based on the merit system. The Korean career civil service is also based on the merit system, but the advantages of the merit system may also be its weaknesses. Therefore, various reforms are required, and such reforms are being prepared. In particular, an insistence on the merit system and dependence on political neutrality or a guarantee of status may go against administration's ideology of democracy and efficiency in the case of officials belonging to the senior executive service. These officials are deeply involved in policy decisions along with ministers and vice-ministers, meaning they are already engaged politically in their daily work. A "flexible" merit system rather than a strict and "rigid" merit system is applied to civil servants in Korea who belong to the SES. Lastly, Korea is gradually reinforcing elements of position classification. The base of the public service is being strengthened so that job analysis can be reinforced, but the pace of expanding the position classification has been very slow.

Below are some of the recent reform efforts in the Korean career civil service.

- Expanding the term employees: term employees (including part-time civil servants) were formerly contract employees. The Korean civil service is actively working to expand term employees in order to strengthen professionalism and competitiveness. The total number of term employees was only about 900 in 2004, but the number increased to 2,000 in 2013.

- Operating the open position system and job posting: the open position system was introduced in 1999, and job posting was introduced a year after in 2000. Job posting breaks away from the convention of closed human resource management within a department. It selects qualified people through public offerings and assigns them to positions. This system has increased fairness, and the open position system with strong position classification characteristics has made a contribution to raising the professionalism of administration by inviting outside specialists.

- Implementing performance-based pay: performance-based pay is a system where pay is commensurate with the performance of a civil servant. In the case of the central government, performance-based pay was first introduced for chiefs and director-levels officials in 1999. Annual income is given based on a graded pay system that follows each individual's target management performance results. Performance-based pay was expanded to manager-level officials starting in 2005. The system was applied below the manager level starting in 2001, connecting pay with performance. Yet, the assessment of performance pay has not been so positive. Thus, successfully rooting the system within Korean personnel administration still remains a task.

3. Merit system

The merit system refers to appointing and removing civil servants based on individual capacity, performance, and qualification rather than taking their partisanship or other favoritism into account. In the early days, the main task given to the merit system was to overcome favoritism. Achieving objective public office employment, equal opportunity, political neutrality, and guaranteeing job security were the vital points. However, as time passed, the merit system has allowed individual capacity and performance in addition to fair participation, which enhances administrative efficiency and improves the government's productivity through a civil service conducted by experts. In other words, the merit system is an important system that makes possible administration for all citizens instead of making administration serve only certain groups of people.

However, people should be aware that the merit system is not always universal. The merit system can cause rigidity when managing human resources when it is excessive. It is possible to miss competitive individuals when following a strict merit system. Plus, a number of leading companies have been raising the importance of interviews rather than written tests since written measures of performance and capacity are not always accurate. Table 5.2 summarizes the advantages and disadvantages of the merit system.

The Korean government officially adopted the merit system as its basic personnel administration system from its establishment, but it is hard to say that the government has sincerely followed it, considering some practices that were completely out of the system's boundaries (Kim, 1999: 21). The most severe

Table 5.2 Comparison of the merit system's advantages and disadvantages

Advantages	Disadvantages
Opens more opportunities for participating in the civil service via open competition	Causes rigidity of human resource management due to complex human resource management structure
Improves administrative efficiency with capacity and performance	Unable to provide valid measurement for talented individuals
Secures the fairness of administration through political neutrality	Declining responsibility due to weakened political control
Secures the stability of administration through a guarantee job security	Causes complacency
Contributes to preventing corruption	Corruption remains due to secretiveness

violations of the merit system occurred during the First Republic and the Second Republic. Violations have been on a downward trend ever since, but problems such as local favoritism still exist in present personnel practice (Oh, 1993: 32).

The constitution and government officials regulate equal opportunity when holding civil service office in Korea through political neutrality, job security, and appointment by capacity and performance. Nonetheless, excluding the cases of new recruitments through open competition, career tenure is highly emphasized in addition to school, regional, and kinship ties in promotions and personnel changes. In addition, Korean civil servants are often advanced by the power structure, or they themselves intermittently show opportunistic inclinations, expecting benefits in return afterwards (Yoo, 1997: 67).

The Korean government is strengthening the advantages of the merit system while making up for the weaknesses of the system by making efforts to improve those weaknesses. Above all, rank-limits represent an example that is currently being applied to police officers, firefighters, and military personnel. Rank-limits are thought to have contributed to inspiring civil servants to have an achievement-oriented public consciousness. However, it can bring anxiety and lower morale when it is excessively applied. Next, there is the argument that strict laws regarding political neutrality should be relieved. Considering the reality where civil servants already take advantage of political interests, relieving political neutrality regulations to a certain extent is thought to be okay. Lastly, there are a number of voices that raise the need for extensive job analysis for the merit system. That is a strict job analysis needs to be implemented so that the fairness of performance evaluation is guaranteed. Korea has been intermittently executing job analyses for particular goals since 1995, but it is necessary to carry out a more extensive job analysis.

4. Rank-in-person classification system

The rank-in-person system refers to a system where public office is classified according to each individual's status and rank. Here, status and rank are normally decided by level of education, work experience, and other qualifications. Therefore, rank is inevitably related to status. An individual's level of education and work experience become important factors that decide their rank. Similarly, level of education and career are still considered as important factors when classifying ranks in the case of an individual appointed with a certain qualification after passing the test. Those with a certain rank are expected to be in charge of various tasks that correspond to their rank.

Rank-in-person classification contrasts with the position classification system. First, a rank-in-person system is appropriate for promoting talented individuals with general ability. The rank-in-person system is based on the philosophy of fostering amateurs or all-around administrators, and public officials gain extensive insights and experience under the system, which promotes cooperation among departments and institutions. Second, changing jobs and career transfers are very flexible under the rank-in-person system. Therefore, the efficiency of utilizing human resources can be improved as limited manpower performs various types of duties. Third, the structure of offices in the rank-in-person system is fundamentally based on closed recruitment. Under a rank-in-person system, a series of personnel changes are occur frequently when high-ranking officials move. Fourth, the rank-in-person system provides strong drivers that incorporate people and the organization, creating an organizational atmosphere where members of the organization are attached to the future of the organization. Fifth, status is thoroughly guaranteed unless officials voluntarily resign or are involved in legal issues, disciplinary actions, or are sentenced. Table 5.3 compares the characteristics of position classification and rank-in-person classification.

Table 5.3 Comparison of position and rank-in-person classification characteristics

Classification	Characteristics	
	Rank-in-Person	Position
Classification unit	Rank	Position
Employment standard	Potential and general capacities	Professional ability
Career growth	Generalist	Specialist
Recruitment system	Closed	Open
Guarantee of status	Strong	Weak
Personnel realignment	Extensive, flexible	Limited, rigid
Career civil service system	Advantage	Disadvantage
Vision of civil servants	Comprehensive, extensive	Fragmentary, narrow
Administration specialization	Hindrance	Contribution
Fairness of duty performance	Low	High
pay	Same pay for same rank	Same pay for same duty
Human resource management (education and training, promotion, evaluation, wage, etc.)	Seniority-focused, easy for boss to intervene arbitrarily	Capacity and performance-focused, provides objective standards

Source: Ha et ai. (1999: 6).

The Korean civil service fundamentally follows a rank-in-person system, but it has occasionally added a considerable number of elements of position classification. The Korean civil service once established a position classification system in November 1963, although it was abolished in 1973. This accounts for the clarification of the principles of the position classification system in today's Government Officials Act. The Second Amendment to the Government Officials Act classifies civil servants into types, and the Fifth Amendment provides a definition of the position classification system.

Korea abolished the rank of senior civil servants in 2006 and started running the SES, which adopted a job-grade system. Positions in the Diplomatic Service and affiliated organizations to which foreign service personnel belong are classified following the job-grade system. The appointment of duty classes is carried out based on the results of job analysis.

The Korean government has also been consistently reinforcing open employment in order to relieve the elements of the rank-in-person system. The open employment system contrasts with the closed employment system that has the career civil service system as its basis. Open employment, in principle, allows new employment from the outside for every government position. Up until recently, almost 99 percent of civil servants above Grade 6 (excluding Grade 5) have been appointed according to the process of promoting insiders. Seven out of ten new Grade 5 appointments every year are promoted from inside in the annual open recruitment. The Korean government revised the Government Officials Act on May 24, 1999, as the government found in Article 28 a need for an efficient policy or a need for professionalism in regards to director-level positions and the chiefs of central government organizations. Accordingly, the government has allowed certain positions that require appointment of personnel from inside or outside to be designated as open positions.

5. Senior Executive Service (SES)

Since the 1949 enactment of the Government Officials Act, reforms of the civil service have mostly maintained the frame of the rank-in-person system. The old personnel system's problems form the background of the institution of the SES. Under the old personnel system and customs, chief- and director-level senior executives were rotated every year, reducing their professionalism and responsibility as they enforced policies. The old system also failed to provide incentives for them as performance management was done in a loose fashion, mainly focusing on seniority. Education and training programs were not systematic either, putting limits of trying to raise abilities and job performance. Besides, the old system excluded other department employees or external personnel when filling senior positions, making it difficult for departments to cooperate and to coordinate policies (Park et al., 2014: 131; Park and Cho, 2013).

In short, the SES abolishes Grade 1–3 chief and director-level senior positions and tries to manage human resources by focusing on duty and performance in an openly competitive setting. The Korean SES has four important features.

First, the open position system, which enables outsiders to flow in, and the job posting system, which fosters competition among departments, are all meant to enhance the opening and the competition of senior positions. Second, the SES tends to improve the abilities of senior executives through evaluation of competence, education and training, and setting a minimum appointment period. Third, the service secures the performance and responsibility of senior executives through eligibility screening, the job-grade system, and the job performance contract system. Fourth, the service uses an integrated management system when managing senior executives so that they can perform their duties to the national interest from a broad perspective, away from the narrow perspective of their affiliated department (Park and Cho, 2013).

In the current situation, outcomes from the introduction of the senior executive service can be evaluated by looking at whether each of the following goals were realized: improvement in openness to senior executives from outside, improvement in the mobility of senior executives among departments, reinforcement of the performance-based system when managing senior executives, and strengthening the abilities of senior executives.

First, looking at the openness of senior executives, the number of open positions was 129 when the open position system was first established in 2000, but the number in June 2012 went up to 286 in 40 different departments. Among these 286 positions, 179 senior executives and 107 managers were designated as open positions. In the case of the mobility of senior positions among the departments, the number of posted positions was 199 when the job posting system was first introduced in 2006, but this number declined significantly to 89 by March 2012. This decline seems to be motivated by the reduction in positions caused by integrating ministries that happened according to the 2008 government reorganization.

Second, the reinforcement of the performance-based system in managing senior positions has seen some progress as well. The importance of performance-based pay has grown gradually, and the introduction of relative evaluation components in 2009 when evaluating the performance of senior executives has limited the ratio of the highest rankings to 20 percent. Performance evaluation and screening tests were enhanced so that executives with low performance levels get weeded out.

Third, in the case of strengthening abilities, the ratio of those who failed the competency evaluation rose from 10.4 percent in 2006 to 28.1 percent in June 2012 (Park and Cho, 2013). Prior education that prepares people for the competency test has the effect of improving core competencies and management capacity.

The Korean SES, as can be seen above, is identified as having obtained desired system and output results. In fact, a recent Organisation for Economic Co-operation and Development (OECD) report (2011) also says that Korea, France, Israel, and the UK have had mechanisms for managing potential senior executives from the very beginning. The report ranked Korea 6th out of 34 nations in the area of applying special HRM for the senior executive service, and Korea is ranked higher than the OECD average. Nonetheless, in order to achieve the desired effects of the SES, there is still a significant number of tasks left that need to be improved in terms of both the system's content and management.

For instance, regarding system management, the decreasing ratio of external recruiting for open positions and posted positions is problematic. In the case of open positions, the level of remuneration is still very low compared to that of the private sector. The contract term is also short, which provides less motivation for talented individuals from the private sector to apply.

Maybe it is too early to talk about the senior executive service's outcomes. Organized performance evaluations are needed for whether departmental parochialism is overcome by the integrated pan-government perspectives of the SES, whether qualified people are going through the right employment process, whether the closed service is being overcome by a flow of outside manpower and personnel exchange among departments, whether senior leadership capacity is being reinforced through systematic education training, whether the connection between compensation and outcomes is providing motivation, whether a performance-based culture is being implanted while breaking away from the old rank- and seniority-focused culture, and whether responsibility is being strengthened through performance evaluation and tests of qualification.

III. Recent reforms

1. Action-based learning and performance-based training

The change in the paradigm of civil service training is what mainly accounts for the introduction of action learning (AL) to the Korean civil service as the main means of training. The Korean government made groundbreaking changes to the structure and method of the civil service training in the last decade. These changes include the following: 1) from a teaching approach to voluntary learning approach, 2) from accumulating individual knowledge to achieving organizational goals, 3) from delivering knowledge to solving problems, 4) from classroom-based training to field-based training, and 5) from supplier-focused to consumer-focused (CSC of Korea, 2004).

The next background for the introduction of action learning is the expansion of training for performance. As performance-oriented training is expanded and becoming more emphasized, it is highly likely that participatory and problem-solving training will be enhanced. Training will avoid the old lecture-led education that used to focus on knowledge delivery but will rather actively expand education that focuses on discussion, rewards, and problem-solving.

Third, as training becomes more field-focused, action learning has to be emphasized consistently. The need for the action learning is becoming stronger as learning about both the successful and unsuccessful cases of the government's main policies is emphasized along with field-focused training, in which learning and tasks are closely related to one another.

2. Employee–employer relations

Due to the special political circumstances including the division of the Korean Peninsula and the confrontation between North and South Korea, it has been impossible for Korea to expand collective action to the civil service in general service. However, the government has recently taken two actions related to collective action by the civil service. One of them is the establishment of civil service labor unions, and the other is the legalization of such labor unions.

The civil service labor union is a form of labor-management association that has been enforced since January 1, 1999. Public employee labor-management association is a consultative group within the workplace that deals with improving the working environment, improving work efficiency, and addressing difficulties. Korean public employee labor organizations are now run in a dual system with the labor union and the labor-management association.

The dominant perception in the past was that civil service labor unions could not be formed due to the distinct characteristics of civil servants and their status. However, the perception of acknowledging the nature of civil servants as employees has recently spread across many countries, and it is becoming the tendency to allow the formation of public-sector labor unions for civil servants.

Although a number of citizens agree with extending permission in regard to the problem of collective action by civil servants, it is still the dominant perception that it is not acceptable for civil servants to exercise their rights and pursue their interests as employees since civil servants always need to maintain justice and neutrality when performing as public servants. Acknowledging the fact that society sees a civil servant as a worker, however, it is now time for Korea to examine how to change the popular perception of civil service collection (union) activities. Therefore, successful management of the Public Official Labor Unions Act, which was established in 2006, will be an important indicator that estimates the development of the labor rights of civil servants in Korea.

Although civil service labor unions have been legalized, Korea also needs effort to model civil service labor relations. Collective action and union activities by civil servants can act as a mirror of national labor relations, so now is the time for a model of cooperative group activity (Cho, 2003).

3. Work–life balance

It has not been that long since the Korean civil service started to take an interest in the quality of life of civil servants. Initial actions to improve quality of life were taken at the beginning of the Kim Daejung Administration when the government established a special task force in the Blue House to deal with improving the quality of civil servants' lives. It is not an exaggeration to say that no administration has actively dealt with quality of life from a national public personnel policy perspective since the Kim Administration.

However, there has certainly been some interest during periods of regime change in a comprehensive policy approach attempting to maintain a balanced

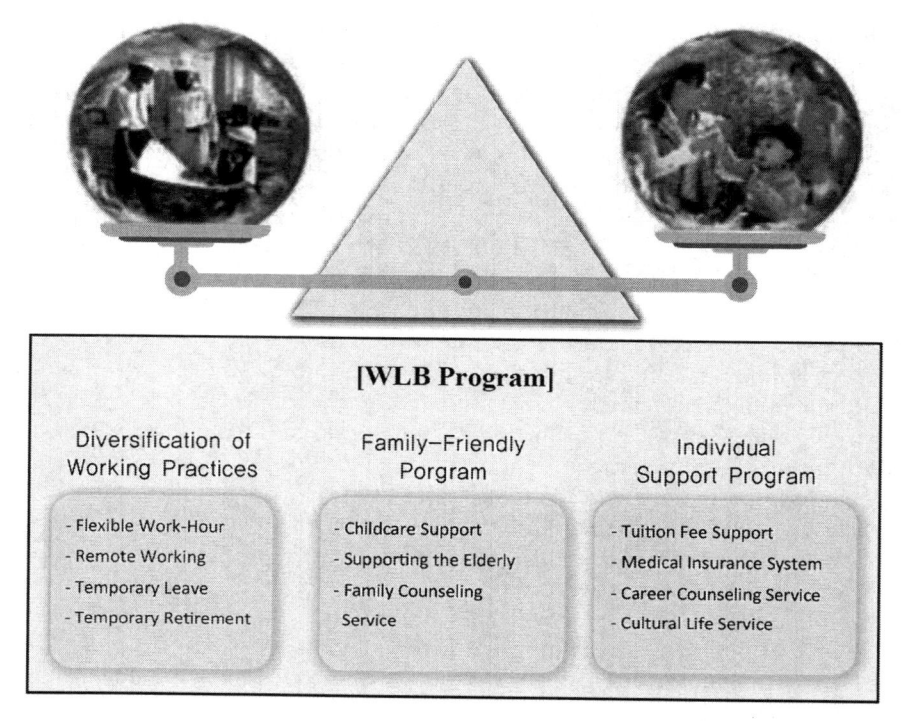

[WLB Program]

Diversification of Working Practices	Family–Friendly Porgram	Individual Support Program
- Flexible Work-Hour - Remote Working - Temporary Leave - Temporary Retirement	- Childcare Support - Supporting the Elderly - Family Counseling Service	- Tuition Fee Support - Medical Insurance System - Career Counseling Service - Cultural Life Service

Figure 5.3 Policy frame for work–life balance and the three major quality-of-life policy frameworks

quality of life for public employment, individuals, and families. This perspective is developing into the Work–Life Balance (WLB) perspective, and three major policies for the quality of life in the diverse fields of working patterns, family-friendly personnel policies, and improving the personal welfare of civil servants are being developed within the WLB frame. Figure 5.3 explains the three major policies for the quality of civil servants' lives using the WLB program.

First of all, the diversification of working patterns is developing into flexible working policies. Next, programs targeted to families are developing into what is called family-friendly personnel policy (FFPP). Lastly, programs supporting personal information are developing from the perspective of welfare and quality of work life.

The WLB policy is a system or policy that supports settling conflicts between work and life. In particular, the policy restores the control of organization members over their lives through increasing positive transfers and reducing negative transfers among different domains of life. The policy can be also defined as a system for supporting people's lives and forming a culture that balances between work and life, all of which are necessary for improving the quality of life (Kim et al., 2005).

A mandatory requirement for achieving a balance between work and life is the proper distribution of time and workload. Therefore, saving time through working efficiently is vital when converting time distributed for work to life spheres. Similarly, it is necessary to manage work efficiently when converting time for private life to other areas as well as to the sphere of work. The flexible working system aimed at civil servants allows the government and public workers to adjust their work shift or workplace so that the balance between work and life can be maintained. A flexible working system is also known to contribute to the improvement of the efficient of human resource utilization. As can be seen in Table 5.4, flexible working systems include different types such as flexible hours and working at home (Lee and Kang, 2010: 115). The Korean

Table 5.4 Types of flexible work systems in the public sector

Types	*Idea*	*Example*
Working at home	• Complete the given tasks at home, not at the office	• Tasks that can be completed individually such as the development of computer programs • Disabled, people caring for children, long distance commuters
Remote work system	• Use of mobile devices, working at places other than the office	• Tasks such as inspection and investigation
Flexible work system	• Maintain the working system of 8 hrs/day (40 hrs/wk) • Self-adjust the office-going hour (07:00–10:00)	• All tasks available • People caring for children, students who need to attend classes after work
Optional work hours	• Self-adjust working hours each day disregarding 8 hrs/day as long as the total is 40 hrs/wk	• Research position • People caring for children, students who have classes to attend after work
Intensive work system	• Maintain the total working hours (40 hrs/wk) and work less than 5 days/wk due to intensive work (e.g. work 4 days/wk if working 10 hrs/day)	• Research positions • Long-distance commuters
Core work system	• Set the core working hours (e.g. 10:00–12:00) and focus on the task to maximum ability during these hours, avoiding meetings, business trips, phone calls, etc.	• Planning organizations

Source: Lee and Kang (2010: 115).

government has recently enhanced work–family compatibility for both men and women by enforcing a flexible working system from a perspective that allows flexibility when building career. Moreover, a flexible work system implies three levels of flexibility, which are flexibility in work schedule, flexibility in workload, and flexibility in workplace. These three levels of flexibility are becoming an important institutional base that improves the work efficiency of both male and female civil servants as well as their quality of personal life.

Emphasizing the perspective of balanced work and life in the Korean civil service is becoming mandatory rather than optional. First of all, even though today's civil servants gain satisfaction from their public career, they simultaneously pursue mental space for developing their capacities as well as having enough time to spend with their family. Thus, it is necessary to broaden policy perspectives through decisively adopting American and English family-friendly personnel policies or WLB policies in order to improve quality of life in the Korean civil service. One study has shown that the level of a civil servant's satisfaction with family life and work drop significantly when their family has a sick family member (Cho and Lee, 2000). This suggests that personal family life can directly influence a civil servant's performance in the public service.

Second, the proportion of female employees in the Korean service is increasing every year, and values are changing towards individualism and family (Cho, 1997). In this sense, policies for quality of life need to change accordingly in a way that closely connects both family and public service. As of 2008, the proportion of female civil servants had exceeded 40 percent. Considering the reality that the proportion of civil servants who are working parents exceeds 50 percent, each department will have to put enormous efforts into implementing the flexible work even though it may seem to be a little late to do so.

Third, the fact that the quality of life of Korean civil servants is determined according to quality of work life (QWL) should not be overlooked. Heavy workload, low goal definition, low trust, and an oppressive bureaucratic organizational environment are some of the main factors that seem to drop the QWL of Korean civil servants.

Finally, as permanent part-time workers are starting to flow in due to the expansion of part-time work, the government has to lead the way and adjust work hours as various forms of work discretion spread. A detailed job analysis is also necessary so that no civil servants are isolated or receive unfair treatment when distributing tasks.

IV.   Lessons learned and future prospects

The importance of personnel administration in the Korean civil service is becoming stronger day by day. Until recently, the Korean civil service effectively utilized position classification, based on the rank-in-person system, and efforts have been made in the last ten years to institutionalize the social equity in personnel systems to fulfill the democratization of administration. The civil service has also been striving to understand social issues and administrative demands from a customer perspective in order to deal effectively with rapidly changing administrative demands. Plus, it has been concluded that the civil service has been putting efforts into dealing with administrative demands that prioritize the public interest rather than private interests. Although some deviant behavior has been recorded (e.g. fraud by local government workers), it is fair to say that civil servants provide a great deal of service in order to protect civil rights. However, there seems to be considerable room for developmental change in Korean personnel administration to determine the nation's future social and environmental and to adapt effectively to various future environmental changes.

1. Institutional aspect

Above all, it is projected that open public service will be emphasized even more in Korea in the future and that internal exchanges will be expanded accordingly. However, in the case of open external personnel, the career official's morale should be maintained, and the rigidity of the civil service should be complemented.

The issue of guaranteed job security is a topic that needs to be discussed from a more aggressive perspective. Korea's current job security guarantees could lead to employment reductions. Therefore, a creative system needs to be developed that can address this issue.

Civil service classification should gradually expand the position classification system's elements while effectively taking advantage of the rank-in-person system's tradition. Later, when job series is reformed, it is necessary to adjust the position system and integrate small and minor job series to improve flexibility in personnel management. In this sense, personnel management's flexibility and professionalism need to be adjusted, and it is also necessary to institutionalize the career development system.

A public institution needs to be able to conduct job analysis and process re-engineering through developed techniques. Virtual job performance, job sharing, automation of civil affairs, job expansion, mentoring, and flexible position classification need to be institutionalized in order to prepare an institutional basis for flexibility in personnel management. Establishment of the flexible work system and part-time work is definitely going to be the main task for Korean public personnel administration in the future. In particular, the conservative and collective culture of the civil service is expected to change in order to establish flexible work and part-time public employment. This implies that changes to the organizational culture and examinations of these changes need to be done on an ongoing basis.

2. Operational aspect

The diversification of the civil service screening test should not be overlooked in personnel administration. Inflation of academic background is expected to grow even more, which forecasts an increase in the unemployment rate of college graduates. The decentralization of selection rights will be enhanced, and the screening system for each department and local government is presumed to be diversified accordingly. Thus, a flexible screening system would allow a reasonable supply of manpower in accordance with aptitude and rank rather than consideration of high school graduation for civil service recruitment.

The number of women participating in the civil service as well as the number of female administrators is predicted to keep increasing exponentially. Accordingly, complementary policies need to be reorganized from a macro perspective (e.g. enhancing the administrator development process) while personnel policies promoting female participation in public administration need to be enhanced.

An individualistic public organization culture is spreading across the nation, and therefore, the issue of managing the boundary between work and life is gaining more attention. Accordingly, the issue of quality of life is going to stand out more than ever, and different benefit and welfare systems are expected to be introduced experimentally. An environment of gender equality needs to be created as declining birth rate and aging issues emerge. Establishing incentives for civil servants to have multiple children and improving the childcare environment are expected to emerge as personnel reform tasks in the future.

Multi-dimensional evaluation (also known as the 360-degree evaluation), which was once introduced, is expected to be modified in order to improve the performance and validity of the evaluation. The multi-dimensional evaluation system is also known to be highly useful as a tool for improving individual competency in organizations (Cho, 2008).

It is presumed that labor and employment relations can be improved from a dual perspective. It is likely that Korea's current dual-track labor relations system will have to be maintained and developed so that the labor-management system can be administered to create collaborative, public-sector labor relations.

Appendix

General Schedule Ranks – Administration

Occupation	*Series*	*Sub-Series*	*Ranks*						
			GS3	GS4	GS5	GS6	GS7	GS8	GS9
Administration	Correction	Correction	Third-grade official	Fourth-grade official	Subsection-chief-grade official	Junior official	Junior administrative official	Clerk official	Assistant-clerk official
	Protection	Protection							
	Prosecution	Prosecution							
	Drug Investigation	Drug Investigation							
	Immigration Control	Immigration Control							
	Railroad Police	Railroad Police							
	Administration	General Administration			Subsection-chief-grade official	Junior-official	Junior-administrative official	Clerk official	Assistant-Clerk official
		Legal							
		Finance and Economy							
		International Trade							
		Transportation							
		Labor							
		Culture and Pubic Relation							
		Education							
		Accounting							

(*Continued*)

Occupation	Series	Sub-Series	Ranks							
			GS3	GS4	GS5	GS6	GS7		GS8	GS9
	Occupation Counseling	Occupation Counseling								
	Taxation	Taxation								
	Customs	Customs								
	Social Welfare	Social Welfare								
	Statistics	Statistics								
	Librarian	Librarian								
	Audit	Audit		Comptroller	Assistant Comptroller					
	Custody/Guard	Custody			Subsection-chief-grade official	Junior-official	Junior-administrative official		Clerk official	Assistant-Clerk official
		Guard								

References

Cho, Kyung Ho. (2008). Performance of multi-dimensional evaluation system of government. *Korean Journal of Public Personnel Administration*, 7(1): 229–259.

Cho, Kyung Ho. (2003). A study of collaborative public union relations rules and procedures. *Korean Journal of Policy Science*, 7(2): 301–326.

Cho, Kyung Ho. (1997). *Public Employees' Values in the Transition Era.* (Korean) Seoul: Jibmundang.

Cho, Kyung Ho and Seon Woo Lee. (2000). Family-friendly personnel policies and occupational satisfaction. *Journal of Public Administration*, 4(1): 51–66.

CSC of Korea. (2004). *A White Paper of Public Personnel Reform.* ROK Government.

Ha, Tae Kwon et al. (1999). *Improving Public Service Classification System.* (Korean) CSC Report, 99–8.

Kim, Jeong Un et al. (2005). A study of culture comparison about leisure and quality of life. *Korean Journal of Psychology*, 19(2): 1–15.

Kim, Jung Yang. (1999). *Korean Public Personnel Administration.* (Korean) Seoul: Bobmunsa.

Lee, Minho and Jungseok Kang. (2010). *Personnel Management Reform after Corporate Governance: Change of Public Institutions.* Seoul, Korea: KIPA.

MOSPA. (2013). *A White Paper on Public Personnel Administration: 2008–2012.*

Nigro, Lloyd and Felix A. Nigro. (1994). *The Public Personnel Administration.* Itasca, IL: F.E. Peacock Publishers, Inc.

Oh, Seok Hong. (1993). *Public Personnel Administration.* (Korean) Seoul: Bakyoungsa.

Park, Chun Oh et al. (2014). *Contemporary Public Personnel Administration.* (Korean) Paju, Korea: Bobmunsa.

Park, Chun Oh and Kyung Ho Cho. (2013). Expectations and performance of Korean SES. *Korean Journal of Public Personnel Administration*, 12(1): 147–168.

Yoo, Min Bong. (1997). *Public Personnel Administration.* (Korean) Seoul: Munyoungsa.

6 Budget and financial management

Wonhee Lee

I. Development of the budget system in Korea

1. Budget perspectives

There can be two approaches to understanding the budget. One is the economic perspective, and the other is the political one. From an economic perspective, the budget is seen as a well-designed document showing the revenues and expenditures of a government. In this sense, the budget can help people understand the functions of a government. It can be a good barometer for understanding the dynamic relationship between governments and markets. On the other hand, from a political perspective, various kinds of actors are involved in the process of making a budget. In this context, many kinds of attempts can be made to analyze the level of political development through the budget-making process.

2. Stages of development of the budgetary function in Korea

Korea gained independence from Japan in 1948, and the first republican government was established. After that period, the budgetary function can be understood as developing through three stages: industrialization (1948–1987), democratization (1988–1997), and globalization (1998–present).

a) Industrialization (1948–1987)

The budget was an important instrument for initiating the development of the national economy during the rapid economic development of the 1960s and 1970s in Korea. At that time, the accumulated capital in the market was not sufficient, so government was the last resort for mobilizing capital. In this sense, budgetary priority was given to economic development.

For the government-led development strategy, the budgetary process was highly centralized through a central budget agency called the Economic Planning Board.

b) Democratization (1988–1997)

Following the democracy movement of the 1980s, the focus was placed on fiscal democratization. As political power began to shift from the president to the National Assembly, the process was opened to the public. The legal basis was revised but, as the political aspect was strengthened, attention was paid to pork barrel politics. During the 1990s, fiscal democracy was the focal concept with regard to the budgetary process.

c) Globalization (1998–present)

The financial crisis of 1997 paved new avenues for the budgetary process. First of all, budgetary priority was changed from economics to welfare. New ideologies such as transparency and participation became the focus. The Three Plus One reform was implemented in line with these political and social changes.

3. Resource allocation

There has been a dramatic change in budgetary priority. The focus was exclusively on economic development during the 1960s and 1970s. The budget was an important instrument to support the Five-Year Economic Development Plan, which began in 1962. Defense was also important during that time due to the suspended conflict on the divided peninsula after the civil war of 1950–1953.

The first change was tried in 1994 when new President Young Sam Kim was elected, who was not from the military. The last Five-Year Economic Plan was executed during his administration. In other words, there were no more Five-Year Economic Development Plans after 1996.

Table 6.1 Summary of period characteristics

	Industrialization	*Democratization*	*Globalization*
Policy orientation	• Growth • Efficiency	• Welfare • Control by legislature	• Welfare • Transparency, participation
Legal basis	• Budget Accounting Act	• Fund Management Act	• National Finance Act • National Accounting Act
Major sources of revenue	• From foreign aid to taxes	• Ear-marked tax • Special accounting and special funds	• Extra burdens, fees
Fiscal soundness	• Expenditures within revenue	• Fiscal deficit due to expenditures on SOC	• Fiscal debt due to welfare
Priority	• Economy and defense	• Welfare	• Welfare
Executive and legislative	• Executive initiative (efficiency)	• Legislative initiative (participation)	• Legislative initiative (pork barrel politics)

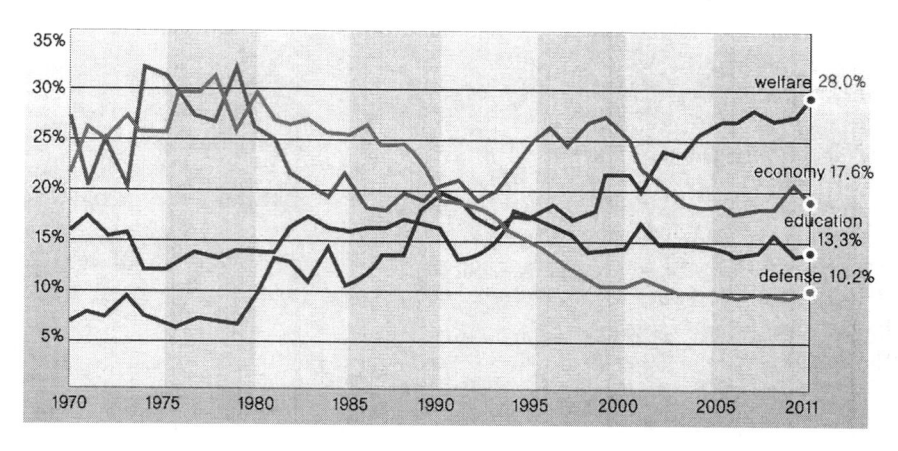

Figure 6.1 Government expenditure by sector after 1970 (%)

A radical new president, Dae Jung Kim, was elected in 2002 and there was a dramatic policy change towards welfare. Since that time, welfare has been the priority as welfare expenditures have downward rigidity.

II.   Characteristics of the budgetary system

1.   *General accounts, special accounts, and special funds*

Korean budgets fall into two categories: general accounting and special accounting. Those two categories must be approved by the Assembly, while the special funds do not need to be approved by the Assembly.

It is very important to understand the role of special funds. Special funds were widely used during the 1960s and 1970s to support economic development policy. Special funds did not need to be approved by the National Assembly during that time, and the law governing special funds was revised in 2006.

The National Finance Act of 2006

Article 4 (Classification of Accounts) (1) The State's accounts shall be classified as general accounts and special accounts. (2) General accounts shall be established for appropriating major revenues, including tax revenues, to the State's general expenditures. (3) A special account shall be established only by an Act when the State plans to operate a specific project, when it plans to hold a specific fund for management, when there is a need to manage an account of certain revenue separately from general accounts to appropriate such revenue to certain expenditure.

Article 5 (Establishment of Funds) (1) A fund may be established by an authority granted by an Act, only when the State needs to manage a specific fund for a specific purpose, in a flexible manner: provided, that no fund may be established with financial resources raised by the Government's contribution or the private sector's contribution or charges received pursuant to an Act, unless there is due authorization by any of the Acts specified in attached Table 2. (2) Any fund established pursuant to paragraph (1) may be operated independently of the revenue and expenditure budgets.

Table 6.2 Comparison of budget and funds

	Budget		Funds
	General Account	*Special Accounts*	
Uses	General fiscal activities unique to the state	• Operation of specific projects • Disbursement of specific revenues for specific expenditures	Operation of specific funds for specific purposes
Source of revenue and management structure	Free of charge projects with tax revenues	Free of charge projects and loans with taxes and copayment revenues	Loans and other specific projects with copayment and contribution revenues
Approval process	• Budget requests by line ministries • Formulation of the budget proposal by the Ministry of Strategy and Finance • Review and approval by the National Assembly		• Plan development by the fund managing entity • Consultation and adjustment with the Minister of Strategy and Finance • Review and approval by the National Assembly
Execution process	Strict legal regulations (prohibition of disbursement for any purpose other than prescribed in the budget)		Independent and flexible based on appropriateness
Link between revenue and expenditure	No link between revenue and expenditure	Specific revenues linked with specific expenditure	
Revision	Through supplementary budget		Requires approval of the National Assembly if the extent of expenditure revision exceeds 20%
Settlement	Review and approval by the National Assembly		

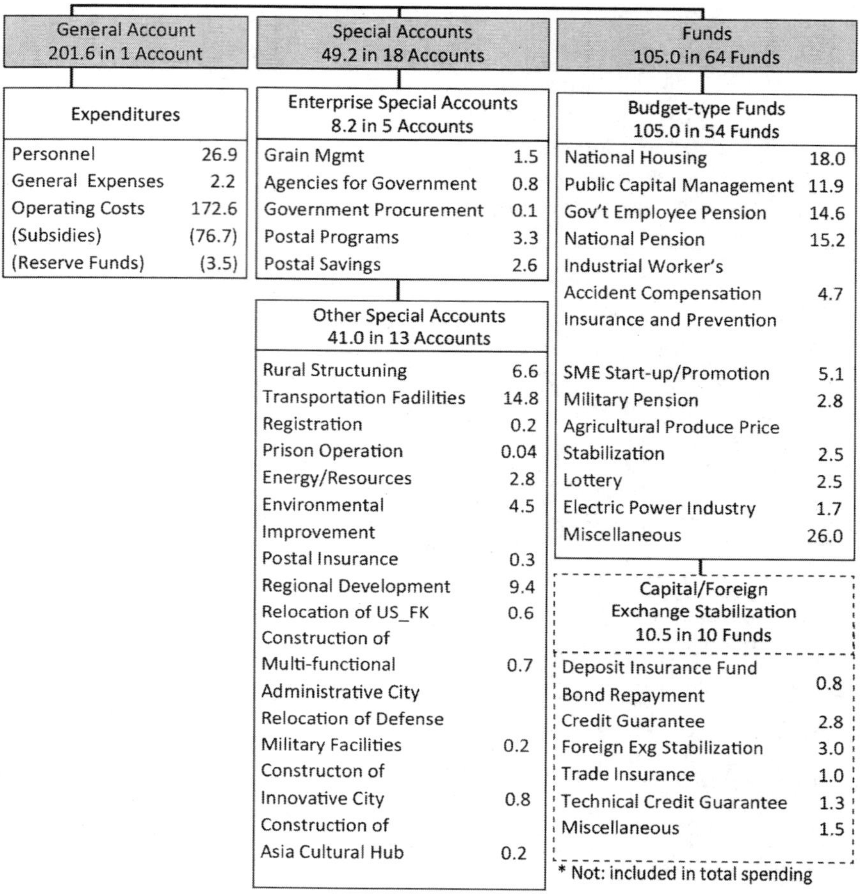

General Account 201.6 in 1 Account	Special Accounts 49.2 in 18 Accounts	Funds 105.0 in 64 Funds

Expenditures

Personnel	26.9
General Expenses	2.2
Operating Costs	172.6
(Subsidies)	(76.7)
(Reserve Funds)	(3.5)

Enterprise Special Accounts 8.2 in 5 Accounts

Grain Mgmt	1.5
Agencies for Government	0.8
Government Procurement	0.1
Postal Programs	3.3
Postal Savings	2.6

Other Special Accounts 41.0 in 13 Accounts

Rural Structuning	6.6
Transportation Fadilities	14.8
Registration	0.2
Prison Operation	0.04
Energy/Resources	2.8
Environmental Improvement	4.5
Postal Insurance	0.3
Regional Development	9.4
Relocation of US_FK Construction of Multi-functional Administrative City	0.6 0.7
Relocation of Defense Military Facilities Constructon of	0.2
Innovative City Construction of Asia Cultural Hub	0.8 0.2

Budget-type Funds 105.0 in 54 Funds

National Housing	18.0
Public Capital Management	11.9
Gov't Employee Pension	14.6
National Pension	15.2
Industrial Worker's Accident Compensation Insurance and Prevention	4.7
SME Start-up/Promotion	5.1
Military Pension	2.8
Agricultural Produce Price Stabilization	2.5
Lottery	2.5
Electric Power Industry	1.7
Miscellaneous	26.0

Capital/Foreign Exchange Stabilization 10.5 in 10 Funds

Deposit Insurance Fund Bond Repayment	0.8
Credit Guarantee	2.8
Foreign Exg Stabilization	3.0
Trade Insurance	1.0
Technical Credit Guarantee	1.3
Miscellaneous	1.5

* Not: included in total spending

Figure 6.2 Structure of public finance in Korea

Source: Ministry of Strategy and Finance (2014). The Budget System of Korea.

2. *Supplementary budget*

The fiscal year in Korea is from January 1st to December 31st. The new budget must be proposed and approved by December 31st for a new budget to start. Even so, unexpected situations not reflected in the original budget can occur during the fiscal year. In such extraordinary cases, the government can employ a supplementary budget. The supplementary budget was widely used during the 1980s and 1990s to adjust the original budget to reflect presidential priorities. The main resource was a surplus resulting from the audit. The problem was that the supplementary budget was not reviewed in the context of its expected overall impact on fiscal outcomes and tended to reduce transparency both in terms of aggregate control and strategic priority setting; as a result, the National Finance Act, newly revised in 2006, prohibits supplementary budgets in ordinary times. It can be justified, however, when managing an economic crisis.

Constitution

Article 56 [Budget Amendment]
   When it is necessary to amend the budget, the Executive may formulate a supplementary revised budget bill and submit it to the National Assembly.

The National Finance Act of 2006

Article 89 (Formulation of Supplementary Revised Budget Bills) (1) The Government may formulate any supplementary revised budget Bill if one of the following events occurs, thereby making it necessary to revise the budget already finalized: 1. A war or large-scale natural disaster breaks out; 2. A significant change in the domestic or overseas situation, such as an economic recession, mass unemployment, change in inter-Korean relations or economic cooperation occurs or is likely to occur; 3. The expenditure the State is obligated to pay pursuant to Acts and subordinate to statutes is incurred or increased.

   (2) The Government shall not allocate or execute a supplementary revised budget in advance before the budget Bill is finally adopted by a resolution of the National Assembly.

III.   Budgeting process

1.   General characteristics

The budgetary process in Korea consists of four stages – proposal, approval, implementation, and audit – which are characteristic of democratic countries.

   The executive proposes the budget draft to the National Assembly within 90 days before the beginning of the new fiscal year. During this stage, the Ministry of Strategy and Finance (MoSF), which is the central budget agency, plays a very important role in coordinating the line ministries. The proposed draft budget is reviewed and approved by the National Assembly within 30 days before the beginning of the new fiscal year.

Constitution

Article 54 [Budget]

(1) The National Assembly shall deliberate and decide upon the national budget bill.
(2) The Executive shall formulate the budget bill for each fiscal year and submit it to the National Assembly within ninety days before the beginning of a fiscal year. The National Assembly shall decide upon it within thirty days before the beginning of the fiscal year.
(3) If the budget bill is not passed by the beginning of the fiscal year, the Executive may, in conformity with the budget of the previous fiscal year, disburse funds for the following purposes until the budget bill is passed by the National Assembly:

   1. The maintenance and operation of agencies and facilities established by the Constitution or Act;
   2. Execution of the obligatory expenditures as prescribed by Act; and
   3. Continuation of projects previously approved in the budget.

The power to propose includes a somewhat unusual meaning in Korea. The executive has the overall power to formulate the budget while the National Assembly only has the power to reduce the budget.

Constitution

Article 57 [Changes of Budget Bill]
   The National Assembly shall, without the consent of the Executive, neither increase the sum of any item of expenditure nor create any new items of expenditure in the budget submitted by the Executive.

The approved budget is sent to the executive and implemented. After implementation, the budget is audited and inspected the by Board of Audit and Inspection. In this sense, budgetary cycle consists of three years.

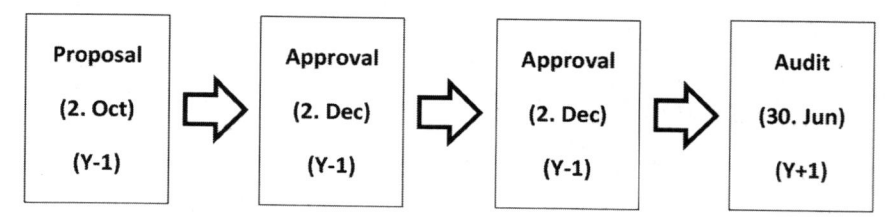

Proposal	Approval	Approval	Audit
(2. Oct)	(2. Dec)	(2. Dec)	(30. Jun)
(Y-1)	(Y-1)	(Y-1)	(Y+1)

Figure 6.3 Stages of the budget process

Table 6.3 Changes in the budgeting timeline from 2014

	2013	2014	2015	2016
Guidelines for budgeting notified (MoSF to line ministry)	April 30	April 20	April 10	March 31
Submission of budget requests (Line ministry to MoSF)	June 30	June 20	June 10	May 31
Submission of draft budget (Government to National Assembly)	October 2 (90 days before the fiscal year)	September 23 (100 days before the fiscal year)	September 13 (110 days before the fiscal year)	September 3 (120 days before the fiscal year)

However, the National Finance Act, as amended in April 2013, requires the budget proposal to be submitted 90 days before the 2013 fiscal year, 100 days in 2014, 110 days in 2015, and 120 days in 2016. This represents the heightened influence of the National Assembly.

2.   *Stages of the budgetary process*

a)   *Proposal*

The budget proposal from the executive can be made through the interaction between line ministries and the central budget agency, which is played by the MoSF. This procedure was dramatically changed through the Three Plus One reform enacted in 2004, which included a top-down system, a mid-term expenditure framework, a performance evaluation system, and a digital accounting system, which is discussed in the next section. It is important to keep in mind that planning and performance have a close relationship to the budget.

A characteristic of the Korean system is the strong power of the central budget agency. The role was given to the Economic Planning Board during the 1960s. The EPB had the rank of deputy prime minister, which meant that it was above the other ministries and had power to control them. A more important thing is that the EPB had both a planning and budgeting role. Planning and budgeting has belonged to the same body from the beginning. It was a very efficient way to support the Five-Year Economic Plan. Even though many developing counties have very ambitious long-term plans created by presidential committees, they are rarely implemented well due to the lack of funds, but it was possible in Korean through this organizational arrangement.

Table 6.4 Time table of the National Fiscal Management Plan

① Budget formation by the administration (Y − 1)	• Guidelines for National Fiscal Management Plan (Dec before the fiscal year) • Submission of Medium-term Project Plan (End of Jan) • Drafting of National Fiscal Plan (Feb–Apr) • Guidelines for Budgeting and Spending Ceilings (End of Apr) • Fiscal Strategy Meeting of the Cabinet (End of Apr) • Budget Request and Performance Plan (May–Jun) • Submission of Budget Request (End of Jun) • Drafting of the Budget Proposal (Jul–Sep) • Advisory Council on Fiscal Policy and Meeting between the cabinet and the ruling party (Sep) • Submission to the National Assembly (Oct 2)

Table 6.5 Time table of the approval by the National Assembly

② Deliberation by the National Assembly (Y − 1)	• Speech on Administrative Policy
	• Pre-evaluation of each Standing Committee
	• Comprehensive Review by the Special Committee on Budget and Accounts
	  1. Public hearing
	  2. proposal enunciation
	  3. review report by a head expert
	  4. comprehensive interpellation
	  5. review by departments
	  6. review by subcommittee on adjustment of figures
	  7. general meeting vote
	• Review and vote at plenary session (DEC 2)

b)   *Approval by the National Assembly*

The budgetary process in the Korean legislature is divided into two stages: the first stage is the preliminary review by standing committees and the second is the review by the Special Committee on Budget and Accounts.

The budget proposed by government is submitted to the legislature by October 2nd and is first reviewed by standing committees. There are 16 standing committees in the National Assembly organized according to their relevant government functions. There is no room for participation by outsiders during the budgetary review in standing committees.

After being reviewed by standing committees, the preliminary revised budget bill is transferred to the Special Committee on Budget and Accounts. The Special Committee on Budget and Accounts can make final amendments to the budget bill that will be presented to the plenary session. In this sense, the Special Committee on Budget and Accounts is the most influential power in the budgetary review process.

National Assembly Act

Article 45 (Special Committee on Budget and Accounts)

(1) In order to examine budget bills, a bill for the operation of funds and the settlement of accounts (referring to the settlement of revenues and expenditures and the settlement of fund accounts; hereinafter the same shall apply), a Special Committee on Budget and Accounts shall be established.

(2) The number of members of the Special Committee on Budget and Accounts shall be fifty. In such cases, their selection shall be made by the Speaker at the request of the National Assembly members representing each negotiating party according to the ratio of the numbers of National Assembly members belonging to the negotiating parties and that of the members of the Special Committee on Budget and Accounts.

(3) The term of the members of the Special Committee on Budget and Accounts shall be one year: provided, that the term of the members first elected after the general election of the National Assembly members shall be from the date of election to the date when it is one year after the commencement of the term of National Assembly member; and the term of members who are appointed for vacancy or reelected shall be the remaining term of the predecessor.

According to the National Assembly Act the Special Committee on Budget and Accounts must hold public hearings.

National Assembly Act

Article 84–83 (Public Hearings on Budget Bills, Fund Operation Plans, and Settlement of Accounts)

The Special Committee on Budget and Accounts shall hold a public hearing on a budget bill, a fund operation plan and settlement of accounts: provided, that in cases of a supplementary budget bill, a modified fund operation plan, or the settlement of accounts, it may be omitted by a resolution of the Committee.

In terms of the legislative budgetary process, the National Assembly Budget Office (NABO) plays the very important role of analyzing the proposed budget draft. The role of the NABO is to support the National Assembly by analyzing and evaluating issues related to the national budget, funds, and fiscal operations. The NABO was founded to help the National Assembly efficiently check and monitor the administration.

The NABO supports National Assembly members by undertaking the following responsibilities. First, it conducts research and analysis of budget bills, settlements of accounts, fund operation plans, and settlements of funds. Second, it carries out cost estimates for bills that require funds or implementation of the budget. Third, it conducts analyses and produces outlook reports on the operation of state finances and macroeconomic trends. Fourth, it conducts analyses and evaluations of major government programs and analyses of medium- to long-term fiscal demands. Fifth, it carries out studies and analyses in response to requests by National Assembly members and standing committees.

There is room for participation by the NABO in public hearings and conferences. The NABO holds public hearings to provide orientations for analyzing the government budget when the budget proposal is submitted by government to the National Assembly. The agenda is focused on very specific methods or professional issues.

c) *Implementation*

Budget implementation or execution refers to all acts that carry out national revenue and expenditure plans. It involves, not only carrying out the budget approved by the National Assembly, but also various acts to counter unexpected situations that arise during budgeting and the process of deliberation. It is necessary to allow certain flexibility to adapt to changing economic conditions while strictly adhering to the fiscal limits and the original intent of the legislation.

(1)   CONTROL MECHANISMS ADHERING TO THE SPIRIT OF THE NATIONAL ASSEMBLY

Balanced execution is important after the budget is finalized. The Ministry of Strategy and Finance deliberates on the budget allocation plan. It is carried out in sequential order after the budget is finalized: budget allocation, budget re-allocation, expenditure-incurring acts, fund allocation, and fund execution.

Table 6.6 Time table for budget implemenataion

③ Execution (Y)	• Budget allocation and re-allocation • Expenditure-incurring acts • Fund allocation • Maintenance of flexibility in execution of the budget (reserve fund, continuing expenditure, etc.) and the funds

The head of each government agency submits a budget allocation request prepared in accordance with the project management plan to the Ministry of Strategy and Finance. The Ministry of Strategy and Finance plans budget allocations based on these requests. Then the budget is allocated to the head of the central government agency for it to be executed as planned and to be subsequently reallocated to subordinate organizations.

(2) FLEXIBLE MECHANISMS FOR ADAPTING TO CHANGING SITUATIONS

The annual budget is subject to the principles of annuality and purpose restriction. First, continuing expenditures, an exception to the principle of annuality, are expenditures on multi-year projects that may be disbursed over the course of a maximum of five years as approved in advance by the National Assembly.

Second, each fund-managing entity consults with the Minister of Strategy and Finance to prepare a revised fund management plan when it intends to revise the expenditures within a main category of the fund management plan. The contents of the budget expenditure are subdivided by (1) chapters (functions), (2) sections (fields), (3) paragraphs (4) sub-paragraphs (5) items. When a revision is tried in chapters (functions), sections (fields), or paragraphs, it must be approved by the National Assembly, but revisions to sub-paragraphs and items can be done without the approval of the National Assembly.

Third, when it is anticipated that a certain expenditure in the budget will not be completely disbursed during the relevant year, such expenditure may be transferred to and used in the following year with the prior approval of the National Assembly by clearly stating the purpose of the expenditure in the revenue and expenditure budgets. This kind of carryover is prescribed in the National Finance Act.

d) Audit and inspection

Coming after implementation, the audit system is important not only for closing the account but also for preparing for the next year. It is carried out in sequential order as seen in Table 6.7.

Table 6.7 Time table of the audit

④	• Statement of Accounts submission to MoSF (End of FEB)
Settlement and evaluation (Y + 1)	• National Statement of Accounts submission to Board of Audit and Inspection (APR 10)
	• Review of Board of Audit and Inspection (APR 10–MAY 20)
	• National Statement of Accounts submission to the National Assembly (End of MAY)
	• Self-assessment of fiscal projects, in-depth evaluations of fiscal projects, performance goal management

The Board of Audit and Inspection (BAI) is important for the audit. The supreme audit institution in Korea is the Board of Audit and Inspection, which belongs to the executive, even though the constitution specifies that it is independent. The BAI has two roles: auditing and inspection. Auditing is an accounting review while inspection is related to detecting corruption.

There had been little room for participation by civil society in such investigation activities until the situation began to change in the 1990s. Public officials at the BAI are professionals, though their capacity is limited. As they are in the bureaucratic sphere, they want opinions from outside so they hold ad hoc advisory meetings. The BAI has held advisory meetings to hear civil society voices with professors, consultants, and researchers invited since the mid-1990s.

A significant development for citizen participation in auditing was made with the introduction of the "resident audit request" in 2000. A certain number of residents can request that the BAI conduct audits of specific actions of local governments that are considered against the law, in violation of the public interest, or against the rights of individuals. In addition, residential suits were introduced to enable residents to file suit against local governments with regard to the unlawful execution of the budget or accounting issues.

IV. Fiscal reform in Korea

1. Overall trend of fiscal reform

The budget was considered an instrument of presidential will supporting economic development under the authoritarian regimes from 1961 until the late 1980s, so there were not any significant fiscal modernization reforms. Many meaningful fiscal reforms have been tried since the democratization movement in 1987. The trend has been towards strengthening transparency, participation, and accountability.

2. Three plus one fiscal reform of 2004

The Korean government attempted to reform the budgetary process and its structure to allocate public resources more efficiently. Both the demand for social welfare and the sharp increase in the national debt increased the importance of managing the public debt. The demand from civil society organizations for participation in the budgeting process has also highlighted the importance of fiscal transparency.

To meet public demands, the government began to implement significant budgetary reforms in 2004 called the "Three Plus One reforms," which included the introduction of the National Fiscal Management Plan, top-down budgeting, performance management, and digital accounting. Simultaneous implementation of the interrelated reforms proved to be very effective. All the budgetary reforms were aided by the implementation of the digital IT system, which enabled the public to access budget information.

Table 6.8 Major trends in fiscal reform in Korea

1961–1987	Authoritarian regimes
1987	Democratic transition with direct presidential elections
Since 1987	Budget transparency improves marginally with enhanced review of budget by the National Assembly
1993	Introduction of real-name financial transaction system
1995	Restoration of local autonomy, with election of governors/mayors and provincial/local councils
1996	Enactment of the Freedom of Information Act
1997	Financial crisis; election of opposition candidate, Kim Dae-jung, as president
1998–2002	Improvement in budget transparency, e-government, reform of corporate governance
1998	Introduction of budget efficiency awards
1999	Introduction of Preliminary Feasibility Study in major national projects
2000	Introduction of Resident Audit Request system
2001	Enhancement of Basic Law for Management of Special Fund
2002	Election of a reform-minded president, Roh Moo-hyun
2003–2007	Improvement in budget transparency and participation
2003	Establishment of the National Assembly Budget Office
2004	Three Plus One reforms
2005	Establishment of the Audit and Inspection Research Institute
2005	Amendment of the Local Fiscal Act, which provides the legal basis for participatory budgeting
2005	Opening of a Call Center for Budget Waste Claims at each ministry
2006	Enactment of National Fiscal Act that provides legal basis for the Three Plus One reforms and public participation

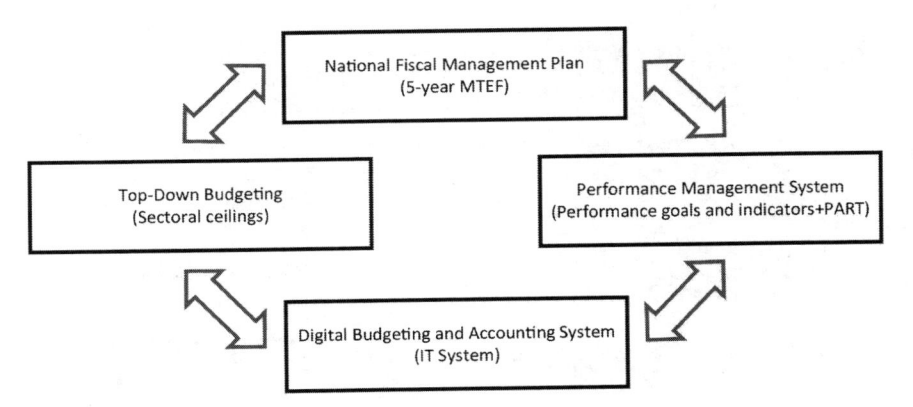

Figure 6.4 Three plus one reform of 2004

The government organized the Budget and Accounting System Reinvention Office to design a new system in consultation with the Ministry of Planning and Budget, the Ministry of Finance and Economy, the Ministry of Government Administration and Home Affairs, and the Board of Audit and Inspection. Many studies have been carried out to set the direction of the new system and prepare detailed plans since the Budget and Accounting System Reinvention Office was established in May 2004. The new governance structure was an efficient way to implement an audacious challenge.

This reform includes an innovative change in budgeting institutions, systems, and behavior. The Three Plus One reform was adopted to overcome issues with the yearly budget, centralized and authoritarian process, input orientation, and dispersed information. It was carried out by a special committee consulting the president, The Committee for Governmental Innovation and Local Decentralization.

a) *The National Fiscal Management Plan*

The National Fiscal Management Plan (NFMP) was introduced to replace the traditional Five-Year Economic Development Plan. The Korean government made Five-Year Economic Development Plans to implement the government-led development strategy from 1962 to 1997. However, as the market economy matured and democracy was embedded, the government-initiated Five-Year Economic Development Plan was officially discarded in 1997 though there was widespread demand for a new macro-economic control mechanism after Korea suffered from financial crisis in 1997.

The NFMP was introduced in this context. The NFMP is a basic plan that represents an aggregate plan for fiscal management. The NFMP is a five-year fiscal management plan designed to present national policy visions and directions as well as sectoral expenditure programs in a medium-term perspective. The NFMP has the following characteristics. First, it is a rolling plan. The plan is subject

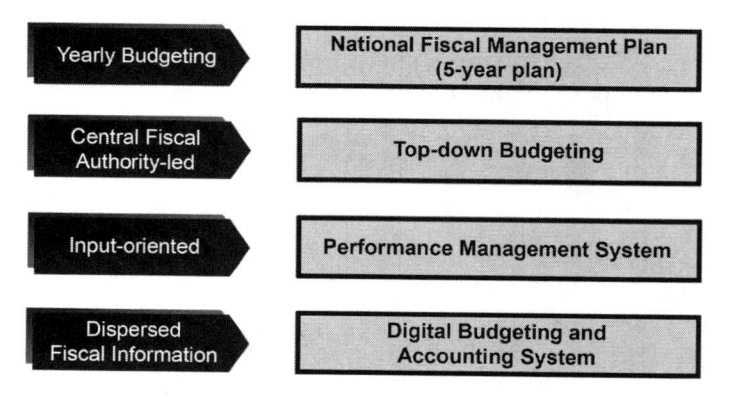

Figure 6.5 Policy orientation of fiscal reform

to adjustment each year. Second, wide participation, including from NGOs and experts, is permitted from the initial formulation stage. Third, it is submitted to the National Assembly as an obligatory reference for budget deliberation.

The NFMP is scheduled to be formulated from February to June. Public hearings are held in the last stage. The hearings are divided into nine sessions in 2014: macro budgetary policy, local finance, the welfare budget, the education budget, the industry support budget, the agricultural budget, and the R&D budget. Each of the nine sessions is attended by about six participants who included professors, researchers, and experts representing civil society and the private sector. The hearings are open to the public and broadcast on TV.

b) The top-down process

The NFMP has a close relationship with top-down budgeting. Before adopting the top-down system, the central budget agency was fully authorized to allocate public spending. It can be said that the budget for each project was determined wholly by the central budget agency. This, however, created perverse incentives for moral hazards on the part of line ministries. They requested many projects for no valid reason and often inflated the total amount required, anticipating substantial cuts by the central budget agency. The line ministries did not worry much about performance because there was no room for performance reviews by or feedback from the over-burdened central budget agency.

After the adoption of top-down budgeting, the budgetary process was divided into two steps. In the first stage, the central budget agency sets ceilings by sector. In the second stage, line ministries allocate the budget for programs in detail within the ceilings.

Figure 6.6 shows the new process of the resource allocation according to the top-down method. The national plan and budget are effectively connected with each other in accordance with the ceilings authorized by the cabinet in this

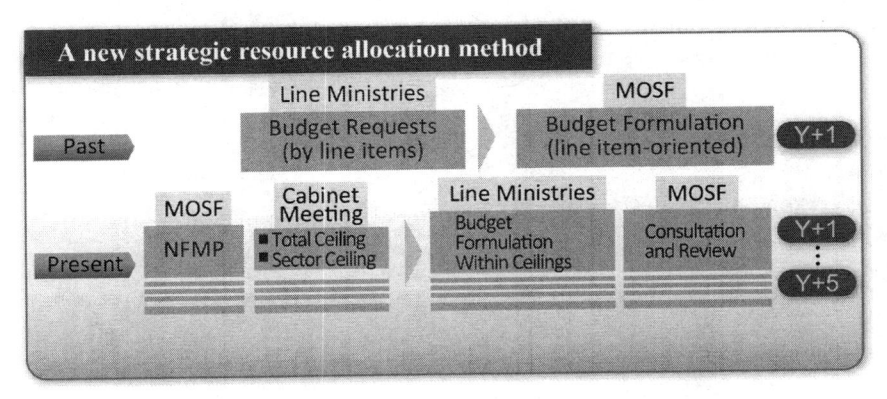

Figure 6.6 The process of resource allocation under the top-down method

Source: MoSF (2009).

system. The budgetary process within bureaucracy was considered a black box before the introduction of this system, but outsiders can now understand the internal process, and such materials between ministries are open to the public.

c) *Performance management*

It was difficult to understand the detailed contents of projects under the old budget system. Fraud, waste, and abuse were not easily noticed. It was widely accepted that the budget was confined within annual projects. The audit was for screening the estimated amount and the implemented amount, not real performance. As there was no performance evaluation process, the budget was considered a blueprint that was only useful for the central budget agency.

Following the introduction of performance management, the main programs and projects are subject to review every three years. The procedure is divided into two stages: self-evaluation by line ministries and meta-evaluation by MoSF. Line ministries carry out program monitoring and program review, which is called self-assessment. There is supposed to be an evaluation committee when each line ministry conducts its self-evaluation with about 20 members included on the committee. Participation is thus open to the public, and committee members have strong power to influence the budgetary projects in the process of deciding the evaluation. Thus, the decision is not limited exclusively to bureaucratic politics but extends to the broader policy community. Then the central budget agency carries out a meta-evaluation, and the results are reflected in the budget for the subsequent year. The Korea Institute of Public Finance, a public think-tank funded by the government, supports the meta-evaluation. Finally, the government performance evaluation report is submitted to the National Assembly.

All of these processes are open to the public on the MoSF website. Citizens can learn about budgetary performance on the Internet. Furthermore, participation is open to experts and NGOs during program monitoring, to review by line ministries, and to program evaluation by the central budget agency.

The MoSF provides a standardized checklist for self-assessment reporting. The checklist contains questions on program design, program implementation, and actual performance and adopts an input–output model, design–planning management, and results-based accountability.

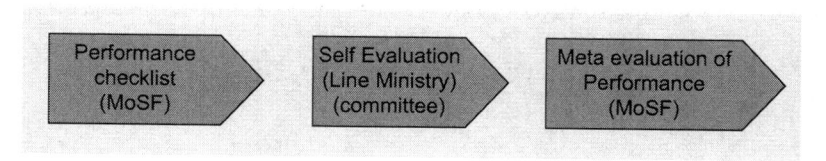

Figure 6.7 The process of performance evaluation
Source: MoSF (2009).

Table 6.9 Scheme of performance evaluation

Design and planning (30)	I.	Program purpose
	II.	Rationale for government spending
	III.	Duplication with other programs
	IV.	Efficiency of program design
	V.	Relevance of performance objectives and indicators
	VI.	Relevance of performance targets
Management (20)	I.	Monitoring efforts
	II.	Obstacles of program implementation
	III.	Implementation as planned
	IV.	Efficiency improvement or budget saving
Results and accountability (50)	I.	Independent program evaluation
	II.	Results
	III.	Satisfaction of citizens
	IV.	Utilization of evaluation results

d)   *Digital brain*

A new infrastructure was created to support the above three fiscal reforms (NFMP, top-down system, performance management).

(1)   REFORMING GOVERNMENT BUDGET CLASSIFICATIONS

The first task was to introduce a program-budgeting system based on performance management. The previous budget system was organized by line items focused on inputs into the unit item within a program and on control rather than on performance and the results of individual programs.

Through the reorganization of the program-budgeting system for policy programs and performance management, individual programs are able to take the central role in all fiscal processes including budget formulation, execution, account settlement, and performance evaluation. This implies the preparation of a fundamental fiscal management frame with the principles of autonomy, responsibility, and performance.

(2)   DOUBLE-ENTRY BOOKKEEPING AND THE ACCRUAL BASIS

The second task was to introduce a double-entry bookkeeping system and accrual accounting system instead of single-entry bookkeeping and cash-based accounting. Accrual accounting focuses on the changes made to the economic resources by recognizing earned economic resources as revenue and consumed resources as expenses. Double-entry bookkeeping is an accounting method that records each transaction as both a credit and a debit in a ledger to measure changes in assets, liabilities, and net assets.

Therefore, government can forecast and diagnose mid- and long-term fiscal risk and soundness. In addition, a comprehensive fiscal stance can be investigated by recognizing assets and debt, and government can improve the credibility of accounting information and can strengthen internal control through self-inspection.

(3) INTEGRATED INFORMATION SYSTEM

The last task was to develop an integrated finance information system for the real-time utilization, analysis, and reproduction of financial information based on advanced information technology. It integrates the budget formulation system of the central government and connects every financial system including local finance, local education finance, and public entities.

The Digital Budget and Accounting System is a government fiscal activity applied to all financial processes including budget formulation, execution, accounting, performance management, and fiscal information.

Thus, fiscal expenditure efficiency and transparency will be increased, and reasonable financial policy decision making can be achieved through analysis based on accurate and timely fiscal information.

(4) IT INFRASTRUCTURE

Information and communications technology in Korea has developed significantly since the 1990s. As a result of information and communications technologies (ICT) development, e-government has been implemented in public administration overall. The Digital Budget and Accounting System was implemented in line with the development of ICT under budgetary reform plans. The digital budget system enables more accurate analysis of fiscal data and information in real time with timely support for policy formulation and the decision-making process.

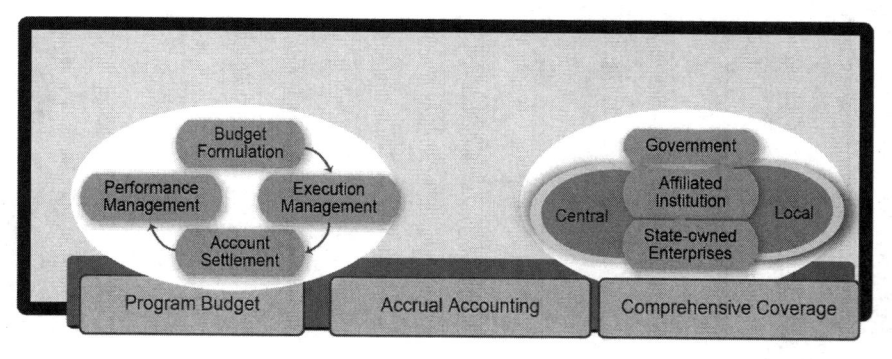

Figure 6.8 Digital budget and accounting system
Source: MoSF (2009).

3. Lessons learned from fiscal reform

After the financial crisis of 1997, the Korean government publicly announced the introduction of an accrual-based national accounting system in May 1998. The Three Plus One reform was put in place in 2004. The results were the National Finance Act in 2006 and the National Accounting Act in 2007. Participation, transparency, and accountability were stipulated under the National Finance Act. The National Accounting Act stipulated that a double-entry bookkeeping and accrual-based accounting system take effect in the central government starting on January 1, 2009.

Korea has experienced dramatic changes in transparency and participation since the democratic transition and the changes accelerated during the early 2000s. On the one hand, enhanced transparency and public participation in the budgetary process is a result of deepening democracy. On the other hand, budgetary participation and transparency has contributed to the deepening of democracy.

Some characteristics can be inferred from fiscal reform in Korea. First, the Three Plus One reform was implemented at the same time. The new system, including planning, performance management, and top-down, have had a synergistic effect. The Korean government devised a road map managing the time schedule. Second, the fiscal reform was implemented in a very short period of time. By then, there had been numerous academic studies on the topic, and civil society offered many ideas. As such, the new government tried to coordinate and harmonize agendas that had already been raised. Third, it was very important to utilize the IT system. The Korean government promoted infrastructure for the purposes of fiscal reform by using e-government. The three reform systems (planning, performance, and ceiling) were implemented autonomously. Fourth, the performance management system was reinforced. This system is related to the feedback system. The results of performance indicators are important as back up data for budget decision making. Fifth, budgetary classification changed from line items to programs and activities. This system made the budget more readable and transparent.

Even so, there are still many barriers to overcome. Institutions have inertial pressures to return to the familiar past. This is why people should watch what is happening with the budgetary process. It is the duty of all taxpayers to guarantee fiscal democracy.

References

Kim, John and Nowook Park. 2007. "Performance budgeting in Korea," *OECD Journal on Budgeting*, 7(4), 1–11.

Ministry of Strategy and Finance. 2009. Global Financial Crisis and Role of Korean Public Finance.

Ministry of Strategy and Finance. 2011. Fiscal Reform and Financial Management Information System in Korea. http://www.mosf.go.kr

Ministry of Strategy and Finance. 2014. The Budget System of Korea.

You, Jong-sung and Wonhee Lee. 2013. "A Mutually Reinforcing Loop: Budget Transparency and Participation in South Korea." In *Open Budgets: The Political Economy of Transparency, Participation, and Accountability*, edited by Sanjeev Khagram, Archon Fung, and Paolo de Renzio. Brookings Institution Press, pp. 105–129.

7 Performance management in Korea

Prospects and challenges

Seok-Hwan Lee

I. Performance in the public sector: how much can measurement cover government activities?

The issue of government performance has long been a subject of debate among scholars and practitioners in the public sector. While the objectives of government are difficult to measure, people have tried to measure what government achieves against its targets. At the same time, people have also worked to identify what makes government productive and effective.

Performance has multiple levels according to Holzer and Lee (2014): individual performance, group performance, and organizational performance. They argue that each level of performance can contribute to higher levels, thereby reaching organization-wide performance.

Furthermore, the term performance has been the subject of extensive discussions of teamwork-based organization, balanced performance measurement, and performance-based management and budgeting. This also means government performance can be investigated from multiple angles. In this regard, it is possible to talk about the term performance in a different way than discussed here. The literature concerning public-private distinctions (Buchanan, 1974a, 1974b; Rainey, Pandey, and Bozeman, 1975; Rainey, Backoff, and Levine, 1976; Rainey, 1983) maintain in a consistent way that compared to the private sector, public-sector goals are more complex, and therefore progress is more difficult to measure. The motivational bases of public employees are different and the layers of rules and regulations often prevent public employees from improving the general public welfare in a timely manner.

It is noteworthy that rules and regulations in the public sector are necessary to protect fundamental rights such as the life, liberty, and property of the general public in a democratic society. Any efficiency-oriented values should be preceded by those fundamental democratic values.

Recognizing those prospects and challenges of performance management, this chapter narrows the focus into the Korean government's performance management at the organizational level, including both central and local entities.

II.   Theories and models of performance improvement in the public sector

1.   *Performance as a comprehensive concept*

The literature argues that performance management is an improvement effort process where sequential activities are interconnected. These include top management support, committed people at all levels, a performance measurement system, employee training, reward structures, community involvement, feedback and correction on budget-management decisions (Buntz, 1981; McGowan, 1984; Greiner, 1986; Halachmi and Holzer, 1986; Werther, Ruch, and McClure, 1986; Holzer and Callahan, 1998). It is important, therefore, to build performance management capacities for performance improvement.

While the terms productivity and performance are intermingled with each other, Halachmi and Holzer (1986) view productivity improvement as an open system. As they posit,

Organizations obtain inputs (e.g., mission requirements as defined by law or public policy; demands for existing services, products or procedures; resources, including materials, budgets and personnel), plans, and schedules from their environment and transform them (using processes or procedures) into outputs (e.g., products or services for individuals and other organizations) that are released back into the environment. Those outputs, in turn, generate feedback regarding performance- feedback that may affect subsequent inputs, processes and procedures. Productivity improvement can, therefore, be perceived as a desired relationship among the components of a given system, one that improves the survivability of the system as such.

(Halachmi and Holzer, 1986, pp. 5–6)

Buntz (1981) argues that productivity requires a variety of factors including technology, staff ability, and motivation and environmental factors such as public attitudes, policy shifts, and client characteristics. In addition, Holzer and Callahan (1998) suggest a comprehensive public-sector productivity improvement model where managing for quality, developing human resources, adapting technologies, building partnerships, and measuring performance combine to improve productivity in the public sector.

2.   *Performance management models: MBO and BSC*

Drucker (1954), while mentioning importance of Management by Objectives (MBO), emphasizes that MBO must measure both tangible and intangible goals. According to Drucker, the goals of an organization have to be measured in eight areas: (1) market standing, (2) innovation, (3) productivity, (4) physical and financial resources, (5) profitability, (6) managerial performance and development, (7) workforce performance and attitude, and (8) public responsibility.

Following Drucker's MBO, Kaplan and Norton (1992) suggested the performance management model called the Balanced Score Card (BSC) which measured four dimensions (customer perspectives, financial perspectives, internal process perspectives, learning and growth perspectives). Based on their experience consulting with CEOs in many successful organizations, they concluded that effective CEOs do not make important decisions simply based on a financial perspective. Effective CEOs place an emphasis on how their customers see them (customer perspective), how they look to their stakeholders (financial perspective), what they must excel at (internal process perspective), and how their employee's capacity are increasing (learning and growth perspective). In other words, they considered balanced information when they make important decisions that require a high level of risk in uncertain situations.

3.   *Importance of citizen-driven government performance*

Citizens are the key to government performance and productivity in every dimension. Many scholars agree that productive government is responsive government and that responsiveness requires government at all levels to seek how citizens feel about current public services and conditions in their neighborhoods (Schachter, 1997; Geczi, 2007; Mathers, 2008; Robbins, Simonsen, and Feldman, 2008).

There have been a variety of perspectives on how the concept "citizen" is to be defined among practitioners and scholars in the public sector. Some scholars argue that "citizens" should be treated as "customers" to improve government services. Other scholars argue that "citizens" should be viewed as "owners" who make a final judgment on how government is doing as well as have the right to be informed about every activity done by governments (Schachter, 1997; Denhardt and Denhardt, 2000; Vigoda, 2002). It should be noted that there is a growing number of scholars and practitioners placing more emphasis on the "owner" concept for citizens. Where "active citizen participation" is regarded as an important element for improving services in the public sector, the fundamental idea is that citizens are owners, not customers.

Both customers and owners can also get involved in the process of producing services as co-producers, while providing their opinions to the government as final users. However, when citizens are viewed as customers, citizens do not have to show interest in every service provided by government, while government focuses only on people who are getting direct services. Meanwhile, citizens as owners should be able to tell government how they are doing rather than simply evaluating services in terms of what government is doing.

Much of the literature points out that decision making by public managers without public participation is ineffective (Schachter, 1997; Weeks, 2000; Irvin and Stansbury, 2004; Glaser, Yeager, and Parker, 2006). Although much has been discussed about the importance of citizen engagement, little has been discussed about how citizen engagement contributes to improving government decision making, thereby improving performance and productivity in government at all levels.

4. *Importance of performance management capacity*

In sum, it is very important to have performance management capacity for performance improvement. In this regard, Holzer and Zalk's (see Holzer, 1992, pp. 7–8) capacity building model of ten steps provides a very useful guideline for productivity improvement. They suggest obtaining top-management support, locating models, identifying promising areas, building a team, planning the project, collecting program data, modifying project plans, expecting problems, implementing improvement actions, and evaluating and publicizing results. The step-by-step process is as follows:

> *Step 1. Clarifying Goals and Obtaining Support.* Productivity programs must agree upon, and have commitments to, reasonable goals and objectives, adequate staff and resource support, and organizational visibility. The full cooperation of top management and elected officials is a prerequisite to success.
>
> *Step 2. Locating Models.* Because productivity is an increasing priority of government, existing projects can suggest both successful paths and ways to avoid potential mistakes. Models are available on the Internet, in the professional literature, at conferences, etc.
>
> *Step 3. Identifying Promising Areas.* New productivity programs might select as targets those functions continually faced with large backlogs, slipping deadlines, high turnover, or many complaints as a means of building a successful track record. Improved morale, training, or working conditions might offer a high payoff because personnel costs are the largest expenditure for most public agencies. Organizations might also target functions in which new techniques, procedures, or emerging technologies seem to offer promising payback.
>
> *Step 4. Building a Team.* Productivity programs are much more likely to succeed as bottom-up entities rather than top-down or externally directed entities. Productivity project teams should include middle management, supervisors, employees, and union representatives. They should also include citizens, clients, and representatives of advocacy groups. If employees and citizens are involved in looking for opportunities, then they are likely to suggest which barriers or obstacles need to be overcome: what tasks can be done more efficiently, dropped, or simplified; which workloads are unrealistically high or low.
>
> *Step 5. Planning the Project.* Team members should agree on a specific statement of scope, objectives, tasks, responsibilities, and time frames. This agreement should be detailed as a project management plan, which should then be updated and discussed on a regular basis?

Step 6. Collecting Program Data. Potentially relevant information should be defined broadly and might include reviews of existing databases, interviews, budgets, and studies by consultants or client groups. A measurement system should be developed to collect data on a regular basis, and all data should be supplied to the team for periodic analysis. The validity and usefulness of such information must be constantly monitored.

Step 7. Modifying Project Plans. Realistic decisions, based on continuing team discussions of alternative approaches and data, must be made about program problems, opportunities, modifications, and priorities. For instance, would a problem be solved best through more intensive use of technology, improved training, better supervision, or improved incentives?

Step 8. Expecting Problems. Projects are more likely to succeed if they openly confront and then discuss potential misunderstandings, misconceptions, slippages, resource shortages, client and employee resistance, and so on. Any such problem, if unaddressed, can cause a project to fail.

Step 9. Implementing Improvement Actions. Implementation should be phased in on a modest basis and without great fanfare. Projects that are highly touted, but do not then deliver as expected, are more likely to embarrass top management (and political supporters). Projects that adopt a low profile are less likely to threaten key actors, especially middle management and labor.

Step 10. Evaluating and Publicizing Results. Measurable success, rather than vague claims, is important. Elected officials, the press, and citizen groups are more likely to accept claims of success if they are backed up by hard data. "Softer" feedback can then support such claims. Particularly important in providing evidence of progress are timely data that reflect cost savings, additional services, citizen satisfaction, independent evaluations of service levels, and reductions in waiting or processing times (Holzer, 1992, p. 2–3).

III.   Performance management initiatives in Korea

5.   *Innovation management and its link to performance management*

Responding to the turbulent environment surrounding the public sector, the Korean government launched the so-called innovation management initiative across the public sector in 2003 when the Roh Moohyun Administration took office. The initiative's scope was comprehensive, thereby affecting government at all levels. To make it happen, the Blue House gave the Ministry of Public Administration and Local Autonomy the power to execute innovation management initiatives and to monitor the efforts made by each government body in the public sector. As a major driving force in making the initiative a success, the Blue House believed that performance management should be done in a systematic way to have government focus on innovation in every aspect of delivering public services. The main objective of performance management at that time was to let government agencies have a customer focus. Citizens were not customers in a strict sense, but the Blue House wanted governments to learn more about what citizens really wanted to get from the government. As part of the effort, performance management and evaluation began to receive great attention from both scholars and practitioners in the Korean public sector.

6. Introducing performance management to government at all levels

Before the performance management concept was introduced, public officials had no idea about what vision, strategic goals, core values, and key performance indicators really mean. The Ministry of Government Administration and Home Affairs (MOGAHA) had to spend a significant amount of time educating and training public officials in performance management as well as the need for performance management in the public sector.

At the initial stage, public officials got together to discuss their organizations' missions, visions, strategic goals, performance goals, and key performance indicators after a workshop led by university professors and experts in consulting firms. They learned the so-called cascading procedure in which goals are set from top to bottom. Once an organization's vision was set up the strategic goals followed. Those goals were followed by performance goals, which are narrowed down (see Figure 7.1). The first set of performance indicators that public officials found were mostly output indicators. They were afraid that outcome indicators, despite their importance, might give themselves a disadvantage when their performance is evaluated based on the achievement according to the

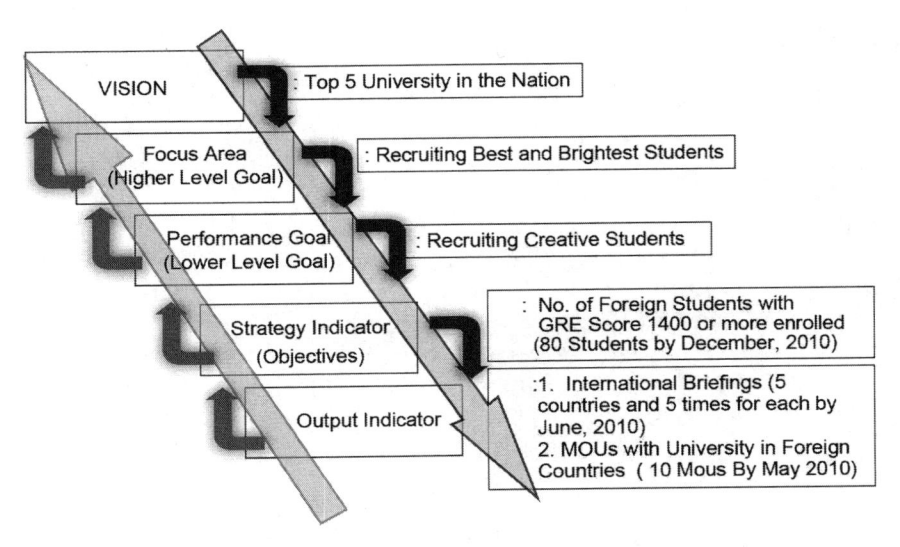

Figure 7.1 Framework for performance measurement and management system

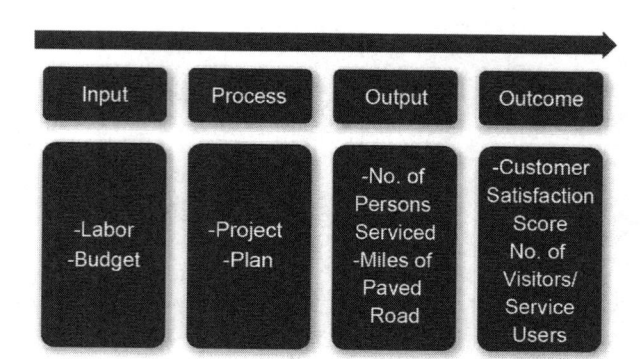

Output: What you produce, What you do
Outcome: What you achieve, Why you do

Figure 7.2 Structure of performance indicators

indicators. They preferred not to have outcome measures as they are difficult to control, so the experts had to persuade public managers to have positive feelings about outcome indicators that lead people to know why they are doing their jobs (see Figure 7.2).

As time went on, public managers began to realize the importance of outcome measures and came to think about how public employees were encouraged to put outcome indicators on the table. The Ministry of Public Administration and Local Autonomy thought that evaluating the degree of challenge and difficulty of the indicators, in addition to evaluating the achievement of the targets, would help people concentrate on outcome indicators. In other words, how challenging the measures were and how difficult the measures were to achieve were included in evaluation items at the department level in government organizations.

7. Structure of performance evaluation in Korean public sector

Performance management and evaluation in the Korean public sector can be categorized into three levels: central, local, and public entities. At the central level, performance evaluations are led by a government performance evaluation committee where the prime minister and one nominated private-sector senior expert (usually a university professor) co-preside over the committee. Following the Government Performance and Results Act (GPRA) in the US, the Korean government initiated a similar law in 2006 called the Government Performance Evaluation Act. According to the Act, the committee of 15 members, including 3 ministers, is in charge of evaluating the performance of central government, local governments, and public entities (see Figure 7.3).

All of the central government is supposed to submit to the committee an annual performance review regarding both a performance plan and the specified

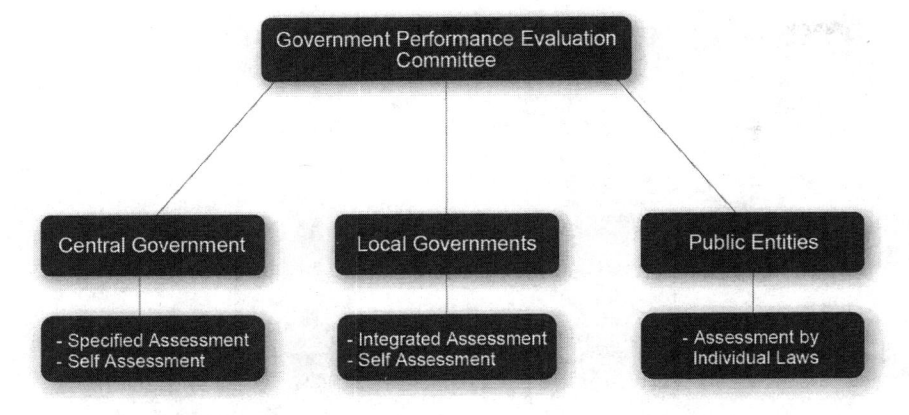

Figure 7.3 Government performance evaluation committee structure

tasks assigned to each entity. Overall, the committee is in charge of monitoring and giving feedback to each agency concerning performance in the public sector. It is to be noted, however, that the result of the performance evaluation is not really linked to next year's performance budget. Furthermore, a low level of performance does not really affect the president's decision as to whether or not to retain top management. Central government agencies pay attention to performance evaluation results as they are reported to the president, but performance information still needs to be utilized more for controlling ministries as well as for improving performance.

Each government at the local level is to conduct a self-assessment of their performance in which a small number of evaluation committee members are involved in local areas. Then these local governments are investigated and evaluated by an integrated group composed of evaluation experts with support from the MOGAHA. Final reviews then go to the government performance evaluation committee for final confirmation.

The committee is also in charge of evaluating the performance of public entities in a limited scope. The performance of these entities is heavily investigated on an annual basis by the large-scale evaluation group under the support of the Ministry of Strategy and Finance on a separate basis. The results of the performance evaluation do affect Blue House decisions on whether or not to retain top management has to be continued unlike for the central-level government.

8.   *Government 3.0 Project and efforts for eliminating barriers among public agencies*

The Park Keunhye Administration declared the so-called Government 3.0 Project when President Park took office in 2013 on the belief that providing customized

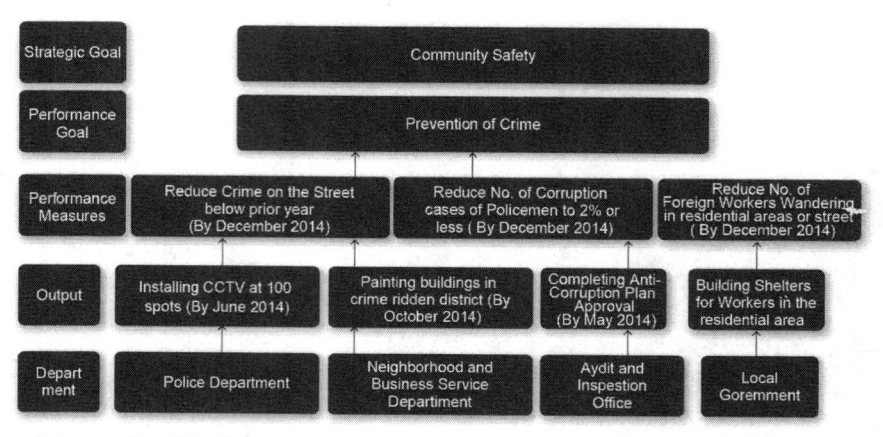

Performance Oivne Police Department Chief

Figure 7.4 Cooperation for achieving organization's goal beyond boundaries (UOFO)

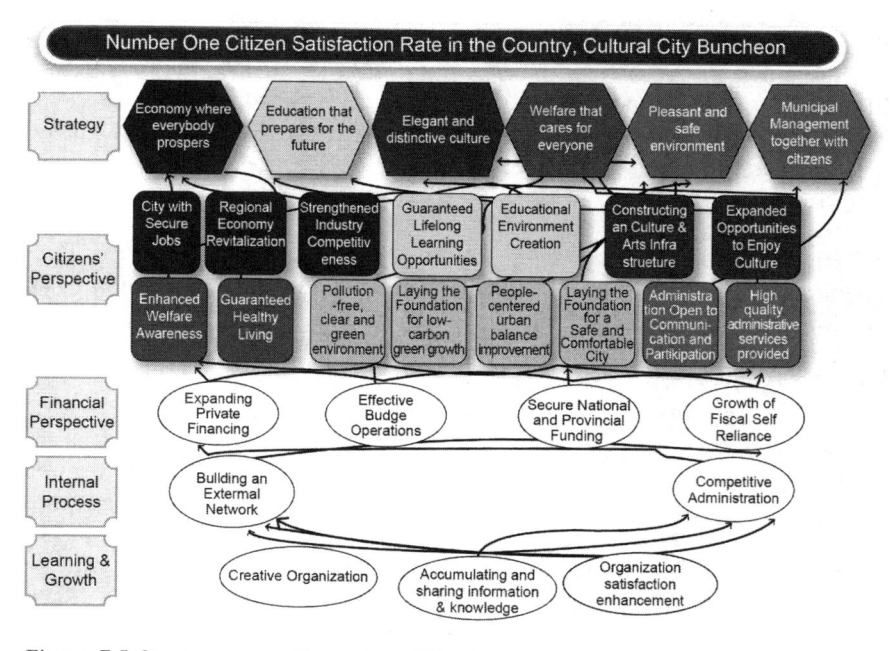

Figure 7.5 Strategy map of the city of Bucheon

public service is critical for enhancing the level of responsibility to citizens and that cooperation and coordination among related departments and agencies are key to achieving upper-level goals. In such an effort, several local governments and public agencies focused on performance management to lead agencies to look beyond their boundaries to get to their goals. The new concept developed by Lee (2008), unreasonable objectives-focused organization (UOFO),[1] was introduced, and people realized that performance management is for managing the white space on the organizational chart. In the UOFO concept, developing performance indicators helps an agency find partner agencies and external departments (see Figure 7.4). As Figure 7.5 indicates, specific multiple performance indicators can be developed under upper-level goals, and these indicators show that multiple organizations have to work together. It should be mentioned that the so-called performance owner has to initiate the process and that top management has to give power to a performance owner agency to evaluate people working together from different agencies that receive requests for cooperation. In doing so, the traditional type of hierarchical organizational structure can be a barrier, but the realization of cross-functional organizations has to be done for a high-performance organization. This UOFO type performance management is now at the initial stage in several organizations, and real performance is expected to come out about a year later.

9. Citizen-driven government performance (the story of the city of Bucheon)

There has been a noteworthy practice at the local level in efforts to disseminate performance management and evaluation across the Korean public sector. The idea was that government performance not only has to be initiated by public officials but it is also has to be agreed to and consulted by citizens.

The mayor clearly defined the organization's vision and strategy after implementing the BSC in 2005. All officials, including the mayor, use it as a strategic management system recognizing the BSC as a system compatible with the organization's strategy formulation and goal achievement. Bucheon was the first local government in Korea to implement the BSC, even implementing it a year before the central government.

In order to put the idea of citizen-driven government performance into practice, Bucheon tried to have citizens directly participate in core strategy establishment, performance indicator development, performance evaluation, results application, and other processes.

Bucheon is also planning to implement the so-called performance objective (CSF) owner system, which enables the city to align a variety of objectives to the city's vision to be the "Number One City in Citizen Satisfaction, Cultural City Bucheon."

The most distinct factor in Bucheon's strategy implementation and goal achievement was strengthening its relationship with the citizens. Bucheon conducts a citizen survey on an annual basis to see if the city is targeting the right performance indicators that citizens also recognize in importance and priority. Questionnaires in the annual survey are administered to both the general public and targeted citizens in each focus area. Each department has different customers in a sense. Therefore, departments pay attention to whether or not their performance indicators meet citizen needs. When department indicators lose support from citizens, there is no need to keep allocating the budget to related tasks and departments, but departments should find new indicators whose importance citizens can agree on in the city's administration.

Performance indicators can be said to be the language for communicating between the city government and the citizens. Bucheon annually measures and reflects on the citizens' awareness of performance indicators through surveys. The mayor particularly emphasizes communication with citizens. Bucheon communicates with different levels of society through the citizen-targeted Citizen's Forum, Citizen's Communication Committee, and the Post-It Forum on the wall of the Mayor's office and, by building CRM, managing a customer group of over 150,000 citizens.

IV.   Lessons learned

There has been considerable improvement in terms of the content of performance indicators and strategy maps in Korean government bodies based on the tremendous efforts of the Korean government. One good thing is that public officials now clearly recognize why they do their jobs and thereby have a perspective when they do their jobs.

Nevertheless, performance management in the Korean public sector still needs to go further. The following are some selective issues that must be considered in order for performance management to contribute fully to making government responsible to citizens.

First, successful implantation of a performance management system requires strong leadership and commitment from the top. As noted in the performance improvement model, the necessary first step is to get top management support and leadership at the initial stage. Since performance management has to be accompanied with change management strategies, organizational resistance from employees is always the issue that an organization must overcome.

Second, middle-level management commitment is also equally important to successful implementation of performance management in any type of organization. Top management commitment without middle-level management support makes an organization mouth the slogan with no action taken at the bottom.

Third, performance at the organization level must be linked to the business unit's performance as well as individual-level performance. Every member in an organization has to be evaluated according to their contribution to organizational performance. In this sense, a well-designed performance appraisal system really matters. This appraisal system must include well-balanced sets of both quantitative and qualitative measures.

Fourth, performance management must lead to cooperation and coordination in an organization. Drawing an organizational chart is an important starting point for making people work. However, employees have to be able to work together beyond the boxes on an organizational chart. Specialization is a very important element for an organization to be effective. It is to be emphasized, however, that specialization can be a big barrier to organizational performance as it is likely to make organizational members look at the function within the box on the organizational chart. A high-performing organization looks at the whole first then considers how parts have to be arranged for getting to the goal at the top.

Fifth, performance measurement and evaluation results have to be utilized for making organizational decisions. The reason why people measure their performance is because they have to improve for next time. Without measuring what one has done, there is no way to improve one's job. In this regard, performance evaluation should not end up rating agencies or employees on a relative assessment basis. Both organizations and individuals have to use performance information for improving their actions and policies.

Sixth, performance management must be understood in the context of citizens' perspectives. There could be a debate over whether citizen input is always right for society as a whole, but when governments develop performance measures, they have to examine whether or not citizens also trust those ones as important to themselves and society. Getting citizens involved in discussing performance measures is a necessary first step for successful performance management especially in a democratic society.

Finally, performance management should be linked to strategic planning in an organization. The fact that current practice does not see the link between performance management and strategic planning indicates performance-based budgeting is not taking place. Important decision making in an organization must be budget based. Strategic planning is not simply a technique dealing with what is going to happen in the future. It is an advanced and scientific skill that examines what has already occurred and what would be the greatest factor to impact society. From such a point of view, performance management has to be operated in conjunction with strategic planning in any type of organization in the public sector.

Performance management is not a panacea for solving organizational problems. It is a problem-defining procedure rather than a problem-solving one. This is a comprehensive, continuing process where public employees, citizens, and interest groups get together to discuss what government has done and what should be done first.

Note

1 For detailed information, refer to the book by Seok-Hwan Lee, *Unreasonable Objectives-focused Organization: Strategic Performance Management for Strong Government and Enterprises"* (Bubmoon-Sa: Seoul, Korea, 2008).

References

Buchanan, B. (1974a). Building organizational commitment: The socialization of managers in work organizations. *Administrative Science Quarterly, 19*, 533–546.

Buchanan, B. (1974b). Government managers, business executives, and organizational commitment. *Public Administration Review, 34*, 339–347.

Buntz, C. G. (1981). Problems and issues in human service productivity improvement. *Public Productivity and Management Review, 5*, 299–320.

Denhardt, Robert, and Denhardt, Janet (2000). The new public service: Serving rather than steering. *Public Administration Review, July/August*, 549–559.

Drucker, Peter (1954). *The practice of management*, New York: Harper and Brothers.

Eran, Vigoda (2002). From responsiveness to collaboration: Governance, citizens and the next generation of public administration. *Public Administration Review, September/October*, 527–540.

Geczi, Emilian (2007). Sustainability and public participation: Toward an inclusive model of democracy. *Administrative Theory & Praxis, 29*(3), 375–393.

Glaser, Mark A., Yeager, Samuel J., and Parker, Lee E. (2006). Involving citizens in the decisions of government and community: Neighborhood-based vs. government-based engagement. *Public Administration Quarterly, 30*(2), 177–190.

Greiner, J. M. (1986). Motivational programs and productivity improvements in times of limited resources. *Public Productivity and Management Review, 10*, 81–101.

Halachmi, A., and Holzer, M. (1986). Introduction: Toward strategic perspectives on public productivity. In A. Halachmi, and M. Holzer (Eds.), *Strategic issues in public sector productivity: The best of public productivity review, 1975–1985*, (pp. 5–16), San Francisco, CA: Jossey-Bass.

Holzer, M. (1992). Mastering public productivity improvement. In M. Holzer (Ed.), *Public productivity handbook* (pp. 1–11), New York: Marcel Dekker.

Holzer, M., and Callahan, K. (1998). *Government at work: Best practices and model programs*, Thousand Oaks, CA: Sage.

Holzer, M., and Seok-Hwan Lee (2004). *Public productivity handbook* (2nd ed.), New York: Marcel Dekker.

Irvin, Renee A., and Stansbury, John (2004). Citizen participation in decision making: Is it worth the effort? *Public Administration Review, January/February*, 55–65.

Kaplan, R. S., and Norton, D. P. (1992). The balanced scorecard: Measures that drive performance. *Harvard Business Review, January/February*, 71–79.

Lee, Seok-Hwan (2008). *Unreasonable objectives-focused organization*, Seoul: Bubmoon-Sa.

Mathers, Earl (2008). Citizen engagement in Gallatin County. *Public Manager, Spring*, 17–21.

McGowan R. P. (1984). Improving efficiency in public management: The torment of Sisyphus. *Public Productivity and Management Review, 8*, 162–178.

Rainey, H. G. (1983). Public agencies and private firms: Incentive structures, goals, and individual roles. *Administration and Society, 15*, 207–242.

Rainey, H. G., Backoff, R. W., and Levine, C. L. (1976). Comparing public and private organizations. *Public Administration Review, 36*, 233–246.

Rainey, H. G., Pandey, S., and Bozeman, B. (1975). Research note: Public and private managers' perceptions of red tape. *Public Administration Review, 55*, 567–574.

Robbins, Mark D., Simonsen, Bill, and Feldman, Barry (2008). Citizens and Resource Allocation: Improving Decision Making with Interactive Web-Based Citizen Participation. *Public Administration Review, 68*(3), 564–575.

Schachter, H.L. (1997). *Reinventing government or reinventing ourselves: The role of citizen owners in making a better government*, Albany, New York: State University of New York Press.

U.S. Department of Labor (1996). *Working together for public service*, Washington, D.C.: Government Printing Office.

Weeks, Edward (2000). The practice of deliberative democracy: Results from four large-scale trials. *Public Administration Review*, *July/August*, 360–372.

Werther, W.B., Ruch, W.A., and McClure, L. (1986). *Productivity though people*. New York: West Publishing.

8 Local government

Young-Chool Choi

I. Introduction

The concept of local government autonomy can be seen as part of the larger concept of the separation of powers between central and local government. Even though local government autonomy has not been defined conceptually in a careful and consistent manner, it is generally accepted that it can be conceptually defined as a system of local government in which local government units have an important role to play in residents' lives and their economy, have discretion in determining policy without undue constraint from higher levels of government, and have the means or capacity to do this.

Korea is a unitary republican state, which consists of three levels of government: the central government, metropolitan cities and provinces (second-tier government), and municipalities (third-tier government). Within the second-tier local authorities, there are a total of 226 municipalities: 75 cities, 82 counties, and 69 autonomous districts. In addition, there are 3,588 administrative areas that have no autonomous status, including *dongs* (similar to urban wards), *eups* (similar to rural towns), and *myuns* (similar to small rural townships) (Choi and Kang, 2011: 122).

The historic roots of local government autonomy in Korea do not go very far back into the past. Local government autonomy in the modern understanding is a result of the Local Autonomy Act in 1949, one year before the Korean government, as currently understood, was established. The Local Autonomy Act of 1949 defined Seoul Special City, province, city, and town (*eup*), as self-governing bodies. However, since 1991, when local elections took place for the first time since 1960 and political turbulence occurred, Seoul Special City, metropolitan cities, and provinces have been recognized as second-tier local authorities, whereas cities, autonomous districts (subdivisions of the metropolitan cities), and counties (subdivisions of the provinces) have been recognized as third-tier local authorities.

What is noteworthy here is that the rules governing the status and scope of the activities of local authorities in Korea are laid down in the Local Autonomy Act and other related acts. However, the general acts do not apply to the capital city of Seoul, which has a special administrative and legal status.

Thus, it may be said that, in the unitary Korean system, metropolitan cities and provinces represent the intermediate level of governance as a second tier between the central government, and the municipalities represent a third tier. The latter could also be seen as the basic level of a system of Korean governance consisting of three tiers of government: central government, metropolitan cities and provinces, and municipalities. Unlike the metropolitan cities, the provinces, the municipalities, and administrative districts, which have autonomous status, administrative units including *eups, myuns*, and *dongs* do not have any local legislative powers and, therefore, are only administrative bodies. An outline of Korea's local government system is shown in Figure 8.1.

The special features of local autonomy, which is protected by the Constitution, are presented in the Local Autonomy Act. The Korean Constitution recognizes the principle of local government autonomy in two ways. On the one hand, it is with regard to the implementation of local autonomy and, on the other, with regard to the existence of local councils for local autonomy. The Local Autonomy Act, based on constitutional principles, stipulates general provisions for local autonomy. Articles 2, 3, and 4 of the Act contain provisions about the type, organization, and territorial sphere of local authorities and about their bodies and functions, and Articles 30 and 31 set out matters relating to local councils. In addition, Articles 93, 94, and 95 of the Act describe elections, terms of office, and roles of local government chiefs.

The constitutional status of local authorities in the Korean system, compared to that of those in Western countries, is not quite clear. Article 117 of the Constitution says that local authorities should pay attention to matters concerning the well-being of local residents, should protect their assets and property, and may enact their own local ordinances and regulations regarding local autonomy as delegated by national laws. This represents a contrast with the situation in Western countries, in which more detailed requirements regarding local autonomy are stipulated in the Constitution. In Korea, local autonomy-related matters are essentially stipulated in the Acts concerned. For example the Local Autonomy Act says that the municipalities are recognized as third-tier local authorities.

As mentioned above, the Local Autonomy Act was enacted in 1949, and local council elections took place even during the Korean War of 1950–1953. However, following the political turmoil of 1961, a lively political discussion took place concerning the status of municipalities, after which local autonomy was not implemented until 1991 when local elections took place again for the first time in 30 years. The Local Autonomy Act, which was completely redrafted in 1988 and which came to represent the legal foundation the 1991 local elections were based on, contains provisions regarding overall matters relating to local autonomy.

The Act contains general provisions regarding local government and stipulates how these principles are to be implemented. Of course, the Act is the result of a political compromise, given that an agreement on the legal status of the municipalities could not be found easily. With some modifications, the provisions contained in the Act are still today the relevant legal foundation of municipalities.

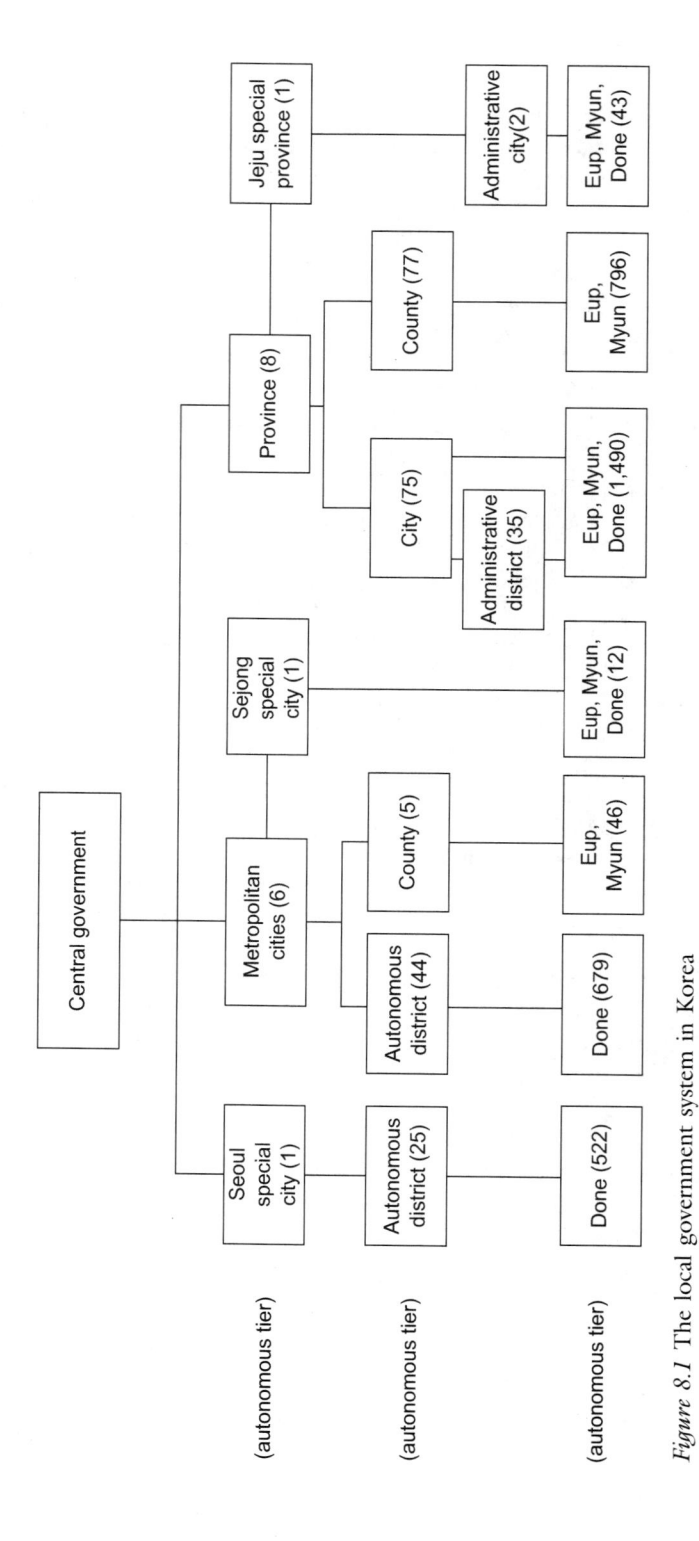

Figure 8.1 The local government system in Korea

Source: Local Government Information Service (as of January 1, 2014).

Article 3, Paragraph 2 of the Act implies that each province is divided into municipalities and that each municipality is a territorial and administrative body of its own, enjoying the right to self-government. In contrast to the administrative bodies of *eups, myuns,* and *dongs,* municipalities enjoy a certain amount of autonomy, since they are – within their autonomous sphere – not subject to instructions from the central or provincial governments. In this way, they operate outside the concept of ministerial responsibility. At the same time, they are subject to supervision by the Board of Audit and Inspection, the central government, and local councils in order to ensure the democratic legitimacy of their administrative actions.

The sphere of competence of local authorities includes two types of responsibilities: those that belong to the autonomous sphere of local authorities and those that are delegated to the local authorities. The first type comprises of matters that are concerned exclusively or predominantly with the local community and are appropriately handled by it. Local self-government in this sense includes the right and the ability of local authorities to regulate an important component of public affairs under their own responsibility and in the interests of the local population.

Only those powers delegated to the municipalities by the central government are bound by instructions from the delegating authority. Within this sphere of delegated action, municipalities can be qualified as common administrative authorities, which are bound by instructions of the highest authorities in the relevant field (Choi and Kang, 2011: 94).

Since the *eup* (rural town), *myun* (small township), and *dong* (urban neighborhood) are only administrative bodies, they have no right to create local legislation in a formal sense, unlike provincial and municipal governments. Administrative bodies cannot enact ordinances that are general administrative acts. They need a legal basis in each case and are only entitled to implement the relevant legal provisions in their jurisdiction. By contrast, both the provincial and the municipal government, the other two levels of the Korean unitary system, exercise local legislative and administrative powers.

The existence of an autonomous sphere of competence can be qualified as the core element of local self-government in general. Behind this element lies the idea that the handling of state functions affecting matters that affect the exclusive or preponderant common interest of local residents can be delegated to local government itself, insofar as these matters can be handled by it.

The territorial dimension of municipalities shows a high degree of variation. The smallest municipality (Ulrung-gun) occupies 72.87 square kilometers, while the largest (Hongcheon-gun) has an area of 1,819 square kilometers. Changing municipal boundaries or merging and splitting municipalities require a local referendum after a special decision by the local council. From a legal point of view, the changes take place via the act. The public may need to be consulted depending on the policy measures enacted by the central government. In the mid-1990s and the late 2000s, a number of "area forums" were created in respective areas, and many special acts were passed that amalgamated smaller municipalities into bigger units, thus abolishing these former local communities. Local government and the local council have to consider the public interest when abolishing a municipality as well as the ability of each municipality to carry out its functions (both those belonging to its autonomous sphere and those that are delegated). Furthermore, the economic and cultural interests of local residents have to be taken into account. Ultimately, according to the Local Government Act, residents and the local council may determine the number and the territorial dimension of the municipalities.

II.   The internal organization of local authorities and their democratic dimension

1.   *Internal organization*

The Local Autonomy Act (Articles 93, 101, and 103) lays down detailed requirements for the organization and operation of local self-government. Furthermore, according to Articles 22 and 23, local government may lay down detailed local legislative frameworks for local authorities, in accordance with the principles of the Act. In this respect, the Constitution and the Local Autonomy Act usually determine the administrative arrangements of local authorities, local electoral processes, local taxes, representation of local authorities in the administrative and legislative process, and local authorities' right to initiate local legislation or specific forms of direct democracy, such as referendums.

The National Assembly and the central government have passed a number of ordinary laws in order to implement the rules established by the Constitution and the relevant acts. These concern issues such as local government acts, local councilors, inter-municipal associations, and election statutes for local communities and cities.

The Constitution and the Local Autonomy Act do not distinguish between different types of municipality but refer to the concept of "uniform municipality." This means that local authorities that perform the same tasks must be granted equal legal treatment, irrespective of their size, economic situation, population, or legal status, with the exception that local authorities with more than 500,000 residents have a particular status in some respects and are required to perform specific tasks of administration. This kind of administration is usually operated by larger authorities and, to a certain extent, is situated at a level between that of the central government and that of the municipalities.

The capital city, Seoul, has 10 million residents and occupies an area of 605 square kilometers. Seoul today has a special statute according it privileged status. Because of its privileged status both as the capital and a metropolitan city, Seoul has specific rights in many respects. As a local authority, Seoul is subdivided into 25 municipal districts, which have their own district councils headed by elected district mayors.

Articles 30 and 93 of the Local Autonomy Act recognize two main bodies of local self-government: the local council and the mayor. These are discussed in turn.

2. Local council

The local council can be qualified as both the general representative body and the highest authority of the municipality. Pursuant to Article 31 of the Act, councilors are directly elected for four years by all local citizens, according to the same electoral principles as are applied to the election of the National Assembly: equal, direct, secret, and individual suffrage on a proportional basis. The number of members of the local council usually depends on the number of residents. The total number of local councilors in 2014 was 3,687.

Article 39 of the Act says that local authorities are responsible to the local council for the performance of their functions within their autonomous sphere. Thus, the local council serves as the supreme local body overseeing the functions exercised in the autonomous sphere. Most of the Acts regarding local government entitle the local council to perform all the tasks that no other body is explicitly competent to manage. The local council has the power to pass ordinances within its autonomous sphere of authority, and it decides on the local authority's draft budget.

3. Mayor

In practice, the most important political entity of a local authority is the mayor, who represents the municipality externally. The Local Autonomy Act provides that mayors be elected by local residents to a four-year term of office. The mayor is the chief of the local administrative office and of local government employees and also manages local property and the local budget. The mayor has the right to table motions and to issue instructions. Mayors are accountable to local councils regarding matters relating to their sphere of competence. In the performance of all tasks delegated to the local level, municipalities are subject to the instructions of either central government or provincial governments, depending on whether the task in question involves central or provincial competence. In the event of illegal conduct, mayors may be dismissed by the Court or by a citizen recall.

4. Local authority and democracy

Democracy at the local government level has – just as it does at central government level – a strong representative element, which means that instruments of direct democracy are not very important. The strengthening of these instruments has become an increasingly pressing political demand. Article 13 of the Act provides for direct participation by citizens. Residents of local authorities have various opportunities for participating directly in the decisions of their communities, such as through voting, initiatives, citizen consultations, and recalls. These all share the common feature that they trigger the democratic participation of the local population with regard to issues of general interest. The Act has developed certain requirements for these instruments. More specifically, direct democracy instruments enjoyed by local residents cannot operate more strongly than the same type of instruments at the central level.

Local authorities are – as for all other administrative bodies – bound by the law according to the principle of legality. Ostensibly, the Constitution and the Acts regarding local government permit local authorities slightly more autonomy in establishing rules without being bound completely to a strict interpretation of the principle of legality. Nevertheless, it is clear that they are bound by law, unless other legal provisions provide specific autonomy for certain purposes.

III.   Functions of local authorities

Local authorities in Korea discharge a very wide range of functions, except for national defense and diplomatic matters. Basically, a local authority will be responsible for the discharge of all functions within its area. All powers and duties of local authorities are provided for by the Local Autonomy Act and other specific related acts, which give the central government considerable scope to add, remove, or modify functions as it sees fit. The functions of local authorities can usefully be divided into duties (i.e. functions that they are required to discharge by legislation) and powers (i.e. discretionary powers that a local authority will need to exercise in order to discharge its functions and provide necessary services to its inhabitants).

The functions of local authorities in Korea include the provision of welfare services, social care, public transport, environmental services including refuse collection and recycling, and leisure services including libraries, etc. Local authorities also have a role in the financing and governance of fire and rescue authorities. They also deal with many land-use, building, and planning issues and consider applications and issue licenses for a number of activities and trades, including the operation of entertainment venues. They also provide leisure, sport, and recreation facilities.

The Ministry of Security and Public Administration (now the Ministry of Government Administration and Home Affairs) undertook a review of the functions of local authorities. The review sought the views of local authorities and their assistance in compiling a list of the statutory duties that are incumbent upon them.

In general, the constitutional principle of differentiation between state bodies (federal and regional) and local self-government bodies operates in Western democratic countries, and it represents the fundamental guarantee of local autonomy. Unlike in Western countries, there is no constitutional principle of differentiation between central and local government in Korea, and instead the Local Autonomy Act outlines the functions that local authorities have to exercise. As noted above, local authorities in Korea are not merely administrative units but autonomous bodies with a right to self-government. This is demonstrated by the fact that administrative tasks are performed by bodies other than central government. As a characteristic of self-government, their sphere of competence includes autonomous and assigned/delegated functions. In theory, local authorities may not be given strong instructions by the central government perform tasks within their own sphere of competence (autonomous functions). However, they are subject to instructions from the central government when they perform delegated tasks.

Local powers have a sound written basis, not in the Constitution, but in the Local Government Act, which clearly reflects the principle of subsidiarity. Articles 9, 101, 102, and 103 of the Act stipulate that the autonomous sphere of competence of local authorities includes all matters that exclusively or predominantly concern their local communities and may reasonably be performed by the authorities within their municipal boundaries. Articles 9 and 10 of the Act set out an illustrative list of matters for which local authorities are responsible within their autonomous sphere, such as the appointment of local government employees, local economy administration, local welfare, local government management, and local development planning. This list provides an illustration of the most important fields that the general clause in the Constitution comprises in the abstract. The Local Autonomy Act specifies which matters fall within the autonomous sphere of the different tiers of local government. The local authorities' own responsibilities cover issues of local interest as defined by the Act. They include urban and spatial planning, transport, environmental protection, water supply and sewage, household waste collection, construction, and libraries and culture as well as health (municipal hospitals) and welfare.

On the other hand, issues relating to the delegated sphere of competence that are administered by the mayor include the registration of residents, health measures, and others. In contrast to the tasks assigned to the local authorities' autonomous sphere, the central government neither enumerates the tasks falling into the delegated sphere nor entrenches them in a general clause. In addition, the central government and provincial governments share responsibilities with the municipalities in areas such as education and healthcare.

VI.   Coordination of the different levels of governance

It is often not easy to distinguish aspects of coordination of the actions of local government and the central government and aspects of control of local authorities by the central government. Unlike those countries where local authorities enjoy constitutional rights and the allocation of competencies in the Constitution, in Korea, because local authorities exercise only the functions that are granted to them by the National Assembly in legislation, there is little potential for a significant overlap of functions or for legal disputes between the central and local levels of government over the proper allocation or exercise of competencies.

In legal terms, the central government has responsibility for consulting and collaborating with local authorities in exercising plans and policies. It undertakes to progressively remove obstacles that prevent local authorities from pursuing their role, including reducing the burden of appraisal and approval regimes and earmarking funds for specific purposes.

When exercising delegated powers, local authorities are subordinate to the relevant state ministry. The relevant ministries, whose competencies include exercising the power of state administration within the limits stipulated by law, execute their functions by issuing regulations and directives. The Ministry of Government Administration and Home Affairs coordinates directives and instructions relating to the delegated powers of provincial government and municipalities. This ministry is also responsible for monitoring the provision of specialist assistance to municipalities, managing and coordinating (in cooperation with the relevant ministries) the development and implementation of regional information systems and arranging for the management and implementation of projects.

Provincial governments cooperate with municipal authorities when exercising their own responsibilities. They are not permitted to interfere with the exclusive powers of municipalities. Basically, provincial governments will always consult them on issues of regional development that are of concern to municipal organs.

Given the number of small local authorities, inter-municipal cooperation is a key feature of local government in Korea, even though the scale of local government is relatively greater than that of other countries. In practice, there exists a wide range of formal and informal instruments of such cooperation: *de facto* collaboration, mutual assistance, mutual contracts, associations, and companies operating under the relevant laws. Articles 147 and 148 of the Act set out the requirements for and the processes involved in this inter-municipal cooperation in local service provision.

Other forms of institutionalized cooperation include administrative associations. These usually are associations with no legal personality, which are set up to jointly handle a function. One of their main purposes is to deal with administrative matters in a collaborative way, using resources efficiently and effectively. The expectation is that these instruments for collaboration and coordination will strengthen local autonomy.

V.   Supervision and inspection of local authorities

1.   *Supervision by central government*

In theory, self-governing bodies are, from a rule of law perspective, bound by law, but they are not bound by the directives of the executive bodies of the central government. However, self-governing bodies are subject to the administrative supervision of the central government. The main features of this supervision are provided in Articles 166 and 167 of the Local Government Act. This supervision should ensure that self-governing bodies fulfil their functions and do not infringe on the law. The central government may exercise its supervisory powers in relation to the performance of the national tasks that are carried out by local authorities in their autonomous sphere. In general, supervision of the activities of local government organs focuses solely on legality. To ensure legality, a number of supervisory instruments, including preventive measures, the right to information, and even the right to approve local ordinances in some cases, are available to central government. With specific reference to ordinances, the supervisory authority has the power to annul those that are contrary to law. A special instrument of supervision, which shares the features of a legal remedy, is a supervisory authority's power to repeal unlawful local administrative acts. In cases of repeated illegal conduct, a supervisory authority has the power to audit, evaluate, and annul local authorities' decisions.

2. Inspection of local authorities by the National Assembly

a) The significance of parliamentary inspections

The parliamentary inspection system in Korea is a function whereby the National Assembly examines and questions overall state affairs (Lee, 2002: 295). Parliamentary inspections accurately comprehend overall state affairs and elicit data and information required for legislation and for budget examination. Furthermore, by exposing and correcting any mistakes made in the field of administrative affairs, they serve to efficiently carry out the main roles of the National Assembly as designated by the Constitution: legislation, budget examination, and government control.

In addition, parliamentary inspections, as well as parliamentary investigations, enshrine the people's right to know, the principal condition for the realization of popular sovereignty. Those conducting them serve as agents of the people, gathering information about the state's activities that people wish to have. This is a useful means of helping people to make political decisions (Kim, 2008: 1350; Jung, 2011: 134). Nevertheless, although parliamentary inspections have similar functions, stages, and means as those of parliamentary investigations, which are continually conducted by the National Assembly, the fact that they are conducted every year without any special resolution to this effect marks a distinction between them. They are used more frequently than parliamentary investigations in the National Assembly as a means of checking and controlling the administration. In addition, they differ from inspections conducted by the Board of Audit and Inspection in that the inspectors are assemblymen elected by the people, who thus reflect the will of the people (Korea Legislative Studies Institute, 2006: 39).

Following its introduction with the establishment of the first Constitution, the parliamentary inspection system was temporarily abolished during the Fourth Republic as a consequence of the Seventh Amendment of 1972. It was revived in 1980, during the Fifth Republic, via the Eighth Amendment; and in 1988, during the Sixth Republic, the Ninth Amendment divided it into two parts, parliamentary inspections and investigations.

Article 61 of the Constitution provides grounds for the National Assembly to inspect or investigate specific administrative affairs. Articles 127–129 define the basic data for parliamentary investigations and inspections, and more specific details are included in the law on parliamentary investigation and inspection. According to this, the first clause of Article 2 of the law on parliamentary investigation and inspection determines that inspections of overall state affairs will be conducted 20 days a year on a periodic basis. They are conducted by the responsible standing committee mentioned in Article 37 of the National Assembly law and, in principle, are targeted on all aspects of administrative affairs: legislation, administration, and jurisdiction. Under Article 12 of the law on parliamentary investigation and inspection, the findings are also made public, and duties are given to the inspected agencies such as the administration. Meanwhile, the law has the legal force to guarantee implementation.

As long as specific regulations on reports, document submission, requests for witness attendance, and verification relating to parliamentary inspections do not exist, the relevant persons or agencies must oblige, and accusations can be made in cases of disobedience, noncompliance, oath swearing, or perjury. The administration or related agencies must also report the results of parliamentary inspections to the National Assembly when correction or disposal of information is requested, and the National Assembly can take adequate measures to implement these reports (Jang, 2004: 45).

Parliamentary inspections by the National Assembly are essentially policy inspections aimed at the central government, and corruption inspections are aimed at frontline enforcement institutions. Local government inspections by the National Assembly contain a strong element of compulsion and control that is aimed at uncovering corruption and illegal behavior on the part of local authorities (Park, 2002: 52). As a result, they are conducted in accordance with regulations set out in the Constitution so as to reveal and correct errors made by local authorities, where more than half of the national budget is spent (Bae, 2002: 143). According to research on the attitudes of assemblymen toward parliamentary inspections by the National Assembly, including judgment of bills, budget and account examination, parliamentary inspection, and activities including district activities, civil complaints and petitions, 30.28 percent of assemblymen selected parliamentary inspection as being the most important activity in which they engaged (Lim and Ham, 2000: 70).

b)   *Practical operation of parliamentary inspections*

Under the law on parliamentary investigation and inspection, the standing committee independently decides upon enforcing the results of the investigation in the 30 days prior to the date of the ordinary meeting. The place where parliamentary inspections are to be carried out is decided by the committee and is usually at the National Assembly or at the site of the inspected agency.

The committee can conduct preliminary investigations with experts who are not members of the Secretariat of the National Assembly or the inspected agencies (Article 9 of the Act, line 2). The committee can also request the submission of related reports and documents by the responsible agency or personnel and the attendance of witnesses, appraisers, and testifiers and may conduct examinations. However, the approval of at least one-third of the committee members

Table 8.1 Enforcement period for parliamentary inspections (16th and 17th Assemblies)

National Assembly	Year	Total Number of Inspection Days per Standing Committee	Inspection Days per Annum	Number of Agencies Conducting Inspections
16th Assembly	2000	189	20	357
16th administration	2001	191	20	392
16th administration	2002	160	20	365
16th administration	2003	171	20	362
16th administration	AVG.	177.75	20	369
17th Assembly	2004	193	20	457
17th administration	2005	179	20	461
17th administration	2006	181	20	510
17th administration	2007	159	19	488
17th administration	AVG.	178	19.75	479

Source: Adapted from Kwon and Lee (2012: 19).

Note: For specific data on changes in parliamentary inspection system regulations, see Jung (2011). According to Lim and Ham (2000), the most important percentages of assemblymen considering parliamentary inspections, legislation evaluations, budget and settlement evaluations, and other activities were, respectively, 30.28 percent, 21.19 percent, 18.73 percent, and 29.80 percent. In other words, parliamentary inspections were considered to be the most important function of the National Assembly.

is required should the committee wish to make a request for documents relating to the investigation or inspection. The committee can open a hearing to select evidence from the documents relating to inspections or investigations or conduct investigations (Article 10). A hearing consists of summoning witnesses and listening to them when a committee of the National Assembly screens an important issue or conducts a parliamentary investigation or inspections and is held in order to obtain information or data that will be used as a basis for judgment prior to the making of decisions.

Hearings, both private and public, can take place when requested by at least one-third of the members in the case of standing committees. Data, such as the issue in question, date, time, place, and the names of witnesses, should be announced five days before the opening.

The stages relating to the appraisal and testimonies of witnesses, appraisers, and testifiers are specifically defined in the Law on Testimonies and Appraisal in the National Assembly. They include the obligation of witnesses to attend (Article 2), refusal to give testimony (Article 3), problems regarding testimonies, and document submission of official secrets (Article 4), along with attendance requirements for witnesses (Article 5).

V.   Local finance

The major provisions on local government financial and fiscal autonomy are set out in the Local Government Act, the Local Finance Act, and the Local Tax Act. In general, according to the Local Government Act, local authorities must meet the expenses incurred in the performance of their tasks, whether they belong to their autonomous or their delegated sphere of competence, unless central government legislation stipulates otherwise. Pursuant to the Local Tax Act, local authorities are entitled to levy either exclusive local taxes or shared taxes.

The financing of local authorities is achieved through a variety of sources. These might be divided into three main sources: grants from central government, local taxes, and other forms of income generated by the activities of local government. The most recent statistics suggest that local authorities rely on central government grants for around 60 percent of their income. Local authorities also have the main means of levying local taxes, which account for around 32 percent of total government tax revenue. The remainder of local income comes from sales, trading activities, and rents, which constitute around 8 percent of local authority income. As a portion of the sales, trading activities, and rents of income, many authorities generate some income through issuing civil penalties relating to matters such as littering or minor traffic and parking violations.

As noted above, the largest portion of local income is derived from central government grants. This has always been a source of central government control of the activities of local authorities, since the central government has always maintained powers to limit tax sources, requiring that money be spent on particular activities or the provision of particular services. It is arguable that the current central government financial deficit, as a result of different forms of administrative and financial monitoring and inspection measures, has placed local authorities in a position of tougher constraints and greater dependence on the central government. At all times, the fact that central control of the use of money received from the central government is being gradually reduced is undoubtedly positive for local autonomy. However, such autonomy may prove to be limited, since the amount of matching-grant projects paid for by local government has increased significantly over past years owing to the government's austerity program.

Figures 8.2 through 8.4 show fiscal relations across levels of government in Korea.

A fiscal reform was undertaken in 2005 that established the Special Account for National Balanced Development, transforming many specific-purpose grants for regional development that were otherwise scattered throughout central government accounts into integrated national grants (OECD, 2012: 140). The Special Account for National Balanced Development was then reorganized, and the Regional Development Special Account was established in 2009 to expand fiscal spending for local municipalities. As a result, 200 projects were merged into 24 comprehensive projects, and block grants were adopted to give local municipalities the authority to design projects autonomously (OECD, 2012: 141).

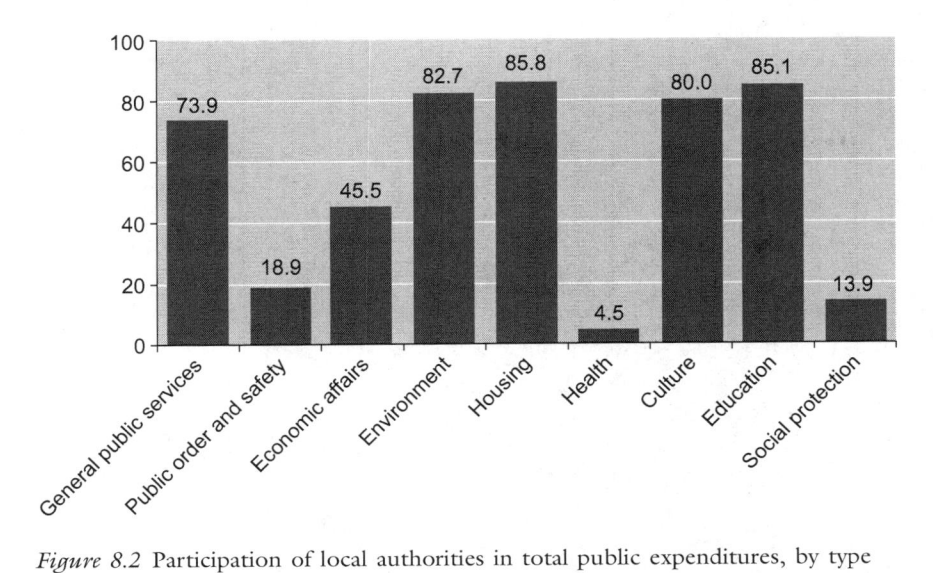

Figure 8.2 Participation of local authorities in total public expenditures, by type
Source: OECD (2013: 140).

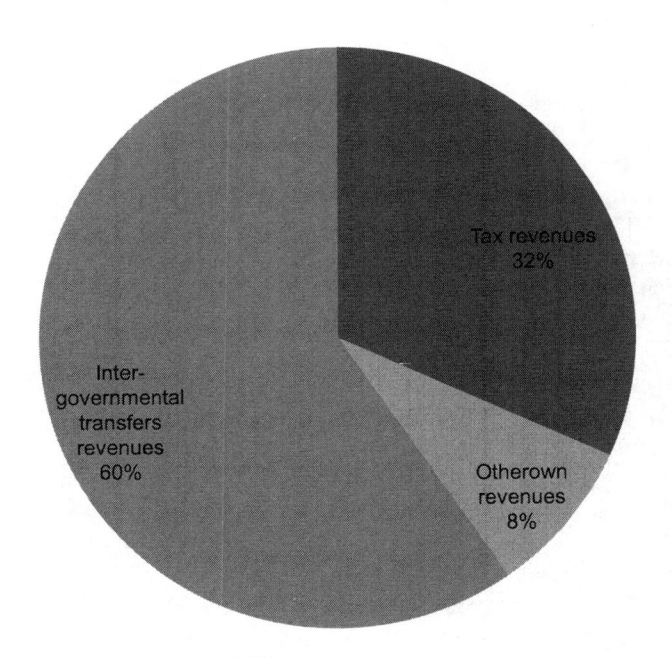

Figure 8.3 Sources of revenue below the central government
Source: OECD (2013: 140).

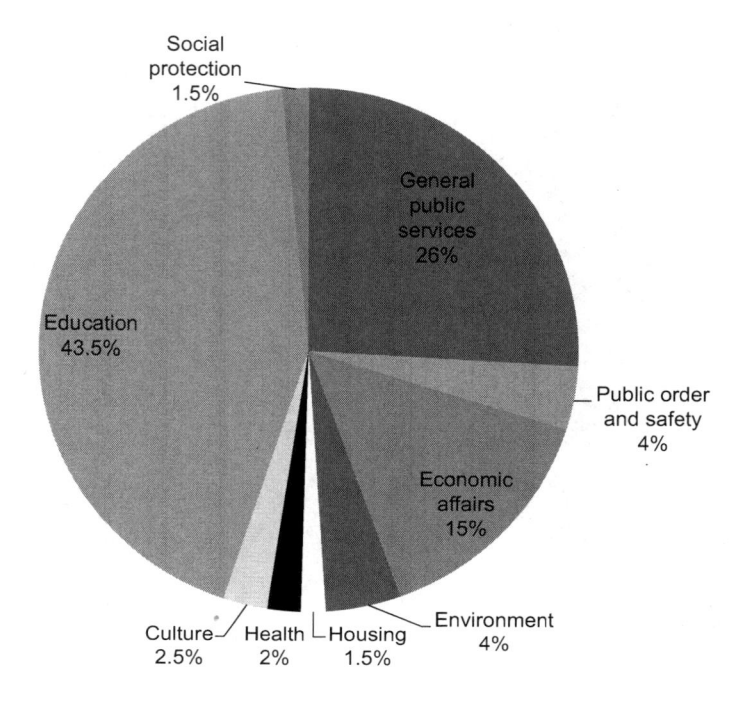

Figure 8.4 Distribution of local government expenditures
Source: OECD (2013: 140).

What is particularly important here is establishing the level of fiscal autonomy enjoyed by local government in Korea. For this purpose, the values for tax decentralization and expenditure decentralization levels used by the Organisation for Economic Co-operation and Development (OECD) can be used to measure Korea's decentralization levels, and the value of the tax autonomy index can be applied to calculate such values. As a first step, the weighted values of central and local government discretion on taxation as calculated by the OECD may be used. Table 8.2, employing the OECD indicators used to measure the degree of local government fiscal autonomy, presents the findings regarding taxation autonomy.

Table 8.2 shows that the average tax autonomy weighted value for the 26 OECD nations is 0.76, while the value for Korea is slightly lower, at 0.67. Meanwhile, the table shows the ratio, in 2012, of local taxes to total taxation. As the table shows, the average for the 26 nations in 2012 was 17.40, while the average for Korea was slightly lower, at 15.81.

Meanwhile, since it is also necessary to examine local expenditures, the proportion of local expenditures in 2012 can be simplified, as seen in the table. While the average for the 26 countries was 34.08 percent, the ratio for Korea was higher, at 43.25 percent. The results of multiplying the taxation autonomy

Table 8.2 Weighted value of tax autonomy, proportion of local tax, and expenditure levels

Country Name	Weighted Taxation Autonomy Values	Proportion of Local Tax	Proportion of Local Expenditure	Taxation Autonomy	Expenditure Autonomy
Austria	0.49	4.75	30.50	2.34	15.05
Belgium	1.00	9.92	36.39	9.88	36.24
Canada	0.93	49.52	66.45	45.84	61.51
Czech Republic	0.80	1.26	23.01	1.01	18.41
Denmark	0.84	26.52	61.63	22.17	51.52
Estonia	0.43	13.07	25.07	5.67	10.88
Finland	0.85	22.81	40.34	19.29	34.12
France	0.85	13.23	20.66	11.20	17.49
Germany	0.48	29.81	38.72	14.41	18.72
Hungary	0.69	6.27	18.71	4.31	12.85
Iceland	0.75	26.67	28.79	19.97	21.56
Italy	0.66	16.63	29.45	10.98	19.44
Korea	0.67	15.81	43.25	10.52	28.77
Luxembourg	0.79	3.99	11.60	3.16	9.18
Mexico	1.00	3.57	45.34	3.57	45.34
The Netherlands	0.87	3.59	32.12	3.14	28.06
Norway	0.79	12.58	33.65	9.91	26.52
Poland	0.55	12.45	30.98	6.86	17.06
Portugal	0.65	7.12	12.42	4.66	8.13
Slovak	0.81	3.02	16.78	2.45	13.62
Slovenia	0.38	11.12	19.86	4.22	7.53
Spain	0.80	41.92	40.49	33.66	32.51
Sweden	0.90	36.62	48.65	32.96	43.79
Switzerland	1.00	39.76	57.94	39.76	57.94
UK	0.80	4.90	26.08	3.92	20.86
US	1.00	35.47	47.25	35.47	47.25
Average	0.76	17.40	34.08	13.89	27.09

Note: Some countries were excluded owing to a lack of data on the ratio of local expenditure although they had taxation autonomy values.

weighted values by these ratios and considering certain constraint factors are shown in Table 8.3.

Since tax autonomy values and expenditure autonomy values range differently, the average of each indicator was calculated to derive its relation to the average. Then, these two values were added and divided by 2, giving the value that will be utilized. Thus, if the OECD average was 100, the relative positions of different countries can be calculated. Levels of taxation and expenditure decentralization levels were derived using this method, and the decentralization scores calculated by adding these two values are shown in Table 8.3.

Table 8.3 Decentralization scores

Country	Taxation Decentralization	Expenditure Decentralization	Decentralization Level
Austria	16.88	55.56	36.22
Belgium	71.12	133.79	102.46
Canada	330	227.04	278.52
Czech Republic	7.24	67.95	37.59
Denmark	159.6	190.19	174.89
Estonia	40.84	40.16	40.5
Finland	138.9	125.96	132.43
France	80.64	64.57	72.6
Germany	103.77	69.12	86.45
Hungary	31.01	47.44	39.23
Iceland	143.79	79.59	111.69
Italy	79.03	71.75	75.39
Korea	*75.73*	*106.2*	*90.97*
Luxembourg	22.75	33.8	28.32
Mexico	25.71	167.38	96.55
The Netherlands	22.6	103.58	63.09
Norway	71.37	97.88	84.62
Poland	49.39	62.99	56.19
Portugal	33.56	30	31.78
Slovak	17.62	50.26	33.94
Slovenia	30.36	27.8	29.08
Spain	242.3	119.99	181.15
Sweden	237.28	161.63	199.46
Switzerland	286.27	213.88	250.08
UK	28.21	77.02	52.62
US	255.35	174.42	214.88
Mean	*100*	*100*	*100*

Source: Choi (2014).

As Table 8.3 shows, the decentralization level of Korea considering taxation decentralization and expenditure decentralization is 90.97, lower than the average of 26 OECD nations, which is set at 100.

In conclusion, the results of the analysis show that the fiscal decentralization level of Korea is estimated to be around 90 percent of the average OECD level. When one uses the weighted values of taxation autonomy related to taxation discretion as standards, Korea's score becomes 88 percent of the OECD average (100 percent), similar to the aforementioned score. Since the tax decentralization levels are also lower than the OECD average relative to expenditure decentralization, there is a need in particular to strengthen decentralization in this area, as it is empirically and theoretically accepted that decentralization can influence national competitiveness and national happiness.

VI.   Future policy directions

Local government in Korea has faced enormous changes in the past 20 years. The Local Autonomy Act of 1988 has brought about significant changes to the system of local government in Korea, expanding the powers of local authorities in a number of respects. The increase in the powers of local authorities must be balanced against increasing practical constraints on freedom of action as a result of significant reductions in central government support and cuts to government spending.

There are a few future policy issues to be raised in relation to local autonomy. First, there is the question of how to increase the role of local government. The role of local government in Korea may be under threat from a number of central government initiatives, owing to financial crisis, which has recently become serious at both the central and local level. Although the implications of the government's objectives and plans for policy implementation in relation to strengthening local autonomy are clear, it may be that local government may not see a further increase in certain of its functions as a result. In addition, the lack of clear constitutional protections for local government, combined with the ease with which central government may add or remove powers, obligations, and functions from local government, may leave local government in something of a vulnerable position.

There is no doubt that local government remains an important mechanism for the commissioning and delivery of local services, but the significant level of central government control that remains over both the tasks entrusted to it and the level of financing received from the central government and potentially raised in the form of local taxes remains a significant limitation on the freedom of local government.

Second, decentralization at the local level is an issue to be addressed progressively. In spite of policy efforts made by previous Korean administrations to strengthen local autonomy and decentralization, the outcomes have been insufficient so far from the system of local government. The evaluations that various groups, including academic ones, have conducted regarding the local autonomy and decentralization policies of past administrations have largely concluded that the original plans have not successfully been accomplished for many reasons and, thus, that the current level of local autonomy is also insufficient for fulfilling its ultimate goal, supporting the development of local government. The Korean government needs to continue conducting in-depth and objective examinations of its overall local decentralization policies to dispel these kinds of concerns, successfully carry out local decentralization, and provide discussion in support of its cause.

The fiscal autonomy of the municipalities is too limited for them to be granted complete autonomy. This explains the political demand that fiscal autonomy be strengthened in a revenue-neutral fashion. The issue of increasing sub-national fiscal autonomy raises the question of which taxes should be assigned to each of the different levels of government. Responsibility for levying taxes would strengthen the accountability of local authorities to their electorates. Local authorities are often believed to be better able to discern the preferences of their residents, more aware of local conditions, and also more accountable to their residents. The political demand for more local autonomy is at present far from being or becoming a reality. As a consequence, the future of local self-government in Korea remains an unfinished issue and is part of current reform discussions.

Third is the consolidation of small local authorities neighboring one another. Some local authorities have been weakened over time, with their population decreasing, and their local economies being devastated. How can they survive? In this case, two or more neighboring local authorities can merge with local council approval. Approval for the merging of local authorities may be concluded on the basis of a local referendum. This merger process was dynamic in the past. However, the success rate for the consolidation of local authorities was not high. The policy issue is how to encourage local authorities with small populations and poor economies to combine into one large local authority so that they can sustain themselves without excessive dependence on the central government.

Finally, there is no doubt that, although recent reforms have delivered a certain measure of autonomy to local authorities regarding the use of monies received from the central government and the management of local government employees, the central government retains considerable control over local government finances, which means that the financial autonomy of local authorities is limited by their need to discharge their functions in an era of increasing financial constraints.

Multilateral discussions aimed at successfully promoting local autonomy are required on the part of central government to address such concerns. In particular, according to the experience of previous governments, unexpected variables are bound to appear in the enforcement process even when policies regarding local autonomy are rationally designed and their promotion strategies are efficiently planned. Thus, the central government should conduct an objective, in-depth examination of local autonomy at the launching of a new administration, since this will not only promote successful implementation of the policy but also provide a supporting argument justifying it.

References and Further Readings

Ahmad, E., G. Brosio and V. Tanzi. (2008). *Local Service Provision in Selected OECD Countries: Do Centralized Operations Work Better?* IMF Working Paper 08/67.

Bae, J.H. (2002) *Analysis Report of Budget Issues.* National Assembly Budget Office.

Baskaran, T. (2011) Fiscal decentralization, ideology, and the size of the public sector, *European Journal of Political Economy*, 27: 485–506.

Bjornskov, C., A. Drehe and J. Fisher (2008) On decentralization and life satisfaction, *Economic Letters*, 99: 147–51.

Choi, C.H. and H.K. Kang (2011) *Local Government Theories.* Seoul: Samyoungsa.

Choi, Y.C. (2014) Analysis of the relationships between decentralization level and policy variables, *Local Government Studies Review*, 17(2): 369–89.

Davoodi, H. and H. Zou (1999) Fiscal decentralization and economic growth in the United States, *Journal of Urban Economics*, 45(2): 222–39.

Fukasaku, K. and L. de Mello (1998) Fiscal decentralisation and macroeconomic stability: the experience of large developing countries and transition economies in democracy. In K. Fukasaku and R. Hausmann (eds), *Decentralisation and Deficits in Latin America*. Paris: Development Centre of the OECD, pp. 105–130.

Hong, J. H., H. S. Ha and Y. C. Choi (2006) Developing indicators for decentralization, *Local Government Studies*, 10(2): 7–30.

IMD (2011) *World Competitiveness Report* (online database).

Jang, Y. S. (2004) How to make the National Assembly work, *Public Law Review*, 32(5): 113–38.

Jang, J. H. (2013) Relationships between infant policy and national competitiveness in OECD countries, *Korea Comparative Government Studies*, 17(21): 73–94.

Jung, J. H. (2000) *How To Evaluate National Competitiveness?* Seoul: Jijung Publishing.

Jung, M.-H. (2011) Reexamining the National Assembly Inspection System, *Public Law Studies*, 10(1): 133–59.

Keum, C. H. (2013) *Future Strategy for Decentralization Policies in Park Administration*. KRILA Conference Proceedings.

Keum, C. H. and Y. C. Choi (2013) Evaluating decentralization policies of Lee Myung Bak Administration, *Korea Local Autonomy Studies*, 27(1): 1–18.

Kim, C. S. (2008) *Studies on the Constitution*. Seoul: Bakyoungsa.

Korea Legislative Studies Institute (2006) *Reforming the Korea Audit System*. Seoul: National Assembly.

Kwon, K. H. and J. K. Lee (2012) *Analysis of the Achievements of the National Assembly Inspection System in Korea and Policy Suggestions*. Korean Policy Sciences Association Conference Proceedings.

Lee, K. H. (2002) Future directions of national inspection of second-tier local government in Korea, *National Assembly Studies*, 9: 295–303.

Lee, S. J. (1993) Management strategies for successful policy implementation, *Local Administration Review*, 8(3): 85–105.

Lee, S. J. (2005) Evaluating local decentralization policies of Roh Administration, *Public Administration Studies*, 43(2): 68–89.

Lim, D. W. and S. D. (2000) *Enhancing Productivity of the National Assembly*. Seoul: Bakyeoungsa.

OECD (2012) *Measuring Fiscal Decentralisation: Concepts and Policies*. Paris: OECD.

OECD (2013) *Institutional and Financial Relations across Levels of Government*. Paris: OECD.

Panara, Carlo and Varney Michael (2013) *Local Government in Europe*. London: Routledge.

Park, H. B. (2001) *Social Capital and Local Government Competitiveness*. KAPA Conference Proceedings.

Park, K. K. (2002) *National Inspection System for Local Government: Problems and Future Directions*. National Assembly Public Administration Committee Policy Report.

Schneider, A. (2003) Decentralization: conceptualization and measurement, *Studies in Comparative International Development*, 38(3): 32–56.

So, J. K. (2004) Measurement indicators for social capital, *Korea Regional Development Studies*, 16(1): 89–118.

Suh, S. T. (2002) Role and tasks of urban planning for strengthening social capital, *Land Studies*, 33(2): 73–87.

World Economic Forum (2011) *Global Competitiveness Report 2010–2011*. Geneva: WEF.

Xie, D., H. Zou and H. Davoodi (1999) Fiscal decentralisation and economic growth in the United States, *Journal of Urban Economics*, 45: 228–39.

Zhang, T. and H. Zou (1998) Fiscal decentralization, public spending and economic growth in China, *Journal of Public Economics*, 67(2): 221–40.

9 Roles and reforms of public enterprises

Sang Cheoul Lee

I. Privatization or reform of public enterprise governance

Public enterprises in Korea have been most prevalent in utilities and network industries whose performance is of great importance to the Korean economy. The success of Samsung Electronics and Hyundai Motors, Korea's leading private-sector global firms, owe a debt to the stable power supply provided by the Korea Electric Power Corporation (KEPCO) and the good-quality steel supplied by Pohang Iron and Steel Corporation (POSCO). These latter two are major public enterprises that have become partially (KEPCO) or wholly (POSCO) privatized in recent years. Nevertheless, privatization is not the predominant case: public enterprises in Korea are still playing an important role, as the estimated expenditures of public enterprises today are almost twice as much as those of the government.[1]

On the other hand, public enterprises in Korea have been severely criticized since the Asian economic crisis of 1997–1999 due to excessive demands by labor unions and budgetary waste by the management. In other words, public enterprises are perceived as suffering from the worst aspects of the private sector (labor) and public sector (budgetary waste).

The Korean government has been reforming the governance of public enterprises to meet people's expectations. The reform of public enterprises is focused on public corporate governance rather than full-scale privatization, as the government has placed a priority on changes to governance systems rather than transferring these operations to the private sector. Korea's newly reformed public corporate governance systems, such as the evaluation system, have been widely disseminated to other countries and have been actively accepted by many developing countries.

This chapter will review the history and development of Korea's public enterprise governance reform experiences with relevant theoretical issues. It explores how and why public corporate governance has shifted to the current model in Korea.

II. Growth of public enterprises

1. *Economic development and market failure*

Public enterprises, also known as state-owned enterprises (SOEs), have conventionally been established to lead national economic development or to remedy "market failure." Profit-oriented businesses in the private sector have brought about problems related to urbanization, mass unemployment, and unfair social conditions. Economic development is principally associated with developing countries, while addressing market failure is frequently associated with so-called advanced countries, as depicted in Figure 9.1.

2. *Administrative reform and government failure*

Not a few bureaucratic governmental agencies have been privatized or transformed into public enterprises under the modern pressures to downsize bureaucracy: these new public enterprises have created numerous "government failures" due to relaxed regulations or inefficient supervision.

The dominant idea underlying transforming the bureaucracy is that private "management" is inherently superior to public "administration." The subject of business management focuses on enhancing the values of efficiency and profit in organizations. Managerial values such as market, customer, rationality, output, and development are different from the traditional administrative values of bureaucracy, input, exclusiveness, and maintenance. Privatization and organizational transformation are based on the belief that management is more efficient and effective than administration. The differences in values between administration and management are summarized in Table 9.1.

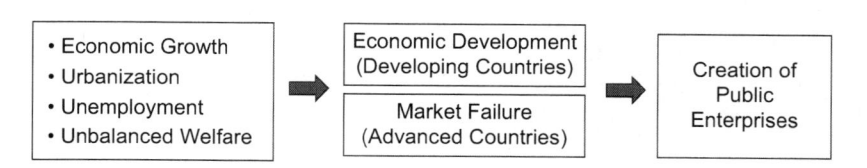

Figure 9.1 Creation of public enterprises

Table 9.1 Values of public administration and private management

Public "Administration"	*Private "Management"*
Bureaucracy, input (constituent-oriented), exclusiveness, maintenance, political significance	Marketability, output (customer-oriented), development, rationality

Administrative reform focusing on institutional transformation stimulates the increase of public enterprises.

3. NPM and the growth of public enterprises

Both bureaucracy and public enterprises have been growing steadily since the Administrative State[2] of the early 1900s. Many bureaucratic agencies have shifted into diverse types of public enterprises since the appearance of the New Public Management (NPM) reforms in the 1980s. The number of public enterprises is now greater than that of bureaucratic agencies.

New Public Management emphasizes results, outcomes, and effective use of public-sector resources – the "management" orientation indicated in Table 9.1. Government departments with a strong trading functions[3] have been privatized or corporatized (incorporated), under the premise that such services could be more efficiently provided by commercially oriented organizations. Corporations are (theoretically) subject to autonomous management rather than immediate ministerial controls and government interference. Such organizations have self-funding obligations with commercial boards.

The validity of NPM reform is premised upon the inefficiency of government as a provider of commercial services, where "commercial" is defined rather broadly, i.e. good/services that could be provided by commercial entities.

III. Concept of public enterprise

The many diverse types of public enterprises have various terms.[4] There is little agreement on definitions or categorizations of public enterprises. Here it is only possible to suggest that a dizzying array of public enterprises rests between the polar extremes of public bureaucracy (government) and private implementation (firm) (See Figure 9.2).

The first characteristic of the public enterprise is hybridization.[5] They gain some of the freedom from rules and regulations that the private sector enjoys but retain some of the accountability and responsiveness of government agencies (Michell, 1999: 6–7). Several key elements can be extracted from the concept of the hybrid. The concept is composed of "public ownership" and "public control"

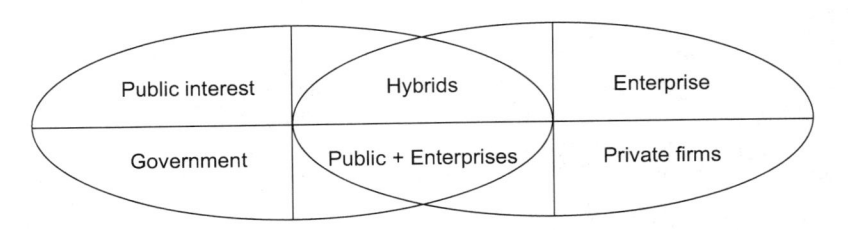

Figure 9.2 Array of public enterprises

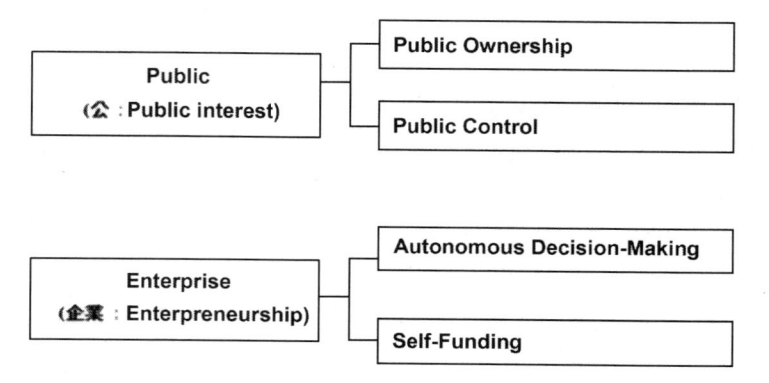

Figure 9.3 Concepts of public enterprise

to maintain the "public interest," alongside "autonomous decision-making" and "self-funding" to enhance "entrepreneurship," as shown in Figure 9.3.

1.   Public ownership and control

Public enterprises have diverse experimental types. The main idea is that public services or national necessities are provided by institutions owned or controlled wholly or substantially by government but that operated in the manner of businesses.

The term "public enterprise" refers to both state-owned enterprises and state-invested enterprises. A state-owned enterprise is a wholly state-owned entity, and a state-invested enterprise (also known as a government-invested corporation) is an entity whose majority or controlling shares are held by government. Unfortunately, there are a number of other terms also in use, and there is much disagreement among scholars as to the precise boundaries of the various terms.

2.   Autonomy and self-funding

Public enterprises should have significant independence from the politicians and governments who retain ownership. The enterprises should be operated with considerable levels of self-generated funds.

They have autonomous decision-making systems such as a Board of Directors, which deliberates and resolves budgets and other important issues. The Board of Directors in public enterprises assumes the deliberative role of the legislature in government. In the classic (Western) design, members of the Board of Directors have no individual authority but may act only as a vote in decisions by the Board; however, in Korean systems individual "Directors" may carry strong personal influence over operations, particularly those assigned to the board as representatives of powerful ministries.

IV   Trends in public enterprise governance reform

The Organisation for Economic Co-operation and Development (OECD) produced the Guidelines on the Corporate Governance of State-Owned Enterprises in 2005. The OECD Guidelines have encouraged many governments to demand new accountability from their public enterprises. These guidelines have been widely endorsed and warmly welcomed by OECD and non-OECD countries alike (Witherell, 2006). The guidelines accentuate centralized departmental control and robust evaluation systems for public enterprises.

The Korean government has attempted to modify its public enterprise governance system based on the guidelines and cognizant of contemporary trends.

1.   *Trends in public enterprise reform*

Every state has its own legal and regulatory framework for public enterprises. English-heritage countries, including New Zealand, underwent significant administrative reform in the 1980s with the intention of increasing efficiency and effectiveness within the public sector (Luke, 2010). He views New Zealand as a "poster country" for New Public Management due to the success of its "sweeping reforms" of public enterprises. Socialist states, including China, have also pursued marketability and management accountability in public organizations during this period.

The following is an examination of the trends in public reforms focused on public enterprise governance in key countries.

a)   *The United Kingdom*

Executive agencies and SOEs in the United Kingdom represent the core themes of public reforms. The executive agencies of the United Kingdom create overall efficiencies for the central government but have further exacerbated the problems of departmentalism, an enduring problem in the functional section system of government. The UK has more recently been considering a public enterprise system to take the complementary roles of agencies: the Shareholder Executive was created in the Cabinet Office in 2003.

The relationship between the state as a controlling or significant shareholder and the minority shareholders has been a particularly challenging topic in public enterprise management. As a dominant shareholder, the state may be in a position to abuse minority shareholders as it is able to make decisions without the approval of minority shareholders. It is also usually in a position to control the board's composition. Moreover, the state is likely to have other political and policy objectives that might be implemented at a cost to the minority shareholders.

b)   *New Zealand*

New Zealand has been called the "Experimental Country," though it only has a population of about 4.4 million people, as it has continued to playing the role as a leader in public administration reform.[6]

Prior to reforms, there were some efficiency and accountability problems in many kinds of public organizations in New Zealand. Seeking the most desirable design in the evolution of the public sector has become the foremost issue in administrative reforms. Public organizations have moved from being departments or executive agencies to public corporations, which have "legal person" status. Being a legal person means that it has autonomous decision-making power through the Board of Directors and is not subject to government interference.

New Zealand has state-owned enterprises and crown entities in the legal person style along with departments and non-public-service departments in a bureaucratic organizational style. These SOEs are fully commercialized organizations: government-owned but commercially focused.[7] SOEs are subject to the SOE Act (1986), which specifies generic objectives for SOEs and the duties and obligations of directors and shareholders. It provides legal authority for the establishment of SOEs. At the same time, SOEs are also companies registered under the Companies Act. SOEs run side by side under those two Acts. The SOE Act is all about transparency in the operations of SOEs: separating duties between managers and owners and specifying accountability for the various roles.

However, plenty of problems have been found in governing and managing these SOEs. The issue of multiple reporting systems in a managerial context gives rise to two issues: first, the risk of over-reporting and, second, the added task of educating authorities as part of the reporting process (OECD, 2006). New Zealand's SOE sector is vulnerable to such an over-reporting risk, which the OECD notes as the most inefficient element in public-sector management frameworks.

Adequate regulatory frameworks and the removal of duplication and blurred lines of accountability are important lessons from the New Zealand context (Luke, 2010).

c)   China

The indirect and three-tier ownership structures displayed in Table 9.2 have emerged in China since the implementation of the Modern Enterprise System in the mid-1990s. That is to say, the ministries of the state, as a representative

Table 9.2 Three-tier ownership structure of SOEs in China

Level	Structure	Role
First	Ministries of state	Formal representative of central government
Second	State-asset shareholding companies or non-corporate organizations	SOEs' direct shareholders
Third	SOEs	Practicing a special purpose mission

of central government, are theoretically located at the first level of the hierarchy and practicing their ownership rights. The public enterprises' direct shareholders, state-asset shareholding companies, or sometimes non-corporate organizations lie at the second level. Public enterprises themselves are placed at the third level of the hierarchy.

The Chinese government decided many years ago to extend the SOE sector in some fields while readjusting in others in order to rationalize state-owned enterprises. In line with this principle, the State-Owned Assets Supervision and Administration Commission of the State Council (SASAC, 國務院國有資產監督官理委員會) announced in 2010 that it had ordered 78 SOEs to withdraw from their core business as these had not been developed properly.

SASAC introduced a set of performance assessment measures for SOE managers and board members in 2010. It also asked listed SOEs to standardize their mission practices and the disclosure of information affecting share prices.

The SOE share of China's production economy has declined enormously compared to what it had been in the early reform period. It is reported that SOEs currently account for about one-third of production in the Chinese economy. In contrast, it was reported in 1978 that SOEs represented 77.6 percent of overall industrial production. Marketization[8] is the primary reason for this change.

Large cross-border Chinese SOEs such as oil exploration companies have brought about competitive neutrality problems. SOEs have more concessionary profits in finance and national resource usage than private companies operating on a level playing field. Not a few SOEs at the national level in China are criticized for various in-kind benefits and highly paid employment.

2. Lessons from global public corporate governance reform

Some lessons may be drawn from the governance reform of global public enterprises in OECD and non-OECD countries.

a) Dual leading system centered on the Minister of Finance

Almost all of the countries discussed here have two shareholding ministers, a Minister of Finance and, typically, a Minister for Public Enterprises. Both ministries jointly hold all the shares on behalf of the public: they are accountable

Table 9.3 The dual monitoring model in public enterprises

Ministry of Finance		Sector Ministry
National account perspective	Public enterprise ownership	Individual commercial perspective
Balance sheet perspective		Political perspective
Risk-averter perspective		Risk-taker perspective

to the Assembly under the relevant public enterprise act, i.e. there is no formal division of ownership.

Managerial monitoring under the dual system results more from the power and importance of the Ministry of Finance than from sector ministries, while sector ministries are traditionally in charge of public enterprises in view of their role in industrial policy.

The decentralized dual system was reformed and converted to a centralized model in France in 2004–2005[9] and is progressively evolving towards a centralized system in Australia. A more radical shift has been witnessed in Finland, where they moved directly from a decentralized to a centralized ministry in 2007.

b)   Robust performance evaluation and contract system

Some enterprises have produced desirable results, but not a few enterprises have been disappointing, with no apparent pattern of improvement in productivity or profitability. The OECD has emphasized strict performance evaluation and performance contracts for separating good managements from bad ones.

It is not easy to appraise diverse public enterprises with the same yardstick. Trade-offs between public interest and commercial entrepreneurship make evaluation of the public enterprises difficult. Pursuit of profit is apt to sacrifice social interests, and vice versa. The success of an evaluation and contract system depends on the following elements: first, the quality of performance indicators selected to monitor performance and, second, thoroughly independent management based on contracts, free from political interference.

c)   Autonomous management by ex-ante direction and ex-post facto results

Autonomy and accountability are the keys for successful management in public enterprises. A number of OECD countries have been changing the way in which they control public enterprises. Instead of checking specific actions, such as personnel or procurement, they are controlling management accountability. Day-to-day oversight of management, derived from the past history of close supervision of public enterprises, has been shifting to a more result-oriented monitoring. Such monitoring can be understood as an evolution towards operational autonomy of public enterprises with mandatory *ex-ante* direction and *ex-post facto* results.

d)   Minority shareholder rights

As a dominant shareholder, the state is usually in a position to control the board's composition. Moreover, the state is likely to have other political and policy objectives that might be implemented at a cost to the minority shareholders.

The Company Law in Greece allows the by-laws of companies to contain provisions regarding minority shareholder rights. A number of listed companies have a general assembly of minority shareholders in which all shareholders except the state may take part.

The state's track record in terms of respecting minority rights has a significant impact on share value and the future capacity of the company to raise further funds on the market. Having diverse kinds of shareholders introduces market pressures and may become an important means of monitoring public enterprise management.

Another minority rights issue is the excessive rights of the state. A "golden share" allows state rights beyond those of an ordinary shareholder's *pro rata* vote,[10] to include rights such as the veto of board decisions, (dis)approval of budgets, and the appointment of the CEO and/or a significant number of board members.

e)   *Competitive neutrality problems*

Competitive neutrality refers to the issue of allowing public enterprises the same level playing field as private companies. Creditors and the board often assume that there is an implicit state guarantee on public enterprise debts. This situation has in many instances led public enterprises to excessive indebtedness and wasted resources. This is detrimental both to bondholders and to the ultimate owners, the taxpayers. Definitive removal of the implicit state guarantee on public enterprise debts is a kernel issue in terms of competitive neutrality. Governments should treat public enterprises and private companies fairly.

For EU countries, the Community Law regime for state aid is supposed to prevent governments from subsidizing losses, thus strengthening the credibility of their commitment not to intervene and thereby allowing unhealthy public enterprises to go bankrupt (OECD, 2006).

V.   Role and reform of public enterprises in Korea

1.   *Role of public enterprises*

Public enterprises in general fill the need to overcome the operational constraints of government agencies or to deliver public services outside of the government. Public enterprises in Korea have been able to lead the recovery from past economic crises. They also acted as the facilitator of economic development by venturing into the fields where private enterprises have found it difficult to penetrate. They construct and manage infrastructure such as roads, railroads, and airports designed to serve as the basic foundations of national and industrial development (Korea Institute of Public Finance, 2014).

Korean public enterprises have always been at the forefront of the debate over public management efficiency, since their performances have usually affected the country's overall competitiveness. Though numerous public enterprises have led private-sector companies with managerial best practices for many years, not a few problems have recently been found in their management. New Public

Management adherents insist that public enterprises should be privatized to enhance managerial efficiency and customer satisfaction.

However, privatization is apt to bring about violent resistance from labor unions who fear job losses and from consumers who wish to avoid utility rate increases. As a result, the Korean government has preferred reform of public corporate governance over the shift from government to privatized ownership.

2.   Reform of public enterprises

a)   The government-invested company Basic Act of 1983

A series of public enterprise reforms were launched in the 1980s to increase productivity and the competitiveness of Government-Invested Corporations (GICs) in Korea at the time when the NPM trend prevailed in the public sector. Major reforms began with the enactment of the Basic Act for Government Invested Company Administration in 1983.

The 1983 Act stipulated that the government would only be allowed to set the objectives for public enterprises and to evaluate their performance but not control the way they pursue those objectives. Moreover, the Act entrusted GIC boards with the authority to finalize the budget in line with government guidelines but without the obligation to submit the budget to the supervising ministry. GICs also acquired the power to make decisions that had previously been decided at the central government level over purchasing goods according to their own discretion. Only a central body of Audit and Inspections was permitted to do external audits. Other governmental or political interference with day-to-day management was strictly restricted. Moreover, a newly structured nomination process for directors allowed the CEOs of public enterprises to play an active role without administrative interferences. Professional expertise was put in place as an element of a well-arranged nomination. The ultimate selection criterion for the manager is competence.

The Act was the starting point for independent and autonomous management through *ex-ante* direction and *ex-post facto* results of public enterprises.

b)   The Act on the Management of Public Institutions of 2007

The Korean government enacted The Act on the Management of Public Institutions in 2007 based on the OECD Guidelines for the Corporate Governance of State-Owned Enterprises in 2005.

The 2007 Act classified existing public enterprises in a new way according to their characteristics, established a committee for management to exercise centralized ownership of public institutions, strictly enforced management evaluation, and strengthened the transparency of the public disclosure system, though the Act did not consider minority shareholder rights and competitive neutrality.

The Act on the Management of Public Institutions has defined public institutions[11] as "organizations that are established or financially supported by the government to provide public services." They possess both public and business traits. Subsequently, there are various types of public institutions, from those whose business is as commercial as private-sector enterprises to those whose functions are as public as government entities. Such characteristics may vary depending on each institution's role and financial structure. The types of public institutions in the Act are classified into three groups by personnel, size of assets, and self-generated revenue. A total of 304 institutions were designated as public institutions in 2014: 30 state-owned enterprises, 87 quasi-governmental institutions, and 187 non-classified public institutions.

Korea's national state-owned enterprises are composed of market-based and quasi-market-based public corporations. Quasi-governmental institutions are divided into fund-management-based, quasi-governmental institutions and commissioned-service-based, quasi-governmental institutions. Non-classified public institutions are designated as neither public corporations nor quasi-governmental organizations.

The classification criteria of Korea's public institutions are shown in Table 9.4.

Table 9.4 Classification of public institutions

Classification (number of institutions)	Classification Criteria
1) Public corporations (30)	• Institutions whose prescribed number of personnel are at least 50 people and whose self-generating revenue accounts for at least 50% of their total revenue
○ Market-based public corporations	○ Institutions whose self-generating revenue accounts for at least 85% of their total revenue (with a minimum asset size of 2 trillion won)
○ Quasi-market-based public corporations	○ Public corporations other than market-based public corporations
2) Quasi-governmental institutions (87)	• Institutions whose prescribed number of personnel are at least 50 persons and whose self-generating revenue accounts for less than 50% of their total revenue
○ Fund-management-based quasi-governmental institutions	○ Institutions that manage (or are commissioned to manage) funds in accordance with the National Financial Act
○ Commissioned-service-based quasi-government institutions	○ Quasi-governmental institutions entrusted by government with the implementation of its plans
3) Non-classified public institutions (187)	• Public institutions other than public corporations and quasi-governmental institutions

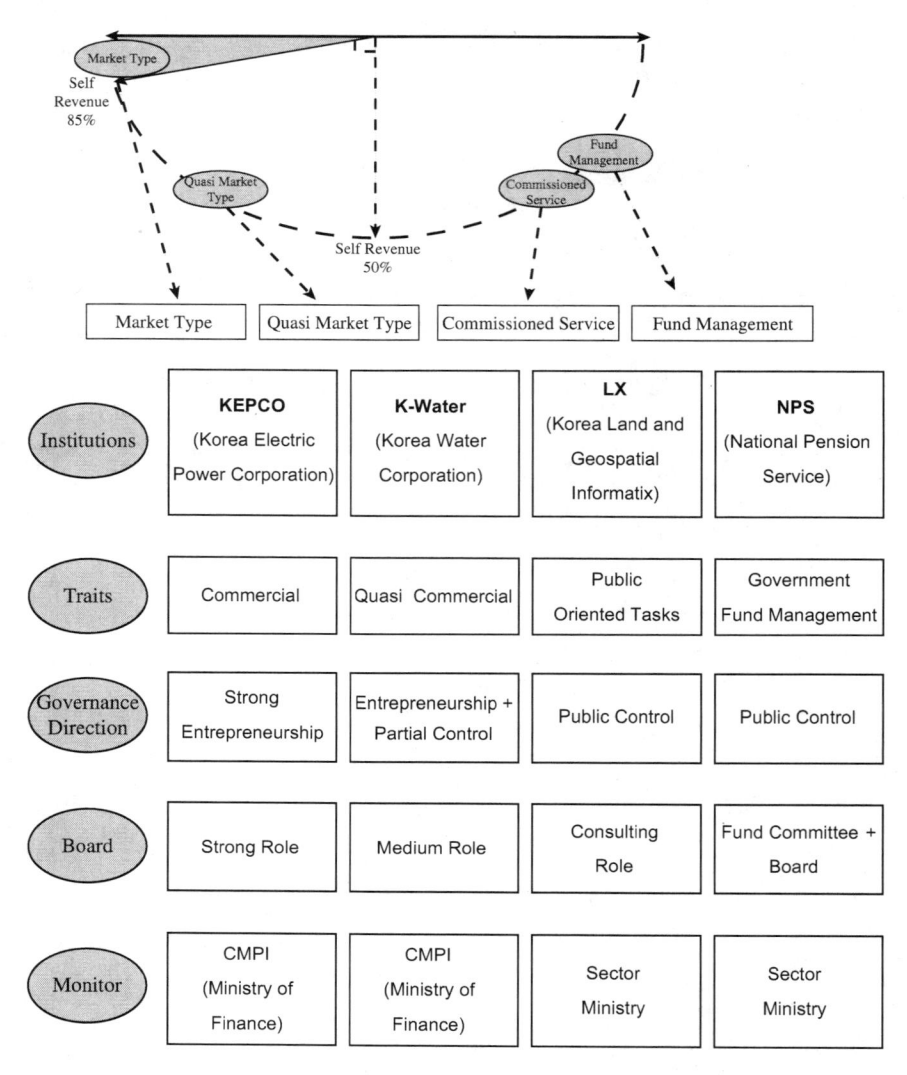

Figure 9.4 Characteristics of each type of public institution

A representative institution and the characteristics of each type of public enterprise are illustrated in Figure 9.4.

II)   COMMITTEE FOR THE MANAGEMENT OF PUBLIC INSTITUTIONS

The rights and authority of ownership over public institutions has been centralized under the Committee for the Management of Public Institutions (CMPI; 公共機關運營委員會), which is governed by the Ministry of Strategy and Finance while half of its members must come from the private sector. Its main functions are making recommendations for CEOs, auditors, and non-standing directors; setting management guidelines; and evaluating each public institution. The fundamental rules and principles for managing public institutions are made and confirmed by the CMPI. The CMPI supervises public institution management, but competent ministries still influence the public institution business as through administrative regulations and informal networks. Korea, in the context of administrative structure, has a dual monitoring system over its public institutions.

III) ROBUST MANAGEMENT AND INSTITUTIONAL EVALUATION

The management evaluation and contract system has been encouraging performance improvement by linking results to personnel appointment and remuneration. Performance-based payments, derived from the evaluation results, are known as the effective system by tailoring the system to each enterprise's missions and characteristics. It also has been strengthening competitiveness by introducing global indices that make comparison with the world's top enterprises possible.

Evaluating the performance of public enterprises can be characterized as a process[12] in which the annual performance of public enterprises is objectively assessed according to evaluation indicators.

The major purposes of the management evaluation are as follows:

- Enhancement of management efficiency and provision of accountability and motivation for goal achievement
- Setting clear targets and effective control over principal–agent problems
- Introduction of competition and pressure to stimulate management innovation
- Improvement of management based on feedback from evaluation results
- Improvement of management transparency in public enterprises

With the strict evaluation system, public enterprises' management responsibility has been enhanced by offering ex-ante direction and ex-post facto result assessment. However, labor unions and boards of directors in public enterprises are asking for the relaxation or the abolition of the evaluation system, as evaluation scores affect bonuses and other compensation.

IV) TRANSPARENT PUBLIC DISCLOSURE SYSTEM

The management publication system is designed to publicly disclose information regarding business performance, the status of personnel, and the financial conditions of public institutions with a view towards establishing a public monitoring system and, ultimately, towards improving their management efficiency.

The Act obligated all public institutions to disclose management information on their official websites and publish the same set of information on the comprehensive public information system, All Public Information In One (ALIO).

V)   NEED TO SECURE MINORITY SHAREHOLDER RIGHTS
      AND COMPETITIVE NEUTRALITY

The Act has not considered the issue of minority shareholder rights yet, nor have other stakeholders, such as the representatives of labor unions, been permitted to participate as members on the boards of public enterprises. The Act should be amended to include the proportional representation of minority shareholders. A general assembly of minority shareholders, as in Greece, could also be imported.

The Korean government supports and encourages public enterprises to expand across borders, just as China does. In order to become global companies, Korean public enterprises should respect issues of competitive neutrality. At present the Korean government implicitly or explicitly guarantees the debts of some public enterprises. For example the government stands as surety on the Korea Land and Housing Corporation, which carries out housing projects. The Korean government should treat all public enterprises equally whether they work domestically or abroad and in public areas or private fields.

New Zealand's issue of duplicated and blurred lines of accountability among government departments for public enterprises has been a chronic problem in the management of Korean public enterprises as well. Korea needs to clarify each stakeholder's role to secure accountability in public enterprises, whether governmental ministry, private shareholder, employee, consumer, or taxpayer.

Notes

1 Korean public enterprises are composed of national (central government) and local public enterprises. The budget of the 304 national public institutions is 655.4 trillion won in 2014, and the budget of the 394 local public enterprises is 49 trillion won. The ratio of the budget of national public institutions to GDP is 43.2 percent. If the budgets of local public enterprises are included, the ratio of the total budget of all public enterprises to GDP increases to 46.4 percent. The ratio of total budget expenditure of public enterprises to that of the government reaches approximately 200 percent (Korea Institute of Public Finance, 2014).
2 "The Administrative State" suggests that the administrative role surpasses that of the legislature or the judiciary.
3 The trade function is the voluntary exchange of goods, services, or both. Trade is also called commerce or the benefit principle. The benefit principle means those who benefit must bear the cost of paying for a service.
4 The many terms referring to public enterprises include quasi-autonomous non-governmental organizations (Quangos), quasi-autonomous governmental organizations (Quagos), state-owned enterprise or state-owned entity (SOE), non-departmental public bodies (NDPB), wider state sector (WSC), parastatals, and public corporations (Lee, 2012).
5 Variations of the term hybrids include Third Party Government, Intermediate Sector, Mixed Public/Private Sector, Nonprofit Sector, Non-Governmental Sector, Twilight Zone, Grey Area, and Contracted Sector (Lee, 2012).
6 New Zealand is a constitutional monarchy, with the British sovereign as head of state.

7 They include New Zealand Post, Airways New Zealand (air traffic control and navigation), New Zealand Railways Corporation, and four corporations in the business of energy production and distribution.
8 China rejects the term "privatization" at this time (as does Vietnam). Tian (2000) suggests that China, reflecting on the problems of privatization in Eastern Europe, sees privatization of state-owned firms as only appropriate after suitable competing firms have been established, including purely private, collective-owned, and other types of businesses.
9 A centralized agency for state shareholdings, the Agence des Participations d'Etat (APE), was created in France at the beginning of 2004 (OECD, 2006).
10 Pro-rata: percentage based on another percentage, e.g. if you own 20 percent of stock, you have 20 percent of votes on the board of directors.
11 The Act used the term "public institution" instead of "public enterprise" or state owned-entity, which had previously been used.
12 The evaluation procedures each year are (1) delivery of the management performance evaluation manual by Ministry of Strategy and Finance and CMPI (January) → (2) formation of a management evaluation team (February) → (3) execution of the management evaluation (March to May) → (4) deliberation and resolution of the Committee for Management of Public Institutions (June 20th).

References and Further Readings

Korea Institute of Public Finance. (2014). *Public Institutions in Korea*. Seoul: KIPF.

Lee, S.C. (2012). *Understanding Korean Public Enterprises*. Seoul: Tae-young Publishing Co.

Luke, B. (2010). "Examining Accountability Dimension in State-Owned Enterprises." *Financial Accountability & Management*, 26(2, May), 417–424.

Michell, J. (1999). *The American Experiment with Government Corporations*. Armonk, New York: M.E. Sharpe.

Ministry of Security and Public Administration. (2014). *Local Public Enterprises in Korea*. Seoul: MSPA.

OECD. (2006). *OECD Comparative Report on Corporate Governance of State-Owned Enterprises*. Paris: OECD.

OECD. (2010). *SOEs Operating Abroad: An application of the OECD Guidelines on Corporate Governance of State-Owned Enterprises to the cross-border operations of SOEs*. Paris: OECD.

Tian G. (2000). "China's Reforms: Past, Present and Future." *American Review of China Studies* 1, 1–8.

Witherell, W.H. (2006). *Preface of the Guidelines on the Corporate Governance of State-Owned Enterprises*. Paris: OECD.

10 Urban development

Jong Youl Lee and Chad Anderson

I. Urban development and urban development issues

There are several concepts that fall under urban development. Urban development itself is a broad term that first referred to the expansion of cities into natural areas (Park and Burgess, 1984). However, it is now also used to mean new growth more generally and may be used to mean redevelopment in low-density areas. Blakely (1989) explains local economic development as the process of stimulating business activity and employment. Blair draws a distinction between urban economic growth and urban development, even though they sound similar. They are related in that economic growth may be considered an element for development. His distinction is made between increase in the economy and increase in the welfare of residents. Growth increases the economy but may not improve the economic situation of residents or may actually even hurt it (Blair, 1995). Growth often brings pollution, destroys traditional and historic culture, and also leads to overcrowding whether or not it improves the welfare of residents.

Problems of growth are often related to urban decline, where the urban economy shrinks. Excessive growth that damages welfare may be a cause, especially in situations where increasing industry leads to pollution or where a greater population density comes with higher rates of crime. The growth that may have developed the urban economy may undermine it, encouraging residents to leave for other areas (Hirsch, 1984). These problems are addressed with renewal, regeneration, and redevelopment.

Renewal means land redevelopment in moderately to highly dense urban areas. Urban renewal is associated with business-oriented housing redevelopment projects that have been the source of controversy as older neighborhoods have been displaced by new development (Spates and Macionis, 1982 pg. 421; Jacobs, 1993; Halle, 2003 pg. 22). Urban renewal frequently evokes strong reactions that depend on the perspective of the listener. Regeneration refers to "the promotion of the social, economic, and environmental well-being of an area" and is a term with more neutral or positive associations than urban renewal (Davies, 2001 pg. 2). Regeneration has become more common in recent years. Restoration, on the other hand, is a more specific architectural term that refers to a broad array of processes from building cleaning and repair and refurbishing to complete rebuilding to return a space to an original form (Spates and Macionis, 1982 pg. 421). Redevelopment is a general term that covers any development that occurs over an area that has already been developed (Anderson, 2010 pg. 13).

1. Critics of growth

The pro-growth school of development addresses issues like the city's role in industrialization, and the clustering and concentration effects that create efficiency and economies of scale. In contrast, the mobility approach looks at how urban households and businesses make decisions where to move within and between urban areas (Bluestone et al., 2008).

The very concept of urban development is not without controversy. There are critics of general concepts of development, of the growth school, and the concepts of mobility in general, and of typical development tools in particular. The predominant pro-growth school has attracted considerable criticism. It is criticized as promoting artificial wants, not addressing questions of equity, contributing to the fluctuations of the business cycle, and depleting finite resources. The advocates of the growth model particularly receive criticism from those who point out that infinite growth is not possible on a finite planet.

The concept of growth itself has been attacked from two directions. The first is the basis of environmental and resource limitations and reality. The second is on the basis of the equitability of growth and the question of who benefits.

2. Limits to growth

Growth critics, and even growth advocates, recognize limits to growth due to limited resources and the finite amount of space that can absorb urban sprawl. The easiest way to grow is to increase the population. More people create more demand and require more products. Therefore attracting more people is an effective way to grow. However, population increase cannot be sustained indefinitely. An increase in the population places more demands on urban infrastructure and intensifies basic urban problems like congestion, overcrowding, and sprawl. There is limited space so cities may not grow indefinitely before they run out of space.

Resources are also limited. More people require more resources. However, even without more people, development according to current technologies and current development models requires major increases in consumption of non-renewable resources like coal and oil and rare minerals. A population that is either growing or becoming wealthier places increasing pressure on renewable and non-renewable resources and is not sustainable forever.

Major environmental problems like pollution and global warming are also worsened by development under current models of growth. Cities generate massive waste, and the problem of dealing with municipal waste is a major problem. Garbage collection leads to huge landfills, incineration, and dumping at sea. These are all solutions to waste on a small scale but become an issue when used to support a metropolis. Larger cities burn more fossil fuels and require significant amounts of power, contributing to manmade climate change. They are also under constant risk of disaster through spills like the BP Oil Spill in the Gulf of Mexico in April 2010 or nuclear plant failures like at Fukushima in March 2011. The logic of growth is contrary to the finite capacity of the planet to care for people.

Sustainable development, in contrast, is development that can continue into the future and that does not compromise the ability of future generations to meet their needs and enjoy their quality of life (Rees, 1998). Development that depends on non-renewable resources such as carbon-based fuels and undeveloped land is unsustainable. Development that requires endless growth in finite space is also unsustainable. Opinion ranges from depending almost solely on growth in a way that basically equates development with growth to opinions rejecting growth, emphasizing sustainability in growth, or emphasizing quality of life in development.

3. Power and equality

Growth is often considered as though it is neutral. However, there is the question of who benefits from growth. There is also the question of the real motives behind specific development projects and development tools. One common view for example sees urban development as controlled by capital-oriented, pro-growth machines that may disagree over many issues but share an interest in driving development and redevelopment (Logan and Molotch, 2007). The leadership of the city competes politically only over details of implementation of a growth program, but not over its existence. Urban regimes are dominated by those who profit from land and construction or by interests allied to them.

Therefore growth may be treated as value-free in that divisions among urban elites are not along a pro- versus anti-growth. Instead, major party politics involve different visions of growth. Elites share in the profits that come from a system driven by urban growth, although they do not agree on particular issues.

Mollenkopf (1975, 1983) sees cities that are "contested" as the site for political struggle for control, where business elites and political elites in urban parties often struggle against broader citizen interests. Wilson (1987) considers the declining inner city to be in the grip of poverty and ghettos based on the class features of urban capitalism. Urban poverty is driven by apparently class-neutral approaches to urban issues that really benefit middle and upper classes at the expense of the urban poor. The underclass is exploited through neglect of their welfare. These critics raise the questions of how development is planned and for whose benefit. They point out that the benefits of urban growth are not shared equally.

4. *Mobility development*

Tiebout (1956) is famous for his hypothesis that residents "vote with their feet" by moving away from an undesirable municipality to one they prefer. This may be due to quality of life, good schools, proximity to work, or levels of taxation and public spending (Tiebout's emphasis). There are some practical issues with this idea. First, individuals and businesses cannot really choose from a very broad range of local governments. In a very centralized system like Korea's, governments have a very limited range of policy choices that are not mandated by the central government. Furthermore, it is unlikely that most workers or businesses have all the necessary information and technical knowledge to make informed choices between different policies along the lines that Tiebout envisioned. Next, even if households and businesses do have full information, there is no guarantee that they are interested in making a rational move as they are not freely mobile. Even if there is a better deal elsewhere, the costs involved in moving may be too high. In addition, non-economic factors like commitment to community may be more important than specific policies. Finally, factors like location, which a municipality has no control over, may be much more important than any policies a city may be able to decide.

Richard Florida (2002, 2007) argues that cities develop by attracting a creative class of talented individuals who innovate in the local economy, providing the labor for desirable high-tech and creative industries. Florida argues that the three elements involved in attracting, creating, and maintaining a creative class are the three Ts of talent, technology, and tolerance. Creative individuals in a creative culture provide the talent who make use of the technology and flourish in an environment of tolerance.

However, Clark (2004) has argued that some of Florida's research can be examined in greater detail in ways where the importance of tolerance is weak or non-existent. Furthermore, the Florida argument makes intuitive sense in many Western societies like Western Europe and North America but seems to be contradicted by the dynamic economies of East Asia. One of Florida's favorite measures of tolerance is acceptance of homosexuals and homosexuality. Many dynamic East Asian nations like Korea, Japan, Taiwan, and China have much lower tolerance in this area, even when coupled with higher levels of education, but all have been excelling in areas of creative innovation. There is a real question whether tolerance is a universal requirement that may be expressed differently in different cultures. Maybe it is a factor unique to Western societies or even not a factor at all.

a) *Inducements to business to relocate*

Offering incentives to businesses to relocate or to stay in an area has become a major trend even though there are several issues with the practice. First, there are usually no guarantees to protect a city in case a business fails to generate jobs or simply takes benefits and leaves. Second, there is little evidence that this method generates significant permanent jobs, particularly when compared to the amount of money spent. Next, there is little evidence that businesses use tax cuts, abatements, and other methods as a factor in relocation decisions, unless they are deciding between a small number of municipalities within a relatively small area. The effect, if any, is mostly that businesses begin to expect such support. The focus of the process can become very political with different politicians assuming that they have no choice but to offer better incentives than other cities in order to attract business. Finally, there is the point that these growth competition strategies are zero-sum strategies where one community gains at the expense of another. There is no possibility that this can be a general strategy for all cities to follow without some losing out (Wolman and Spitzley, 1996).

II. History of urban development in Korea

Korea has a similar urban development history to other countries that developed in the twentieth century. Squatters and their settlements in central cities like Seoul were an obstacle to the economic development of the central city's potential and, at the same time, a housing problem for the squatters. The government decided to resolve the issue through direct intervention after the Korean War (Lee, 2009).

Much of Korea had to be rebuilt after the Korean War, which prompted competition with North Korea and massive aid from the United States, who aligned with the "democratic" non-communist government in the South (Lee and Anderson, 2012). Seoul grew rapidly and drew citizens from around the nation to live in its burgeoning urban slums. From the founding of the republic in 1948 to the mid-1960s, redevelopment worked to displace inner-city squatters and construct large concentrations of apartments (Lee, 1990, 2009; Ha, 1995).

The government decided to resolve the issue through direct intervention after the Korean War. There has been a major evolution in the approaches taken to address urban development and housing in Korea, based on experience, political necessity, and changing resources. The practices can be divided into several general periods with distinct strategies, though most strategies and practices were not limited to the trends of their respective periods (Lee, 2009; Lee and Anderson, 2012).

1. Post-war to the 1960s: shantytown clearance

Impoverished farmers left the land in large numbers during the 1950s and the early 1960s to seek a better life in the cities, which grew rapidly and drew citizens from around the nation to live in burgeoning urban slums. The state demolished squatter settlements without making any provision for the effective resettlement of the residents. Private investment was not available for housing the new urban poor. Private capital was involved in importing and selling basic goods while growing a wealthy entrepreneurial class. While providing some level of development, government policy exploited squatters for the benefit of real estate capital with redevelopment mostly just displacing inner-city squatters as the government and private interests acted together, razing squatter settlements with bulldozers, though squatters protested and resisted (Lee, 1990, 2009; Ha, 1995).

2. *1960s–1970s: legalization and citizen apartments*

As a part of solving Park Chunghee's legitimacy crisis, the government adopted a new policy that called for the relocation of squatters to designated housing areas, the legalization and rehabilitation of squatter settlements meeting certain conditions, as well as the construction of small apartments at the demolished sites with provision for resettlement there for former squatters (Lee, 2009).

Residents and local community members in settlement neighborhoods started to play a role in the process through a system of priority tickets that allowed squatters the right to a small apartment in a new development. The government provided funds for the construction of apartment buildings and gave squatters priority in purchasing units in the form of so-called priority tickets. However, high management costs and limited investment resources forced the city government to start selling the apartments (Kim Won, 1984). Most squatters lacked money to buy in any case, so they sold their tickets and moved to new settlements located on the periphery of the city (Lee and Anderson, 2012). Prolonged tenant protests thus continued.

3. *1970s–1980s: rehabilitation and removal*

Due to the intensive tenant protest provoked by removal, the state promoted more rehabilitation. Removal was still the most common policy tool, though. Residents ultimately bore the entire cost of redevelopment from housing construction and land acquisition. A result, success of the policy depended on resident participation. However, the participation of squatters was almost impossible because they lacked title to their housing, which could not then be sold on the open market, so most residents sold their priority tickets to the more affluent and moved to the new urban periphery, creating new squatter settlements there (Lee, 2009). Redevelopment therefore continued to disrupt existing communities (Sin, 1991).

4. *1980s: joint redevelopment*

New squatter settlements mainly developed at Seoul's urban periphery after 1970. As idle space at the urban center became in ever-shorter supply, the state increasingly turned its attention to this periphery. The relative political strength of the urban poor increased after Park Chunghee's assassination. The state shifted urban development policy to resolve rising urban protests (Lee, 2009).

One of the solutions was joint redevelopment. Under this approach, squatter-owners provided housing lots while construction firms covered all other project costs. The state's involvement was limited. The government only managed and supervised the process. Joint redevelopment was successful and was responsible for many large-scale redevelopment projects. Construction firms and squatter-owners participated due to the major redevelopment profit. The city benefitted from the increased tax base and a reduction in confrontations with protesters due to its reduced role in the process (Lee, 2009).

Although building owners were allowed to form joint redevelopment corporations, displaced tenants received only a small relocation subsidy, limiting their stake in the process (Ha, 1995). Tenants were forced to search for new housing, as their sole benefit was a small relocation subsidy. The anger and resentment of tenants grew, along with their political identity and cohesiveness, eventually erupting into protests as in 1985 in Sanggye-dong and 1986 in Mok-dong (Lee, 1990).

5. 1990s: housing environment improvement program

More space opened up for individual redevelopment projects in the 1990s with the initiation of larger multifamily projects when three-quarters of the residents in an area called for the creation of a redevelopment zone. This led to a "new partnership" between the state, business, and civil society for joint redevelopment. The 1990s also saw the first elected local governments, providing local governments with independence in devising and implementing policy (Lee, 2009). Joint redevelopment led to more housing, but the lack of resident participation in planning, lack of equity in housing allocation, and lack of affordability for low-income residents remained contentious issues. The process remained largely top-down and driven by a combination of state and business interests (Kim, 1997; Lee, 2009). The low cost to the state and the great benefits generated by an increasing tax base (one of the few means of generating revenue not controlled by the central government) as well as high profits for business and building owners kept this method popular (Lee and Anderson, 2012). Urban development protest continued through the period over dissatisfaction with the process.

6. The new millennium

A "new partnership" of state, private sector, and community for economic and physical regeneration has dominated since the 1990s. Sustainable and human development practices are followed. There has been considerable physical improvement since joint redevelopment. However, it has led to various problems such as the lack of resident participation in the planning process, lack of equity in the housing allocations, and a lack of affordability for low-income residents. One facet of this program is that residents of impoverished districts pursue their capital interest by incorporating construction capital (Lee, 2009).

While the same urban development methods have continued into the new millennium, so has resistance. The new liberal governments of Kim Daejung and Roh Moohyun reduced redevelopment conflict by waiting out protests and using the time to allow local actors to negotiate solutions. However, the potential for disaster remained. It came January 19, 2009.

The plans in Yongsan's Hankangno neighborhood, like other joint redevelopments, designated an area for redevelopment by a corporation formed by a construction company and local property owners. The issue took years to negotiate due to problems with the redevelopment compensation. It did not consider the actual costs of moving or starting a new business elsewhere or any long-term investments that had been made. Members of the Federation against House Demolition, including tenants from the area and activists from other parts of the city, demanded that the plan be scrapped. However, instead of negotiating, the police made a raid at dawn after only one day of occupation. Protesters used Molotov cocktails and projectiles thrown by hand or shot from slingshots. Flames ignited almost 370 gallons of paint thinner on the fortified roof and quickly engulfed the building. Five protesters and one policeman died in the fire (Anderson, 2010). Most development schemes were met with protests and evictions though this case is the only one to end in such tragedy (Anderson, 2010).

At the same time, the conservative mayors of Seoul, Lee Myungbak and Oh Sehoon, tried to pursue environmental and cultural projects for urban development while simultaneously approving major redevelopment projects. In this time of increasing interest in and salience of culture, there have been moves in South Korea towards the so-called amenity model of urban development. This model stresses the role of urban amenities and scenes. This model is in contrast to the traditional planning models based on top-down control as well as to the model of luring business through expensive incentive packages. Instead, the concept is to create an urban environment that is more livable for residents that will encourage the development of desired types of human capital and attract and encourage business activity indirectly (Anderson, 2010).

Lee is best known for the restoration of the Cheonggye-cheon and Oh for his design-oriented "culturenomics." Oh ended up suspending most ongoing development projects before the end of his tenure (Lee and Anderson, 2012). The re-election of Mayor Park Wonsoon in 2014 suggested that Seoul would follow a people-oriented development model, while other cities with less independent incomes would continue to pursue place-oriented strategies. Urban leaders in Korea continue to pursue big events like the 2014 Incheon Asian Games and the 2018 Pyeongchang Winter Olympics.

Considerable issues have arisen over the current state of development in Korea, although Joo and Kim (2004) have stood up for the current redevelopment model, despite its flaws, for alleviating the severe housing problems in Korean cities and facilitating dynamic growth, while Sin (1991) found that the reconstruction of apartment buildings in redevelopment had advantages but had unexpected effects on the neighborhood and vicinity while Kim (1997) found joint redevelopment had helped speed up the process.

III.   Development tools

As Korea has a market economy, Korean local governments usually adopt development policies compatible with private markets. Such policies are based on the idea that helping private businesses grow develops and benefits the whole community. Though this may be true, the profits go mostly to private companies even when the money is public (Bamekov et al., 1989). Two general kinds of business-oriented policies are policies that subsidize business and public-private entrepreneurialism. Subsidies work by supporting businesses by lowering their costs while public-private entrepreneurialism supports the creation of new businesses (Lee et al., 2012).

1.   Business subsidies

Some of the most common subsidies to business include offsetting the costs associated with taxes, money, land, and regulations. Specific methods include tax abatements, subsidized interest rates, cheap land, and enterprise zones (Lee et al., 2012).

a)   Tax abatements

A tax abatement is an exemption from local taxes. This exemption may be partial or complete and may be permanent and general or limited to a specific time and specific purposes. Tax abatements are usually used to attract new employers to the community or to discourage current employers from leaving. Either way, tax abatements are criticized for creating competition that results in a "race to the bottom" between localities where each city tries to offer more attractive benefits. They are also criticized for shifting the tax burden to other taxpayers and reducing current and future revenues, with the negative impact that has on the programs that the city can fund. The process does more to shift jobs between communities than it does to create jobs overall (Swanstrom, 1985).

b)   Lower interest rates

Businesses need to borrow money and lower interest rates provide real support to businesses. This can be done through loan guarantees, special bonds to finance public/private development, or even direct loans. This encourages public projects with below-market financing but shares some of the same weaknesses as tax abatements. In addition, many companies come to expect help with financing, which hurts the influence of cities in negotiations. Benefits also usually go to large corporations that do not really need the assistance and can find funding on their own (Squires, 1984).

c)   Cheap land

A major benefit that local government in Korea has to offer is free or cheap land. Major redevelopment projects are usually attractive in no small part because the city even takes on the cost of developing the roads and other public elements necessary to support a private project. Cities provide below-market access to prime real estate to modernize older districts, to provide land for high-tech manufacturing, to reorganize traffic and transportation routes, and to provide upscale housing. As noted above, the personal costs of redevelopment usually affect low-income residents and small business owners who are displaced to make way for projects (Lee, 1990, 2009; Anderson, 2010; Lee and Anderson, 2012).

d) Enterprise zones

An enterprise zone is an area targeted for development and businesses are given incentives to relocate there. These incentives can include tax reductions, loans, land, advertising promotion, technical assistance, training, or reductions in government regulations. Enterprise zones are now a very common form of development assistance. Enterprise zones do not seem to attract new businesses as much as they encourage businesses to move to the zone. Few enterprise zones require that low-income people get preferential treatment in hiring, even though the rationale usually includes increasing employment opportunities for low-income people. Overall, the enterprise zone programs function primarily as tax reduction programs that make it cheaper for businesses to operate within the zone (Burnier, 1992, Wilder and Rubin, 1996).

2. Public-private entrepreneurialism

Local governments may act as entrepreneurs by forming and running businesses. There are two different possibilities for public enterprises run by local governments. The most common examples are convention centers and sports facilities such as stadiums. They may provide profit as well as run in the public interest. The local government invests in these ventures, and then the profits from those enterprises go to the private businesses that run them rather than back to the local government. The public-private partnership, or quasi-public corporation, is a common example. These organizations are usually operated by boards that represent both business and government (Leitner and Garner, 1993).

a) Convention centers

Conventions attract large numbers of visitors to a city and help local businesses that supply visitors with food, lodging, shopping, and entertainment. Even though convention centers often lose money, city officials may use convention centers as anchors for development projects because convention centers create extra demand generated by visitors and their events (Lee et al., 2012).

b) Sports facilities

Sports facilities provide a high-profile amenity that provides similar benefits to convention centers while often adding the prestige factor of being able to host popular athletics. This is particularly an issue where a city hosts a professional team (Lee et al., 2012).

3.   *Problems with subsidizing the private sector*

There are several issues with using private-sector initiatives for development. First, there are often questions about the cost and cost-effectiveness of public-private development programs. Second, inducements to business need to increase to get the same effect as businesses come to expect public subsidies (Wolman and Spitzley, 1996). Cities often have little power to compel businesses to keep promises made in exchange for promised benefits area (Jones and Bachelor, 1993). The benefits provided to businesses are not usually the deciding factor in a relocation decision. Meanwhile, taxes are not a major expense to a business, but lost tax revenue to a city may be very significant (Wolman and Spitzley, 1996). The main reason for private-sector subsidies seems to be that it is a very visible way for urban leaders to be seen to be doing something that reasonably appears to be attracting and creating jobs.

4.   *Other policies for local economic development*

Even though many cities prioritize public subsidies for private interests, there are several other methods commonly used for development. These include planning, retaining manufacturing, public entrepreneurship, and community development corporations (Lee et al., 2012).

a)   Planning

Almost every urban government uses some kind of city planning. City planning departments deal with urban problems produced by market failure, like traffic congestion, air pollution, and inadequate housing. Planning can be very detailed or very broad, leaving more to the market. Either way, planning is usually structured to advance urban development plans (Feagin, 1988). Two planning strategies for doing this in specific ways include equity planning and linkage. Equity planning involves systematically structuring plans to favor redistribution towards poorer residents. Meanwhile, linkage is used in rapidly growing areas to connect (or link) expensive commercial and investment building permits to redistributing benefits to residents in general or to poorer residents in particular (Lee et al., 2012).

b)   Retaining manufacturing jobs

As many areas see a shift from manufacturing jobs towards lower-paying service jobs, localities may take proactive strategies to adjust to the changes. Instead of doing anything to lower the costs for the businesses that are left, localities may identify future-oriented industries and invest in infrastructure and training for the local workforce in order to create a climate where companies will relocate to take advantage of the workforce or to join a cluster through agglomeration. What separates this from the private investment strategies noted above is the future orientation, the focus on developing the workforce for new and rising industries, and an emphasis on long-term infrastructure instead of on short-term cost reduction (Lee et al., 2012).

c) The public entrepreneur

Cities have the alternative of operating their own businesses, owning and running their own public services such as transportation and utilities. While this is not common in Korea, many cities around the world run their own Internet, their own public transportation, their electricity and gas, among other services (Lee et al., 2012).

d) Community development corporations

Communities such as neighborhoods at a level lower than the local government may organize community development corporations (CDCs) for the purpose of addressing the needs of the community in terms of local economic development, although CDCs may also be formed under the sponsorship or in conjunction with local government. This has been particularly the case where poor neighborhoods or districts have been ignored or abandoned by private investors. CDCs are usually nonprofit corporations. CDCs employ a very broad range of strategies, including education, community organizing, and political activism to the founding of for-profit and non-profit enterprises. They are community-owned and are organized to attract or raise capital for investment in the community as well as to provide services that are not provided by the market (Rubin, 1994).

IV. Major projects in Korea

1. New town development

A new town is a new urban community that is deliberately planned and constructed in whole. New towns are designed to overcome some of the problems of organic development. They are planned to be self-sufficient by providing housing, employment, education, entertainment, and shopping for its residents.

Classically, a new town is usually constructed in an undeveloped area and is highly planned to avoid land use conflicts typical of organic communities, as the planning process defines the land use. In Korea, however, there have still been land use issues in some cases, particularly involving agricultural land. The case of New Songdo, involving land reclamation from the sea, is one of the few cases truly absent land use conflict.

New towns have been popular for development because they allow for reducing overcrowded populations, easing urban congestion. Lim (2010) looked at the development of Gangneung and found that new development on the periphery lowered the population density at the old city center even as it created new centers and expanded the city as a whole.

They also provide economic benefits for urban developers who may be among the important actors in the city, not to mention providing for new tax revenue as property values rise. Finally, they provide new sources of housing. On the other hand, new town developments have been roundly criticized for destroying communities and traditions and putting profit ahead of such civic values. New town developments do not treat all actors equally with investors benefitting overwhelmingly, the city benefitting from new sources of revenue, property owners benefitting from rising land values, but tenants losing out and even being evicted, often in a conflict-driven process. New Songdo in Incheon is one recent example of many new towns in Korea such as Ilsan, Bundang, Dongtan, and Haeundae.

Many have criticized the "new town" model for problems such as generating conflict (Jung and Kim, 2009), the failure to resettle large numbers of original inhabitants (Kim et al. 2010), problems with compensation (Yong-Chang Kim, 2010), unbalanced and unsustainable development (Young-soo Kim, 2005), and an inability to become self-contained, particularly in terms of jobs (Jeong and Kim, 2010). Others have found the model, despite its flaws, to help relieve housing problems and advance development (Joo and Kim, 2004).

2.   *Cheonggye-cheon restoration project*

The Cheonggye-cheon represents an alternative to the "new town" model and was advanced under Mayor Lee Myungbak as part of his "new developmentalism" model of urban development that would pay more attention to non-economic factors like image, the environment, history, and broad benefits to stakeholders. The case provided various benefits to the local community, was leadership driven, involved some citizen input, involved some conflict, and was very expensive.

The Cheonggye-cheon is a stream running through the center of Seoul emptying into a larger stream that empties into the Han River. A reorganization of the stream was completed in 1412 to provide water flow and to manage rainwater but became heavily polluted and the site of poor shanties whose occupants used the stream to do laundry during industrialization. The shanties were displaced to make way for a highway leading to the central business district while the paved-over stream itself became a de facto sewer (Anderson, 2010: 86). The restoration project was announced early in Mayor Lee's term as part of a new development paradigm balancing environment and growth to reconstruct the city as a citizen- and eco-friendly space (Lee and Anderson, 2012), developing the downtown into a center of history and culture, business and commerce, and tourism and shopping, providing a new image for the city.

The restored stream has provided benefits to local stakeholders, attracting more visitors to the neighborhood. The environment has improved with better air quality around the stream, cooler temperatures, better drainage, more wildlife, and urban green space. It has provided leisure space for people living and working and visiting the area. The removal of the road and overpass was facilitated with improvements to the traffic system. The restoration appears to have reinforced divided benefits by gentrifying the areas adjoining the stream. Therefore, much of the cost to the community may have been concealed and passed off into the future. Criticisms were sidelined through the restoration with effective positive public relations and the winning over of many critics, including through the direct intervention of the mayor to settle conflicts. Overall, the substance of citizen input often amounted to better PR and salesmanship for the project, and the provision of more broadly shared benefits that opponents could be persuaded to value (Lee and Anderson, 2013).

The project attracted international attention and become part of the new image of Seoul, accompanying an increase in Seoul's global status (Lee and Anderson, 2013). Mayor Lee Myungbak won the presidency in part over the perception of the success of the Cheonggye-cheon Restoration and promised a transnational canal that was quickly blocked by the opposition (Lee and Anderson, 2013).

The focus on design inspired and helped lead to "culturenomics," the design and culture-oriented economic development policy of Mayor Lee's successor, Oh Sehoon, though that model ended with the election of Mayor Park Wonsoon, who has invested more in local welfare spending (Lee and Anderson, 2012).

3. New Songdo

The New Songdo development, part of the Incheon Free Economic Zone, has attracted considerable attention as an example of modern high-tech trends for city development, such as the ubiquitous U-City that incorporates ubiquitous information technology for universal information technology access through wired or wireless networks (Lee et al., 2012). It is also a prototypical example of the "smart city" that uses information technology on both a large and small scale to manage urban processes (Townshend, 2013) including innovations such as LED traffic lights and centralized pneumatic waste collection on top of specialized systems in luxury apartments that automatically dispatch elevators, open and close blinds, and even monitor health (Anderson, 2014). Furthermore, New Songdo is an early example of an "aerotropolis," a city growing up around and shaped by proximity to an airport, in this case, Incheon International Airport, which is consistently ranked one of the world's best, instead of following the traditional relationship where an airport is located close to a growing city (Kasarda and Lindsay, 2011). New Songdo includes major international investment, an international research park, and several university campuses, including satellite campuses for a number of international universities.

Even though the area has not been completed, New Songdo continues to attract attention as a model "city in a box" featuring technology that can be exported and built anywhere in the world to be centrally and efficiently managed (Townshend, 2013). The development has lacked the kind of land use conflicts typical among Korean development projects, in no small part because it is constructed on land reclaimed from the sea (Anderson, 2014). However, the high debt raised by spending on development by Mayor Ahn Sangsu became a political issue and led to the election of Mayor Song Younggil, who favored retiring debt. As Incheon hosted the 2014 Asian Games, New Songdo remained unfinished with large open spaces remaining alongside continuing construction of large commercial and residential projects (Anderson, 2014).

References

Anderson, Chad (2010). "Urban Scenes and Urban Development in Seoul: Three Cases Viewed from a Scene Perspective." Unpublished Doctoral Dissertation, University of Incheon.

Anderson, Chad (2014). "The Scene of Songdo," International Conference 2014 *From Government to Governance: A Paradigm Shift?* Incheon National University, June 27.

Bamekov, T., Boyle, R., and Rich, D. (1989). "Privatism and the Limits of Local Economic Development Policy." *Urban Affairs Review.* 25: 212–238.

Blair, John P. (1995). *Local Economic Development: Analysis and Practice.* Thousand Oaks, CA: Sage.

Blakely, Edward J. (1989). *Planning Local Economic Development: Theory and Practice.* Newbury Park, CA: Sage.

Bluestone, B, Stevenson, M. H., and Williams, R. (2008). *The Urban Experience: Economics, Society, and Public Policy.* New York: Oxford University Press.

Burnier, D. (1992). "Becoming Competitive: How Policymakers View Incentive Based Economic Development Policy." *Economic Development Quarterly.* 6: 14–25.

Clark, Terry N. (ed) (2004). *The City as an Entertainment Machine.* Amsterdam: Elsevier.

Davies, Jonathan (2001). *Partnerships and Regimes.* Burlington, VT: Ashgate Press.

Feagin, Joe R. (1988). *Free Enterprise City: Houston in Political-Economic Perspective.* New Brunswick, NJ: Rutgers University Press.

Florida, Richard. (2002). *The Rise of the Creative Class.* New York: Basic Books/ Perseus.

Florida, Richard. (2007). *The Flight of the Creative Class.* New York: Harper Collins.

Ha, S.K. (1995). "Housing Crisis and Perspectives of Housing Policy in Korea." Housing Studies Review. 3(2): 135–160.

Halle, David (2003). *New York and Los Angeles: Politics, Society, and Culture: A Comparative View.* Chicago: University of Chicago Press.

Hirsch, Werner Z. (1984). *Urban Economics.* New York: MacMillan.

Jacobs, Jane (1993). *The Death and Life of Great American Cities.* New York: Random House.

Jeong, Da Woon, and Kim, Heung Soon (2010). "Analyzing the Levels of Self-Containment and Centrality of the Five First-Period New Towns Built in the Seoul Metropolitan Area." *Korea Society of Urban Geography.* 13(2): 103–116.

Jones, Bryan D. and Bachelor, Lynn W. (1993). *The Sustaining Hand: Community Leadership and Corporate Power.* Lawrence, KS: University of Kansas Press.

Joo, Kwan Soo, and Kim, Joo Jin (2004). "Redevelopment System by Individual Unit Method and Cause of the System's Fixation." *Urban Administration Studies.* 17(2): 3–25.

Jung, Dae Young, and Kim, Jin Wook (2009). "A Study on the Improvement Plan for Resettlement of Original Residents in New Town Project." *Community Development Society*. 34(1): 189–202.

Kasarda, John and Lindsay, Greg, (2011). *Aerotropolis: The Way We'll Live Next*. New York: Farrar, Straus and Giroux.

Kim, Ho Cheol (1997). "The Analysis of Factors Affecting a Period of Completion in Housing Renewal Projects." *Urban Administration Studies*. 10: 45–62.

Kim, K. (1997). "Understanding the Urban Problems and Urban Planning Practice in Korea." *International Journal of Urban Sciences*. 1(2): 248–257.

Kim, Seong-Hee, Cho, Kyung-Hoon, Shim, Kyo-Eon; Kim, Yong-Jin, and Ahn, Kun-Hyuck (2010). "The Determinants on the Original Inhabitants' Intention for the Resettlement Decision in the Redevelopment Area." *Urban Administration Studies*. 23(2): 149–167.

Kim, Won (1984). "A Study of National New Town Development Policy in Korea." PhD Dissertation, Columbia University.

Kim, Yong-Chang (2010). "Issues and Improvements of Just Compensation and Compensation System for Takings in Development Project for Public Use." *Space and Society*. 33: 5–47.

Kim, Young-soo (2005). "A Study on the New Town Development and Urban Redevelopment for Eco-City." *Community Development Society*. 30(3): 23–36.

Lee, Jong Youl (1990). "The Politics of Protest." Unpublished Doctoral Dissertation, The City University of New York.

Lee, Jong Youl (2009). "Urban Development Strategy: Citizen Participation in South Korea." Presented at Seoul Association of Public Administration Meeting, February 7, 2009.

Lee, Jong Youl and Anderson, Chad (2012). "Cultural Policy and the State of Urban Development in the Capital of South Korea." in C. Grodach and D. Silver (eds.), *The Politics of Urban Cultural Policy: Global* Perspectives. London: Routledge, 111–129.

Lee, Jong Youl and Anderson, Chad (2013). "The Restored Cheonggyecheon and the Quality of Life in Seoul." *The Journal or Urban Technology*. 20(4): 3–22.

Lee, Jong Youl, Tao, Jill, and Anderson, Chad (2012). *Urban Administration: Issues and Practices*. Seoul: Daeyoung Moonhwasa.

Leitner, H. and Garner, M. (1993). "The Limits of Local Initiatives: A Reassessment of Urban Entrepreneurialism for Urban Development." *Urban Geography*. 14(1): 57–77.

Lim, Dong-Il (2010). "Analysis of the Change of Urban Structure in Gangneung-City by Urban Development." *Regional Development Studies*. 10(1): 99–128.

Logan, John, and Molotch, Harvey (2007). *Urban Fortunes: The Political Economy of Place*. Los Angeles: University of California Press.

Mollenkopf, John (1975). "The Post-War Politics of Urban Development." *Politics and Society*. 5(3): 247–95.

Mollenkopf, John (1983). *The Contested City*. Princeton: Princeton University Press.

Park, Robert, and Burgess, Ernest (1984). *The City*. Chicago: University of Chicago Press.

Rees, William (1998). "Understanding Sustainable Development." in Bernd Hamm and Pandurang K. Muttagi (eds.), *Sustainable Development and the Future of Cities*. London: Intermediate Technology Press, 19–42.

Rubin, Herbert J. (1994). "There Aren't Going to Be Any Bakeries Here If There Is No Money to Afford Jellyrolls: The Organic Theory of Community Based Development." *Social Problems.* 42(3): 401–24.

Sin, Bum Sik (1991). "A Study on the Development of Living Condition of Old Apartments by Reconstruction." *Urban Administration Studies.* 4: 103–113.

Spates, James L, and Macionis, John J. (1982). *The Sociology of Cities.* New York: St Martin's Press.

Squires, Gregory D. (1984). "Industrial Revenue Bonds and the Deindustrialization of America." *Urbanism Past and Present.* 9(1): 1–9.

Swanstrom, Todd (1985). *The Crisis of Growth Politics: Cleveland, Kucinich, and the Challenge of Urban Populism.* Philadelphia, PA: Temple University Press.

Tiebout, Charles M. (1956). "A Pure Theory of Local Expenditures." *Journal of Political Economy.* 64(5): 416–424.

Townshend, Anthony M., (2013). *Smart Cities: Big Data, Civic Hackers, and the Quest for a New Utopia.* New York: W.W. Norton and Company.

Wilder, M. and Rubin, B. (1996). "Rhetoric Versus Reality: A Review of Studies of State Enterprise Zone Programs." *Journal of the American Planning Association.* 42(4): 473–491.

Wilson, William Julius (1987). *The Truly Disadvantaged.* Chicago: University of Chicago Press.

Wolman, Harold and Spitzley, David (1996)."The Politics of Local Economic Development." *Economic Development Quarterly.* 10(2): 115–150.

11 Electronic government

Seunghwan Myeong

E-government is more than just deploying information technologies. It requires consideration of the various configurations and types of e-government implementation. For example Korea has been driven towards building an information and communication technology (ICT) infrastructure since its government realized that building an information-oriented society is directly associated with national competence. The country has emphasized the development of ICT-related business and information-oriented public administration systems, and as a result, e-government has become more diverse and efficient. Accordingly, the revolutionary aspects of implementing e-government are not reflected because not enough attention is paid to the business mindset, business re-engineering, and reform of work procedures, including the provision of incentives, delegation of rights, and reform of other administrative-related areas. However, it is very difficult to provide a standardized model of e-government since each country has a different historical and political background and also a different level of technical expertise. In spite of this, e-government is implemented in quite a few countries. It is seen as the correct model of government for the future, so e-government should be implemented according to each country's vision and ideas.

I. E-government model

The pattern of adoption of new advanced ICT into organizations varies depending upon organizational factors and external environments (Gorry and Scott, 1971; Huber, 1990; Kraemer and Dedrick, 1994, Kraemer, Gurbaxani, and King, 1992; Martin, 1994; Norris and Moon, 2005; Rupnik, Kukar and Krisper, 2007; Simon, 1977; Van Bruggen, Smidts, and Wierenga, 1998). It has now become common wisdom that the success of new systems needs strong leadership and a clear vision by the executive leader as well as citizen support. As Bozeman and Straussman argued (1991), the effective use of ICT requires a senior manager's vision of the system as a useful tool for the improvement of government's capacity. Dutton and Kraemer's reinforcement politics theory (1977, 1978) also pointed out that computing policies are greatly controlled by the dominant local political system and its specific configuration of dominant of values, interests, and actors. E-government is more than just deploying information technologies. It requires consideration of the various configurations and types of e-government implementation. E-government projects overall have had a very large failure rate, even in countries with relatively advanced ICT infrastructure though there have been a number of successes in the implementation of e-government projects and initiatives. An excess focus on technology, a piecemeal approach, and wrong sequencing have failed to address the challenges associated with the transformation process leading to the successful introduction and implementation of e-government.

The 2010 United Nations E-government Survey presented various roles for e-government in addressing the ongoing world financial and economic crisis: (i) the public trust that is gained through transparency can be further enhanced through the free sharing of government data based on open standards; (ii) the ability of e-government to handle speed and complexity can also underpin regulatory reform; and (iii) empowering citizens to question the actions of regulators and bring systemic issues to the fore. During the last decade, the costs associated with telecommunications infrastructure and human capital have impeded e-government development. Nevertheless, effective strategies and the legal framework could compensate significantly, even in the least developed countries. Those who are able to harness the potential of e-government have to understand the specific goals of e-government to gain achievement forward (UNDPEPA and ASPA, 2002: 6).

First, e-government has to increase productivity and efficiency by utilizing information technologies in public administration. However, it should improve citizen quality of life as its highest objective by reconsidering the transparency of democracy and public administration. Second, e-government should provide adequate and efficient civil services by applying information technologies in the right places. In order to make this happen, civil services have to be reformed in favor of citizen-oriented work processes. Third, e-government must re-engineer public administration processes and should include a systematic effort to change public administration models. Finally, e-government should refer not only to information-oriented civil services. It also has to be an advanced model of government in an information society and consider society's equilibrium through an extended civil service under democratic ideals.

In sum, social, political, and economic elements greatly influence the implementation of e-government, and these include the information infrastructure, human resources, leadership and vision, maintenance of the legal system, and a revolutionary public administration system.

1.   *Basic elements for implementing e-government*

Figure 11.1 shows the configuration and elements of e-government. These elements enable the analysis required of factors for implementing e-government. In the input stage, leadership can be evaluated as to whether it can provide a

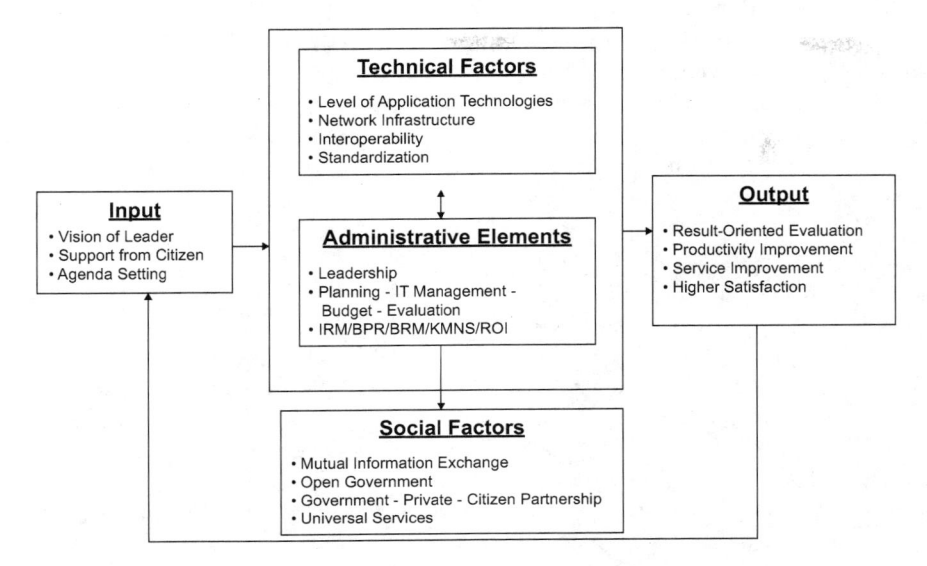

Figure 11.1 Elements for implementing e-government

vision with citizen support. In the meantime, technical factors can be evaluated by variables including interoperability, level of application technologies, network infrastructure, and standardization. Administrative elements can be assessed by leadership, level of planning integration, management of information resources, budgeting, evaluation, level of public administration reform, business process re-engineering (BPR), and return on investment (ROI). Societal elements for building e-government include information sharing with private industry, research institutions, and citizens; level of engagement with citizens through open government; and level of universal services and programs to reduce the digital gap.

a) Input/output

Input/output is a very important element in building e-government. Aspects of input/output do not seem important enough to drive e-government initiatives. However, they are key factors in the success of implementing e-government.

VISION PROVIDED BY LEADERS

Vision provided by leaders is critical in e-government. It is necessary to be able to explain why e-government is so important, and the reason must be adequate and persuasive. The most successful cases of e-government are in the US, the UK,

Korea, and Singapore. What these nations have in common is that the leadership has a rich set of knowledge about e-government in each case. The leaders provide direction and strategies for implementing e-government based on their knowledge. In addition to emphasizing technical factors, they also make attempts to reform public administration. Therefore, implementing e-government and public administration reform are not done separately. They should be done together with close interaction between the two.

LEADERSHIP AND STRONG DRIVING SYSTEM

It is a mandatory that top leadership and a strong e-government driving system is in place to implement e-government successfully and consistently. Countries that have successfully implemented e-government have a strong information orientation and a driving system. This means that power should not be concentrated in one place. Instead each department must have distinct roles and functions under the control of the highest organization such as the Office of Management and Budget (OMB) in the US. Doing so, the establishment of an action plan and its implementation is controlled efficiently under consistent guidelines and management policy, with benefits arising from execution of the plan.

CITIZEN CONFIDENCE AND SUPPORT FOR E-GOVERNMENT

It is very important for the leader to attain citizens' support and confidence for e-government as well as a vision. The foremost problem when implementing e-government in developing countries is that the government's information policy may not be communicated effectively to the public. Citizens may not even know if their government has a plan to implement e-government. Most information through the press has commercial characteristics. Information regarding the building of a network infrastructure and a blueprint for the future may not be expressed in an understandable language and format. The government, therefore, needs to secure citizen support and confidence through events and prior work for a nationwide information orientation.

EVALUATION OF RESULTS

There must be a measurement standard prepared to evaluate the entire process of deploying e-government. For the most part, an input-oriented evaluation is performed during the early phases. This results in different departments competing for budgets and makes it difficult to tell who is responsible for any failures that might occur. Therefore, adequate funds need to be invested to appropriate areas prior to deployment in order to implement e-government in an efficient manner. A CIO also needs to be deployed in each government branch, thereby allowing each area to be adequately managed in terms of efficient use of resources. Furthermore, each government has to set its own goals, and the project should end if these goals are not achieved.

b) Technical factors

E-government should deploy a backup office to support various services for citizens at front windows with networked resources. In order to do this, the system has to be mutually interoperable, and data and information should be shared so that information can circulate seamlessly among the government branches. Therefore, standardization is a very important factor for deployment and application. It is mandatory to plan IT architecture for future advancement. A security and authentication infrastructure also needs to be established in order to provide citizen services securely.

c) Internal public administration factors

E-government requires re-engineered government operations including changing the image of government, eliminating bureaucratic factionalism, and re-engineering work processes. E-government initiatives are performed for a variety of reasons, and thus government must provide adequate support and clear guidelines. In other words, efficiency and productivity are not increased just by adopting ICT. Therefore, re-engineering public administration, business process re-engineering (BPR), and reforming the legal system should be advanced prior to implementation. E-government should be looked at from a wider vantage point than just from its technical aspects.

d) Social aspects

Different social patterns need to be considered to implement e-government. The government needs to secure justice and equilibrium and guarantee the provision of universal services to its citizens. Government needs to create opportunities for citizens through ICT education programs, job training centers, and platforms that anyone can easily access government data and create and exchange apps and cultural values.

2. Contingency model of e-government

In Figure 11.2, the vertical axis (e-government for what) indicates the objective values for building e-government, which include efficiency or productivity, transparency, and power, and the horizontal axis (e-government for whom), whether e-government systems and services are citizen-oriented or designed for the sake of government itself. To illustrate how the model of e-government has changed according to the shifting social paradigm, one can now classify six types of e-government and e-democracy based on the conceptual model of e-government:

Target / Values	EG for Whom?	
	Gov't/Nation	Citizen
EG for What? — Efficiency Productivity	Type I Technocratic G	Type II G for Efficient Service
Transparency	Type III Monitoring G	Type IV Transparent G To Citizen
Power	Type V Big Brother G	Type VI Democratic G

Figure 11.2 Contingency model of e-government

Industrial society-based e-government (Type I, II)

E-DEMOCRACY WITHIN A BUREAUCRATIC SYSTEM AND TECHNOCRATIC
E-GOVERNMENT (TYPE I)

E-democracy is in a stage where it has little direct connection with civil society and is still very passive as applied to the decision-making process within the government. The type of e-government at this stage, then, can be defined as technocratic e-government.

E-DEMOCRACY CENTERED ON INFORMATION DISCLOSURE AND
INFORMATION MANAGEMENT-CENTERED E-GOVERNMENT (TYPE II)

E-democracy in this stage, where the level of social pluralism is still fairly low and the civil society still rather passive, should be classified as "e-democracy centered on information disclosure." E-democracy is applied, in other words, to disclose government-held information to civil society and thereby honor citizens' right to know. The type of e-government pertaining to this issue, then, can be classified as information management-centered e-government.

Information society e-government through mutual transaction-centered e-democracy and transparent and participatory e-government (Type IV)

E-democracy in this stage, where there is an active civil society and considerable progress has been made toward a more pluralistic society, is classified as "mutual transaction-centered e-democracy." In this stage, the scope of application of e-democracy is extended so that civil society takes an active part in the government's decision-making process. In other words, there is a two-way exchange between the government and citizens. The e-government model in this stage can then be called transparent and participatory e-government.

Next-generation e-government through pluralistic society e-democracy and democratic- and governance-type e-government (Type VI)

In this stage of social development, society is highly pluralistic, and civil society is highly active. E-democracy in this stage is, therefore, a "pluralistic e-democracy" enabling active electronic exchange, not just between different sections of the government, but also between the government and various sectors of society. An optimal level of democracy and transparency is reached in the government's decision-making process, and opinions are exchanged by people from all walks of life through a far- and wide-reaching network. In this stage, e-government systems finally assume a model adapted for the next-generation society and may be defined as democratic and governance-type e-government.

With the leaps and bounds made in ICT and the accelerating transition into information society, information media further widened their penetration into the everyday lives of Koreans, becoming embedded into the fabric of Korean society. Going forward, ICT is expected to lead to larger social innovations, playing yet a greater role than today. As ICT opens new avenues of possibilities, it is pushing the limits of human capacities, while increasingly evolving in a direction that will lead to virtual worlds existing side-by-side with the real world. ICT will eventually be mature enough to resolve major social problems. Likewise, in conjunction with economic growth and progress in democratic development, the role of government will evolve as well. Its role is now shifting from the role of a "decision-maker" to that of a "coordinator" who gathers the opinions of people from different walks of life, serving as a mediator to reconcile differences between interest groups. Meanwhile, the evolution of Internet technology, accompanying the shift in the government's role, is causing a shift also in the service paradigm in the public sector. ICT sweeping across society has not only assigned a new role to the government but is also transforming government services and improving accessibility as well as the overall technology environment. Table 11.1 compares the successive models of e-government in Korea in terms of services, accessibility, and technology environment and proposes future strategies.

The Internet has already established its influence as the most powerful information-sharing medium in history, playing an immeasurable role in globalization, in the spread of democratization around the planet, in economic growth, and in education. The evolution of Internet technology, from Web 1.0 to Web 2.0, then to Web 3.0, has been a catalyst for the successive shift in paradigm in the government sector as well (Web 1.0), the Internet has become an open system allowing for content production by users and user participation, and the currently employed (Web 2.0) will soon grow into an intelligent companion for human beings (Web 3.0), endowed with a semantic and logical understanding of information stored within it.

Table 11.1 Evolution and elements of e-government model

E-government generation 변화 양태		Industrial-Society E-Government Government 1.0 World Wide Web	Information-Society E-Government Government 2.0 Web 2.0	Next-Generation E-Government Government 3.0 Web 3.0
Services		• One-way service • Digitalization of services • Limited amounts of information is closed • Services subject to temporal and spatial constraints	• Intersection of government and private-sector services • Creation of new values through new services • Two-way information exchange • Extended range of information disclosure • Mobile services	• Personalized and customizable services • Proactive, Intelligent services • Interactive information exchange • Real-time information disclosure • Uninterrupted supply of services
Accessibility		• Government-centered • First-stop shop • Single portals	• Citizen-centered • One-stop shop • Service integration	• Individual-centered • My Gov • Personalized government service portals
Technological environment	Channels	Fixed Internet	Fixed and wireless Internet	Integration between fixed-wireless Internet and mobile devices (channel integration)
기술환경	Process integration	Processing of unit tasks	Process integration (public-/private-sector collaboration)	Service integration
기술환경	Enabling technology	Browser, web storage	Broadband, rich link/content models	Semantic technology, sensor networks

Source: Kim (2011).

Information society-style e-government systems, based on Web 2.0, constitute the phase in which the main progress consists in enabling active participation by citizens in the affairs of the government and their open communication with it. These systems are expected to be gradually upgraded to Web 3.0-based Government 3.0 systems, espousing the new e-government paradigm for the next-generation society.

II. History and success factors of e-government in Korea

Since the 1980s, Korea has systematically and strategically planned and implemented policies defining, establishing, and improving the national infrastructure and expanding its use. As a result, Korea has become as one of the world's best countries for ICT, ranking it at the top of the United Nations E-Government Readiness Index for the last three surveys done in 2010, 2012, and 2014. Korea has actively implemented e-government as a crucial means to make the government more competitive and transparent by integrating advanced ICT into the administrative system and public service procedures as well as building a broadband Internet infrastructure that has become the fastest and most stable in the world.

1.   *History and development phases of Korean e-government*

The Korean-style e-government initiatives and ICT policies for building a nation-wide high-speed communications network, building a single government portal, and integrating data into a single government data center have seldom been found in other competing nations. The primary goal of the 11 e-government initiatives of Kim Dae-Jung's government (1998–2002) was to build a citizen-centered government service by creating a Single Window e-Government portal that would allow citizens to file online applications for government services and access other information services through a simple and accessible format. Under the single window e-government, government and public offices could share information across their networks and eliminate redundant processes such as the requirements to submit numerous documents for a single government service. Indeed, real-time communication systems between citizens and city governments played a critical role in identifying citizen demands, especially in the period of Roh Muhyeon's government (2003–2007). Personnel and citizen participation were emphasized through various levels of government portals. At the metropolitan government level, the Online Procedures Enhancement for Civil Application System (OPEN) of the Seoul Metropolitan government (1999) is a good example of this effort. This system made the decision-making process in city government open to the public online, thus increasing transparency while avoiding unnecessary burdens or pressures from politics and higher-level governments.

a)   *Building e-government infrastructure*

Korea's e-government was established from the 1970s to 1990s. Reflecting upon changing technologies and society, Korea established the foundation for e-government by computerizing its administrative system in the 1970s, computerizing the national backbone databases in the 1980s, and constructing a high-speed information and communications network in the 1990s. According to a report by Song Hee-Joon, Korea has chosen a stage development strategy for each level of public administration, IT applications, and mid- to long-term planning (2012: 6–8):

> After the 1980s, the Korean government launched various projects, all with different time frames and strategies. These projects were National Basic Information System Project (1987–1996), High Speed Broadband Network Project (1995–2005), Framework Plan for IT Development (1996–current), and e-Government Project (2001–current). The e-government, which was first commenced as an effort to computerize the administrative process, has gone through significant enhancement process with the advancement of information technology, automation of work process, and linkage with process innovation, as well as change in political leadership, implementation organization, and legal basis. In 1983, the Chun Doo-Hwan Administration (1981–1987) established the National Basic Information System Plan for building five major national basic information networks by mid-1990s as a part of the preparation project for the e-government to raise the Korea's IT infrastructure to those of advanced nations' level. The first stage of the e-government (1987–1995) was launched as the 1st (1987–1991) and the 2nd (1992–1996) National Basic Information System Project in pursuant to the Act on IT Network enacted in 1986. [See Table 11.2.] During the process, the IT Network Development Committee lead the automation of government administrative process by building a national DB on information of citizens, real estate, and automobile and by distributing PCs. The 2nd phase of the National Basic Information System Project was pursued by individual ministries and offices through constructing interconnecting computer network environment. The 2nd stage of the e-government (1996–2000) is the e-government growth process through development projects in accordance with the IT Development Framework Plan established in pursuant to the IT Development Framework Act. Particularly, the period is categorized as internet's explosive growth period as the social networking that links the entire nation through mass distribution of internet service and mobile telecommunication service as a result of the high speed broadband network project that was fully launched in 1995. The 3rd stage of the e-government (2001–2007) is the maturity stage. On February 2001, the Special Committee on e-Government under the leadership of the president was established and the importance and priority of the e-government project was elevated as presidential agenda and implemented throughout all the government ministries and institutes.

b)   E-government as a presidential agenda (2000–2007)

The government has focused on promoting e-government as a presidential agenda no matter which administration was in office. Upon recognizing

Table 11.2 Nationwide basic information system and network projects (1987–1996)

Target Task	Provided Services	Date	Area
Residence registration	• Residence registration (Birth, Death) • Document issue	Jan. 1991	3,700 Eup-Myeon-Dong Local Office
Real estate management	• Land change • Change of land property/doc. issue	Feb. 1991	273 City, County, District Admin. Office
Vehicle registration	• Vehicle registration/ doc. issue • Vehicle maintenance, inspection	Mar. 1990	168 related org. (59 registration and inspection offices)
Customs logistics	• Export/import report, inspection • Tax, cash management • Customs/logistics process	Jun. 1990	109 related org. (Seoul custom, 43 transport, 3 banks)
Employment management	• Employment information • Business information/ education	1990	49 related org.
Statistics	• Population, Inflation . . . • Providing access tools to statistics	1991	36 government offices

e-government as a key means for government innovation, the government enacted the Electronic Government Act (2001) and selected 11 e-government initiatives in order to increase efficiency in administrative affairs and dramatically improve public services (See Table 11.3). During 2003–2007, the government selected and implemented 31 roadmap projects in 4 areas aiming to achieve a world-class e-government, as shown in Table 11.4. In summary, Table 11.5 shows the development stages of E-Government in Korea.

c)   E-government project implementation

The government has been engaged in implementing e-government projects focusing on connection and integration to support new value creation (2008–present). E-government services are being integrated to provide integrated citizen- and business-oriented services. For example the Korea E-Government Portal (www.korea.go.kr) provides integrated and customized services for citizens. One-Stop Business Support Service (www.g4b.go.kr) provides integrated services for businesses such as services for founding establishments, enterprises, and venture corporations. Information resources have also been consolidated to

Table 11.3 Eleven e-government initiatives

Purpose	Initiatives
Improved services to citizens and businesses	Four initiatives including innovation of application services (G4C), information system integration of the four major social insurances, and integration of national procurement affairs (G2B)
Improved administrative productivity	Five initiatives including development of a national financial information system, comprehensive informatization of local government administration, educational administration information system, and electronic personnel management system
Solid foundation for e-government	Two initiatives including development of an electronic signature/electronic
	Administrative signature system and an integrated pan-governmental computing environment

Source: MOSPA, (2013b: 18).

Table 11.4 Thirty-one roadmap projects for e-government

Area	Project
Innovating the way government works	Eleven projects – digitalizing the entire document processing procedures, realizing local e-government, and real-time management of national agenda
Innovating public services	Fourteen projects – improving Internet-based civil services, single-window for business support services, and increasing online citizen participation
Innovating information resource management	Five projects – building the Government Integrated Data Center (GIDC), building information security system, and stepping up informatization organizations and personnel
Innovating legal systems	Reforming laws and regulations for e-government and security

Source: MOSPA, (2013b:19).

improve inefficient management of information resources caused by the disconnected informatization efforts made by different ministries. As a result, 4,687 information systems (2008) have been integrated into 2,535 systems (2012). At the same time, a government-wide enterprise architecture (EA) was developed to promote efficiency and avoid redundant investments in informatization projects by ministries. The government has been making efforts since 2011 to achieve a smarter e-government that responds to new IT and social changes in advance. Table 11.6 and Table 11.7 show the e-government implementation bodies and financial support structures in Korea by development stages.

Table 11.5 Development stages of e-government in Korea

Stages	Major Actions
Inception (mid-1980s–mid-1990s)	• Building five National Basic Information Systems (NBIS) • Act on Computer Network Expansion and Usage Promotion (1987)
Foundation (mid-1990s–2000)	• Building foundation for high-speed information and communications and promoting the Internet • Enacting the Framework Act on Informatization Promotion (1995)
Launch (2001–2002)	• Carrying out 11 major initiatives for e-government • Enacting the Act on E-Government (2001)
Diffusion (2003–2007)	• Carrying out 31 roadmap projects for e-government • Laying the groundwork for linking and integrating multiple government departments and agencies
Convergence (2008–present)	• Establishing Master Plan for National Informatization (2008) • Carrying out tasks (12) for e-government based on the principles of openness, sharing and cooperation
Smart Gov (2011–present)	• Initiating the future e-government blueprint, Smart Government

Source: MOSPA, (2013a: 6).

Table 11.6 E-government implementation bodies in Korea

Stage	Plan	Committee	Chairperson	Managing Organization
I	Phase 1 Network	Information Network Supervisory Commission (1987–1995)	Presidential Chief of Staff (1987–1989)	Ministry of Post and Telecommunication
	Phase 2 Network		Minister of the Post and Telecommunication (1989–1995)	Ministry of Post and Telecommunication
II	Framework Plan for IT Development Promotion	IT Development Implementation Committee (1996–current)	Prime Minister (1996–current)	Ministry of Information and Communication
III	Phase 1 E-Government	Special Committee on e-Government (2001–current)	Civilian (Secretary of Policy Planning)	Ministry of Information and Communication, Ministry of Government Administration and Home Affairs, and Office of Planning and Budget
	Phase 2 E-Government		Civilian (Secretary of Innovation Management)	Ministry of Government Administration and Home Affairs

Source: Song (2012: 19).

Table 11.7 E-government financial support structure in Korea

Period	Funding Structure	Managing Ministry	Legal Basis
1987–1992	Invest First, Settle Later	MPT	Act on IT Network
1993–2004	Informatization Promotion Fund	MIC	Framework Act on Informatization Promotion (General Provisions for Informatization)
2005–current	General Budget	MOGAHA	Budgeting and Accounting Act (General Accounting E-Government Investment Fund)

Source: Government Innovation Decentralization Committee (2005: 45).

2.   Success factors of Korean e-government

The success factors are commonly analyzed as below, including a strong government leadership, Aggressive investment based on clear goal-setting, and a collaborative governance partnership (MOSPA, 2013b: 16–17):

a)   Strong government leadership

- Recognizing informatization as a key means for national development, the Korean government established a supervising and coordinating body in the area of informatization policies under the president to oversee and manage the process.

  - The "invest first, settle later" method is an example of presidential leadership.

- Laws for supporting efficient informatization were established in the early stages.

  - Examples include the Act on Computer Network Expansion and Usage Promotion (1987), the Electronic Government Act (2001), the Information Infrastructure Protection Act (2001), and the Informatization Promotion Framework Act (1995).

b)   Aggressive investment based on clear goal-setting

- Based on the principle of "choice and focus," the government first selected areas that are likely to lead economic growth, such as broadband network construction, and made intensive investment in those areas. In the 2000s, it made aggressive investments in e-government projects, which were selected as an integral part of the presidential agenda, and improved administrative efficiency and quality of citizens' life.

- Investment amounts were KRW 23.22 million in the Kim Administration, KRW 92.45 million in the Roh Administration, and KRW 56.61 million in the Lee Administration.

c) Supervising/coordinating body in each administration informatization governance framework

- An informatization governance framework was established for mutual benefit and cooperation between the public and private sectors. Expertise in the private sector was actively harnessed in the development, execution, and review of national informatization projects.

  - Experts in the private sector played important roles in overseeing, coordinating, reviewing, and advising organizations on informatization policy.

Song also analyzed these success factors (Song, 2012: 23):

- The success of e-government is the result of organizing human, material, and technical resources through the backing of the strong determination and leadership of the president, which were efficiently utilized to achieve the objectives of administrative efficiency, improved service to the broad public, improved administrative process transparency, citizen participation, and applied advanced information technologies.
- Simultaneously, information industry promotion, with the objective of advancing the IT industry, was also implemented in each stage of the project as well as applying feedback and research results of previous experience on the next phase of planning.
- In case of the 1st Stage e-government Project, finances were invested first and settled later but supplemented the weaknesses and utilized the positive aspects of the method. The Informatization Promotion Fund, financed by government, loans, traditional and mobile telecommunication companies, as well as by dividends from shares of Korea Telecom or sales of corporate stocks, was established in 1993 (Song, 2012: 83).
- The funds, which were managed by the Ministry of Information and Communication, was provided in the form of matching funds to each government branch for IT development projects and stimulated the incentive system for pursuing risk associated projects. In an environment where success was not proven with a low level of expertise, such a policy-backed system played an important role in promoting implementation of risky projects by each department.

III. Next-generation e-government: issues and agenda

1. Smart society and Gov 3.0

The current smart society suggests the beginning of a post-information society. Although information society can make people's lives more efficient and convenient, it may fail to address technology-driven initiatives sufficiently where government-driven ICT policies often ignore individuals' creative and cognitive processes in response to the government's actions.

A smart society focuses on the process of mutual communication and the incorporation of each individual's thoughts into some social agreement. There are four major attributes of a smart society (Myeong and Hur, 2012). First, mobile users deal with their mobile environments freely, facilitating environments that are "always connected" through mobile devices. Second, personalized social networks facilitate communication between individuals anytime, anywhere as a result of many smartphone users and activated social networks. Third, ethics, trust, and fairness are some of the major values floated as new norms to dominate social activities because the public's rights can be strengthened from large corporations to netizens, groups to individuals, and producers to consumers. Finally, a smart society can foster smart workplace environments where people can work without being limited by time or space through advanced ICT applications.

With the rise of smart society, "smart e-government" has been proposed as a new model for government in a smart society. Smart e-government is a system where cooperative governments strengthen the partnership with the private sector. Intelligent governments provide administrative services that better meet national requirements. Transparent governments facilitate public communication, participation, and trust. People in a smart society are more active than those in an information society. As in the case of smartphones and social media, smart technologies facilitate people's participation in their environments. In the past, it was difficult to disseminate people's voices in spite of their ICT use. However, a smart society enables faster, real-time, and personalized communication. In particular, personalized services are one of the most representative characteristics of smart society. Not only enterprises but also governments can focus more on the provision of personalized services.

In a smart society, based on a model of future government, e-government is connected to Gov 3.0 (Myeong and Hur, 2012). Gov 3.0 is a national administrative system that strengthens the role of individuals by redesigning administrative methods and processes based on highly intelligent ICT applications and social connections. In Gov 3.0, the government shares information and knowledge with firms, citizens, and global communities and provides common platforms that can produce democratic value added by exchanges between members of society.

The government not only governs but also provides public goods. The government requires the public's participation in policymaking and providing public services. In addition, the government manages and provides data for transparency, trust, and added value. In some respects, the issue of "Big Brother" is outdated. Monitoring and participation have become easier because of cross-checking mechanisms enabling people's use of smart technologies. In the initial stages of ICT adoption by the government, the emphasis was on accurate, efficient, and fast public administration. However, innovative ICT applications have changed the world, as illustrated by the "Jasmine Revolution" of 2011 in the Middle East. This event demonstrates that smart technologies can provide citizens with the power to change outdated customs and norms through the process of public discourse. The world's least corrupt countries show a high correlation between the quality of e-government and the level of trust in government. According to a 2007 Pew survey, there is greater confidence in the integrity of political leaders in countries where people generally trust one another. Countries with a high level of e-government maturity tend to show a high level of trust (e.g. Sweden, Canada, and Britain). On the other hand, in low-trust countries, such as Nigeria and Lebanon, political corruption is widespread (Wike and Holzwart, 2008).

Figure 11.3 shows the change of e-government from Gov 1.0 to Gov 3.0 from the perspective of governance including the role of each actor, the goal of e-government services, and environmental changes to ICT and demand. In the era of Gov 3.0, the Internet and SNS have already established their influence as the most powerful information-sharing media in history, playing immeasurable roles in globalization, in the spread of democracy around the planet, in economic growth, and in education. The evolution of Internet technology, from Web 1.0 to Web 2.0 then to Web 3.0, has been a catalyst for the successive shift in paradigm in the government sector as well. During Gov 1.0, the Internet became an open system for user participation and content production by users, and the currently employed Gov 2.0 is now about to grow into an

	Gov1.0	Gov2.0	Gov3.0
Goal of E-Gov.	Efficiency of System	Info. Sharing & Connectivity	Open Big Data Individual-oriented Service
E-Gov. Services	Internal & Info. Provide	Gov. Reform & Single Portal	Platform Based My Gov. Services
Ecology of ICT	Gov. Driven & Outsourcing	Gov. Driven & Outsourcing	Gov.-Private-Citizen Partnership, Deregulation
Role of CIO	System Management	BPR, Intergovernmental Project	Initiator of Reform Communicator
Decision Making Initiatives	Political Elites & Gov. CEO	Gov., Professional, Public Officials	Individuals, Citizen, NGOs
Demand & Method for Decision Making	Political Needs	Policy Needs	Participation & Communication based on Big Data
Role of Central Government	Initiator	Contractor	Mediator
Role of Local Government	Dependent upon Matching Funds System Building	Matching Funds Constructing Local Gov. Portals	Local/Community Demand-based Personalized Services
Role of Entrepreneur	System Provider	New Tech. & System Application Develop	Convergent Services Creating New Services
Role of Citizen	Info. Service User	Partly Participation	Active Participation & Voting
Decision Maker	Top Down Budget Allocation	Policy/Budget Control based on Performance Evaluation	Focusing on Problem Solving Data Analysis & Vision
Demands by Paradigm Shift	Gov./National Informatization	Gov. Reform Local Autonomy	Cooperative Partnership & E-Governance

Figure 11.3 E-governance perspectives and changes toward Gov 3.0

intelligent companion for people (Gov 3.0), endowed with a semantic and logical understanding of information stored within it.

Information society-style e-government systems, based on Gov 2.0, constitute the phase in which the main progress consists in enabling active participation by citizens in the affairs of the government and their open communications with it. These systems are expected to upgrade gradually to Web 3.0-based Government 3.0 systems, espousing the new e-government paradigm for the next-generation society.

2. A new demand is coming, but bureaucratic e-government initiatives continue

E-government initiatives have been quite successful when they come from the government and from bureaucrats. It worked out perfectly at least until the era of the New Public Management (NPM) paradigm. The NPM paradigm suggested various structural or organizational choices that promoted decentralized control through a wide variety of alternative service delivery mechanisms, including quasi-markets with public and private service providers. The Korean government introduced a broad range of public-sector reforms for the revitalization of the public sector through e-government initiatives as illustrated above. In doing so, the NPM prevailed in both the central and local governments. A number of market mechanisms were introduced in the public sector in the late 1990s.

It seems fine to say that democracy cannot function without efficient management, but other arguments of equally significant dimensions, such as values and virtues, are relevant to the nature and dynamics of public administration. Bureaucratic and information management-oriented e-government may prevail when the level of social pluralism is still fairly low and civil society still rather passive, but the bureaucratic e-government model may not work anymore when society is highly pluralistic and civil society is highly active. As explained above, active electronic transactions occur in this stage among various sectors of society. People want to participate in the government's decision-making process and express their opinions via public dialogue in SNS and cyberspace.

The assumptions of efficiency-oriented e-government may not capture the complexity of a phenomenon that involves the public as well as social consequences. Businesslike e-government alone cannot respond to the enormous demands on the public sector. NPM or post-NPM may work in certain countries, but it cannot be universally applied because each society is different. In that regard, a critical analysis of the fundamental and instrumental means of e-government is necessary to go beyond NPM or post-NPM, which rely heavily on economic and management theories (De Vries and Kim, 2011).

Wachhaus (2011) argued that the traditional study of the hierarchical bureaucratic model may not be an appropriate perspective for looking at networks. Instead an anarchist orientation may adjust the way we look at governance networks. He suggested anarchist orientations that include shifting the focus from static structural elements to dynamic processes, recognition of collective action as part of human nature, moving from individual networks to social ones, viewing network stability as a function of the linkages in a network, and robust ties within a network. As he argued, a network is organic rather than mechanical. E-government is already organic and bureaucratic government is only one of the entities in the governance network.

3.   *E-government, transparency, and trust*

In terms of the relationship between e-government and trust, implementing security and privacy policies in cyberspace is critical for building trust (Carter and Bélanger, 2005; Welch, Hinnant, and Moon, 2005). This is also a problem if e-government is an organic life evolving toward anarchy and self-dependence administration and not an automated machine anymore. Who should be the most transparent? Government has been pressured mostly by citizens and the media to be transparent. Must only the government and public officials be transparent? What of others? Sometimes, the hidden agendas of government groups are not shared with citizens, leading to biased public opinions in economic, social, and political affairs. At the same time, lack of privacy for civilians, which means they must also be transparent to all e-government policies, may be criticized for lack of reliable privacy policies. This means the issue of transparency is not simple if you look at governance or the network.

It seems reasonable to suppose that there is a strong relationship between e-government and trust. The role of e-government leads to citizen trust and government transparency. The development of e-government services is necessary for generating trust and transparency. It is at least conceivable that the Scandinavian model of governance, which "combines a high cost of government with high levels of trust and citizen participation," has delivered good public services. The Nordic e-government model is designed to perform the public services of government without increasing costs or losing citizen trust. Transparency is essential for building trust. The Nordic countries (Sweden, Norway, Denmark, and Finland) have maintained a high level of trust through e-government services. Tolbert and Mossberger (2006) show that "e-government can increase process-based trust by improving interactions with citizens and perceptions of responsiveness" and that "e-government has been proposed as a way to increase citizen trust in government and improve citizen evaluations of government" (354). The least corrupt countries show a strong relationship between high trust and a high level of e-government maturity. According to the 2007 Pew survey mentioned earlier, there is more confidence in the integrity of political leaders in countries where people generally trust one another. The countries with high e-government maturity have high levels of trust such as Sweden, Canada, and Britain. On the other hand, in nations such as Nigeria and Lebanon, political corruption with a low-trust society are widespread (Wike and Holzwart, 2008).

The question arises here whether people in Nordic countries trusted government and each other before the e-government regime? Again, it is worthwhile to recall the UN's determination that social, political, and economic elements influence the implementation of e-government greatly and that these include the information infrastructure, human resources, leadership and vision, maintenance of a legal system, and a revolutionary public administration system.

IV. Conclusion

In the era of governance, the study of e-governments should not fall in the dichotomy between "science" or "art." It should entail both consensus building and effective implementation, while selecting a leader good at conducting the good governance orchestra for good performances. The NPM-oriented and bureaucratic e-government models are declining in popularity because of their narrow and managerial perspectives that ignore differences among philosophies, histories, cultures, politics, and governments among countries. Advocates of e-government in the future need the capabilities to predict and analyze in a timely manner, the ability to dialogue with and moderate between local and global clients, and philosophies for balancing democracy and efficiency.

References and Further Readings

Bozeman, B., and Straussman, J. D. 1991. *Managing Information Strategically: Public Management Strategies.* San Francisco: Jossey-Bass Publishers.

Carter, Lemuria, and Bélanger, France. 2005. The Utilization of E-Government Services: Citizen Trust, Innovation, and Acceptance Factors. *Information Systems Journal* 15(1): 5–25.

De Vries, Michiel, and Kim, Pan Suk. 2011. *Value and Virtue in Public Administration.* Hampshire, UK: Palgrave Macmillan.

Dutton, W. H., and Kraemer, K. L. 1977. Technology and Urban Management. *Administration and Society* 9(3): 304–340.

Dutton, W. H., and Kraemer, K. L. 1978. Management Utilization of Computers in American Local Government. *Communication of the ACM* 21(3): 206–218.

Gartner Identifies the Top 10 Strategic Technologies for 2012. 2012. *Gartner* (www.gartner.com).

Gorry, G. A., and Scott, M. S. 1971. A Framework for Management Information Systems. *Sloan Management Review* 13: 64–65.

Government Innovation Decentralization Committee. 2005. *Annual Report for E-Government, Ministry of Government Administration and Home Affairs.* MOGAHA. Seoul, Korea.

Huber, G. P. 1990. A Theory of the Effects of Advanced Information Technologies on Organizational Design, Intelligence, and Decision Making. *Academy of Management Review* 15: 47–70.

Inglehart, R. 1999. Trust, Well-Being and Democracy, in M. E. Warren (ed.), *Democracy and Trust.* Cambridge: Cambridge University Press.

Jee, E.H. 2007. Government 2.0: Public Services in the Era of Web 2.0. *SW Insight Policy Report*, March.

Kim, S. T. 2011. *The Future Strategy of Korea for Building a Smart Society.* Seoul: Beommunsa.

Korea Information Society Development. 2005. *Analysis of the Effectiveness of Public Information Systems on Organizational Structure and Management.* Seoul, Korea.

Korean Association for Local Informatization. 1999, 2005. *Local Informatization Evaluation Report*. Seoul, Korea.

Korean Planning and Budgeting Board. 2007. *Public Hearings for National Finance Plan and Management: Information Policy*. Seoul, Korea.

Kraemer, K. L., and Dedrick, J. (1994). Payoffs from Investment in Information Technology: Lessons from Asia-Pacific region, *World Development* 22(12) 1921–1931.

Kraemer, K. L., Gurbaxani, V., and King, J. L.1992. Economic Development, Government Policy, and the Diffusion of Computing in Asia-Pacific Countries. *Public Administration Review* 52(2): 146–156.

Lee, H. J. 2007. e-Government to u-Government: Government 3.0. *Ubiquitous Society Studies Series*, No. 29, Jul. 2007.

Martin, L. L. 1994. A Model of Impacts of Advanced Information Technologies on Organizational Knowledge, Structure, and Performance of Professional Service Firms. New York University, Stern School of Business, Working Paper.

Ministry of Security and Public Administration. 2013a. E-Government of Korea: Best Practices

Ministry of Security and Public Administration. 2013b. Digital Society Development of Korea.

Myeong, S. H., and Hur, C. H. 2012. A Study on Change of e-Government and Paradigm Based on Gov3.0 Through Shift of Smart Society. In Proceedings of the Korean Association for Policy Studies Spring Conference, Jeonju, Korea, 13 April 2012; Korean Association for Policy Studies: Seoul, Korea, 2012; pp. 325–341.

Norris, Donald F., and M. Jae Moon. 2005. Advancing E-government at the Grassroots: Tortoise or Hare? *Public Administration Review* 65(1): 64–75.

Rossteutscher, S. 2008. Social Capital and Civic Engagement: A Comparative Perspective, in Van Deth, D., Jan, W., and Wolleb, G (eds.), *The Handbook of Social Capital, Castiglione*. Oxford: Oxford University Press.

Rupnik, R., Kukar, M., and Krisper, M. 2007. Integrating Data Mining and Decision Support Through Data Mining Based Decision Support System. *The Journal of Computer Information Systems* 47(3): 89–104.

Shadrach, B. 2002. e-Government for Transparency. International Conference on e-Government for Development, Palermo, Italy, 10–11 April 2002.

Simon, H. A. 1977. *Models of Discovery*. Dordrecht, Holland: R. Reidel.

Song, Hee-Joon. 2012. E-Government of Korea – Achievements & Tasks. *Information Policy*. NIA.

Tolbert, Caroline J., and Mossberger, Karen. 2006. The Effects of E-Government on Trust and Confidence in Government. *Public Administration Review*. May/June 2006.

UNDP-APDIP. 2005. The Key to Increasing Transparency in e-Government Deployments: Public Feedback Mechanisms.

UNDPEPA/ASPA. 2002. Benchmarking E-government: A Global Perspective. UNDPEPA/ASPA. Available online: http://www/unspan/org.egovernment/benchmarking/Egov/2001.pdf (accessed on 15 January 2011).

United Nations Department of Economic and Social Affairs. United Nations E-Government Survey 2010. UN.

Van Bruggen, G. H., Smidts, A., and Wierenga, B. 1998. Improving Decision Making by Means of a Marketing Decision Support System. *Management Science* 44(5): 645–658.

Wachhaus, T. Aaron. 2011. Anarchy as a Model for Network Governance. *Public Administration Review* 72(1): 33–42.

Welch, Eric, Hinnant, Charles, and Jae Moon, M. 2005. Linking Citizen Satisfaction with E-Government and Trust in Government. *Journal of Public Administration Research and Theory* 15(3): 371–392.

Wike, Richard and Holzwart, Kathleen. 2008. Where Trust is High, Crime and Corruption are Low: Since Communism's Fall, Social Trust Has Fallen in Eastern Europe, Pew Global Attitudes Project. Available online: http://www.pewglobal. org/2008/04/15/where-trust-is-high-crime-and-corruption-are-low/ (accessed on 5 April 2014).

World Bank's e-Government Site http://www1.worldbank.org/publicsector/egov/

Part III

Accountability and innovation

12 Administrative control
Ensuring accountable bureaucracy

Sung-Jun Myung

I. Introduction

Administrative responsibility is increasing in importance. Indeed nothing is more basic in a democratic society than holding government bureaucracy accountable. While how responsibility is to be defined is still debated, consensus has been made in ensuring responsibility in all administrative processes. How it is to be achieved has been a critical issue in studying governments and public administration.

As the role of government has become pervasive and the administrative state has become the descriptor for the current governmental system, many fear the domination of the bureaucracy on our lives as consequences of administrative constraints and even of beneficial programs wrapped in administrative red tape. The marked increase in what citizens demand of government has led to a number of administrative agencies, a large number of civil servants, and swelling governmental budgets. That has led to this age described by "the administrative state." The term is meant to emphasize that administrators now exercise so much discretion that constitutional arrangements among branches have been disrupted. While the question of how far decision making by the executive has superseded decision making by the other branches, it is unquestionably true that administrators exercise far more discretionary judgment in eras of more restricted governmental responsibilities. Public agencies in the executive advise legislative bodies on new policies and programs. Even an administrative agency can initiate policies and programs that greatly affect citizens. Discretionary powers are exercised by street-level bureaucracies. As a first contact with citizens, administrative agencies and their employees are criticized for red tape.

Back to discussion on administrative responsibility, it is understandable that administrators should be responsible for the well-being of the public and for effective and equitable service delivery. We can at least agree to this degree of defining responsibility. With the growing importance of the executive branch, ways to ensure administrative responsibility draw more attention, which we call administrative control or controlling bureaucracy.

II.   Administrative control: definition and importance

Every well-developed organization in democratic societies has some systems of holding subordinates accountable to their superiors and customers. An administrative system of government entails the subordination of bureaucrats to mandates, to the constraints of the Constitution and laws, and to hierarchical superiors in the executive branch. The term "administrative control" refers to systems that consist of sets of tools holding the executive branch or the government bureaucracy accountable for their actions. The system forces the oversized government bureaucracy to exercise discretionary power properly, abide by the legal process, and work for their stated goals righteously.

Controlling bureaucracy is a quite complex task. Dimock (1951) sees administrative control as management tools to judge and improve effectiveness in achieving goals. Lee (2011), taking the perspective from administrative laws, defines administrative control as activities to evaluate whether or not the assigned tasks are conducted as planned, to adjust programs to meet schedules, to conduct research on causes of problems in the implementation stage, and eventually to make improvements on governmental performance. These definitions show two key components: evaluation and improvement.

For effective evaluation and improvement, activities for administrative control must be clearly defined by subject of control, criteria of control, tools of control, and actors. The subject of control is the first element. The focus of control differs by the times and the philosophies. The focus may be centered either on the process by which decisions are made, on the services that are delivered, or on outcomes. Recently, with the introduction of the new public management regime, the focus has moved to outputs or outcomes, which is evident in Korea where many programs for performance evaluation are introduced as a part of administrative control (or audit) programs on government agencies and publicly funded institutions. Performance evaluations at a variety of levels from department to branch are conducted all the time. In the tradition of the administrative state, the subject of scrutiny is further extended to publicly funded institutions including public enterprises. In the wave of privatization under new public management, the subject of control continues to extend to almost all organizations supported by public money.

Second, evaluation criteria play a critical role in controlling activities and changing the way in which public organizations, even the whole executive branch, are heading. The criteria includes efficiency, effectiveness, legality, equity, and democratic values, but efficiency takes in charge over other values such as equality and citizen participation. Political orientation and the operating environment of public agencies shift the main venues at which administrative control is aiming. Budget pressures from resource scarcity at this time are likely to give efficiency higher priority.

Third, considering the tool aspect, administrative control has the characteristics of administrative reform. It is not just adjusting and improving rules and policies. The tools chosen for administrative control rather create changes in the fundamental ways by which the executive operates. Furthermore, the tool offers both official and unofficial ways to monitor performance. While a set of official tools has to coincide with the Constitution and the law, unofficial tools affect the administrative process differently from the more popular, public perspective.

Finally, the issue of who initiates the evaluation varies in that the executive branch voluntarily monitors their own operation and works toward improvement. In addition, our constitutional arrangement of checks and balances demands both the legislature and the judiciary to monitor the administrative process and to ask for correction if the administration deviates from the public values set by the legislature.

III. Historic development of administrative control

Even under the monarchy, ways to control the bureaucracy existed. Although they were limited by current standards, "conseil du roi" in France and the equity court in Great Britain were there to check administrative rulings. The same is to our country. Under the Chosun Dynasty, agencies for inspecting corrupt government officials and for advising on policies existed to check royal power and to attack corruption. Also, undercover inspectors were sent to monitor local government authorities.

The arrival of the nation states in nineteenth-century Europe pushed forward the people's sovereignty and limited the exercise of the administrative power. At the time, it was under the nightwatcher state that individual liberty was maximized and that state power was confined to protecting public order and national security. Public bureaucracy played only a limited role in implementing laws determined by the legislature and was not allowed to extend its role, for example to the realization of public interests. Interpretation and enforcement of the law were only allowed to the judiciary, and therefore the executive was strictly controlled by both the legislative and the judicial branches.

In the early twentieth century, the Great Depression and the two World Wars, along with industrialization, turned the tradition of nation states into administrative states. A diversity of social problems at the time demanded an active role of the executive branch. Efficiency in the public bureaucracy was emphasized when economies of scale and professionalism were required to tackle social problems. Again administrative control drew heightened attention as the power of government bureaucracy had grown.

The Japanese occupation prevented Korea from building a tradition of liberal democracy, and after the Korean War, the ensuing authoritative administrations exercised exclusive power for almost 30 years. In the 1960s, when industrialization and economic development were heavily pushed, the government bureaucracy exerted great power without checks by the other branches or by administrative control. Even in the rare discussion of administrative responsibility, the value of efficiency and effectiveness superseded equity and equality as a criterion for administrative control. After the democratization of the late 1980s, the horizontal shift of the political power and the increased voice of the public have raised concerns over the adverse effects of the administrative state and have emphasized empowering both the legislative and judicial bodies, calling for the need for controlling the government bureaucracy.

IV. Legislative control of administration

The Constitution gives the legislature the power to approve the budget submitted from the executive, oversee the organization of the executive, watch the implementation of policies and programs, and ensure the separation of power among the three branches. Legislative control is a sort of feedback device to monitor administrative actions and detect errors to meet the demands of the public. In turn, the active role of the legislature is to improve the representation of government bureaucracy and to help resolve conflicts with stakeholders.

Historically, legislative control is divided into the two periods: before and after 1988. Before the year of 1988, the role of legislature as an administrative controller was almost nonexistent because of the dominance of the executive and the strong power held by the president. The dominance of the ruling party, the monopolization of power and information by the government bureaucracy, the lack of decision-making ability of the congress, and even the political culture at the time prevent the legislature from exercising its power to hold the executive in check. However, as the democratization progressed in the 1990s, the National Assembly has regained its powers and has played its role as a controller.

From the Constitution, our government system provides the National Assembly the legislative power and the power to oversee the executive. Specifically the power includes the right to enact laws, to deliberate and compile the budget, to inspect and investigate state administration, to organize Constitutional institutions, and to impeach public officials including the president. In addition, the National Assembly has diverse ways to press the executive in the process of converging public opinions.

Major tools include the authority to inspect government affairs, the power to investigate government affairs, and the authority to open hearings to confirm government appointees. The authority to inspect government offices has the National Assembly audit the overall operation of the government bureaucracy every year. The National Assembly also has the authority to investigate particular incidences on which a quarter of the members agree.

The Personnel Hearing Act of 2004 gives the National Assembly the authority to open hearings to confirm government appointees. Personnel hearings contribute to securing administrative responsibility by appointing qualified persons. The hearings are needed to get approval for the appointment of prime ministers, ministers, chief justices of the Supreme Court, and chairmen of the Board of Audit and Inspection. In fact, a number of prime minister appointees, appointees for the chairman of the Board of Audit and Inspection, and minister appointees failed to get consent from the personnel hearing.

V.   Courts and administrative control

The judiciary is the last watchdog to hold the executive accountable. It interprets laws and then corrects administrative actions when government agencies have disputes with citizens, abuse discretionary powers, or commit legal errors. While keeping the executive in check, the court contributes to effective policy implementation. Government agencies often ask for judicial relief as legal conflicts occur.

As an administrative controller, the court is able to correct improper administrative actions taken, relieve the damage of citizens, and punish corrupt public officials. For those matters, the judiciary has the power to judge administrative litigation, the authority to examine laws and rules, litigation power over compensation for damage and loss cause by administrative actions, and the power to judge criminal cases. In addition, the judiciary can file constitutional appeals through the Constitutional Court. First, the court can correct inappropriate administrative actions that are filed as administrative litigation. Administrative litigation deals with cases for cancelling the effect of the administrative actions, confirming the invalidation, appealing the litigation over illegality of omission, litigation by parties that stand against the administrative punishment, public litigation on illegal actions by government bureaucracy, litigation between public agencies over their jurisdictional power, etc.

Second, the right to investigate is to examine if administrative actions breach laws and, even, the Constitution and then the court can nullify the illegal administrative actions and any effects of them. Third, the court forces the executive to compensate for damages caused by illegal administrative measures. It can also have the executive compensate for losses caused by any administrative action. That applies even when the action taken is legally legitimate. Fourth, the court can punish the illegal behaviors of public officials through laws.

The Constitutional Court is the supreme judicial body, with jurisdictional power over any political, administrative, and legislative cases with suspicion of unconstitutionality. Citizens can file a petition to the Constitutional Court (or constitutional appeals) when their rights as a constituency are violated by the actions of either private or public parties. Article 68 of Constitutional Court Act allows that citizens can directly appeal to the Constitutional Court once they go through all other procedures legally guaranteed. Constitutional appeals can be viewed as a way to control the executive because the Constitutional Court often sees administrative actions more comprehensively than the Supreme Court in Korea.

Court control over the executive is, while effective, still passive and is taken place after damage is done. The advantages include its ability to correct the administrative behavior and, furthermore, the flaws of administrative procedures. However, it is still a post-control and only interferes with cases where citizens make petitions. In addition, citizens must use all methods for remedies offered by the executive, and that delays the resolution.

VI.   Internal measures of the executive for administrative responsibility

Self-control by the executive lets a government bureaucracy review its own performance and hold itself accountable to its own standard. As a relatively convenient way of administrative control, it focuses on improving efficiency and effectiveness. Measures of self-control include self-audits, evaluations by managing agencies, and audits by the Board of Audit and Inspection and the ombudsman. However, self-control is only effective when all members in the executive share the idea that government bureaucracy is only interested in improving public interests and that bureaucrats should put public interests ahead of private interests. Self-audits involve auditing and inspecting one's own organization. Evaluation by managing agencies are conducted by agencies in charge of personnel and finance.

1.   *Self-audit by the public agency*

Self-audit is an internal control where the principal agents of audit are members of the organization under audit. They analyze and evaluate all their jobs and tasks by their plan and performance criteria. The complexity and technicality of tasks in government agencies make self-audit an appropriate measure. Self-audits are authorized under the Public Act of 2010, which is a successor of the Rules of Government Performance Auditing.

The Public Audit Act is in charge of the system of reviewing the performance of central administrative agencies, local government agencies, and public institutions such as public enterprises. The Public Audit Act stipulates the organization, personnel, and tasks of internal organizations for self-audits and provides a foundation for the independence and expertise that is a basis for an effective audit. For example the Act requires open recruitment of its personnel to ensure independence.

The Public Audit Act requires the person in charge of the audit to make a plan for the audit by demanding responses both in person and through paperwork. The head of the public agency implements the correct measures suggested by the self-audit except on special circumstances and reports the results of the corrective measure to higher authorities. The results shall also be reported to the Board of Audit and Inspection and be open to the public. In turn, the Board of Audit and Inspection may reward agencies and employees for their performance and also conduct inspections on agencies with poor records.

Self-audit is useful and effective because the expertise in an administrative task often makes it difficult for a third-party audit based on actual performance. Thus, self-audit based upon expertise would contribute to improving the performance and accountability of public agencies. Despite the contribution, self-audit has a long way to go. A survey on audit officers in public organizations in 2008 reports that the self-audit was one of the audits with the least burden. Another survey on self-audits in 2009 reports that self-audits were not reliable enough to ensure objectivity and credibility by themselves. In addition, frequent and duplicate audits are often criticized because of the lack of collaboration with the other auditing agencies including the Board of Audit and Inspection.

Protecting whistleblowers is another way of ensuring public accountability. Whistleblowers are the ones who report, appeal, tip off, and accuse public agencies of actions that damage public interests. The Whistleblower Protection Bill, enacted in 2011, prescribes that public officials must notify law enforcing authorities or the Anti-Corruption and Civil Rights Commission when they get to know actions violated public interests during their work. Whistleblowers must report wrongdoing to supervisors or law enforcement officers on public interests and conscience. The government must ensure confidentiality on whistleblowers and reward them when the state is benefitted. While the Whistleblower Protection Bill provides basic protection, many calls for extension of the bill. The protection only applies to the subject of administrative dispositions, leaving laws and regulations closely related to public interests. Some demands extension of whistleblowers' protection to people who disclose private institutions' actions damaging public interests.

2.   *Evaluation by managing agencies*

The managing agencies in the central government are the Ministry of Security and Public Administration whose jurisdiction is personnel and organization; the Ministry of Strategy and Finance, which is in charge of budget and finance; and the Office for Government Policy Coordination responsible for performance evaluations.

The Ministry of Security and Public Administration is responsible for a diverse set of tasks from policy-making on safety and disaster management, e-government, organizational management, personnel management, pension management, policy-making on local government autonomy, inter-governmental relations, to managing referenda. The Ministry controls other agencies by regulating their size and structure. For organizational and personnel management, it works to maintain optimal size and redundancy and to run the government system efficiently. For those goals, the Minister produces a government reorganization plan and a human resource management plan every March and reports to the president after getting prime minister's approval.

The Ministry of Strategy and Finance is in charge of planning long-term national development strategies; making policies on the national economy and finance; compiling data on budgets and funds, performance evaluations, government accounts, and international finance; supervising publicly funded institutions; and managing national properties. The Ministry especially controls other government agencies through their power over budgetary policy-making, performance evaluations, and policy-making on publicly funded institutions. For efficient and sound use of the budget, the Ministry makes a long-term national budgetary plan and submits it to the National Assembly. It is a basis for determining the principles of national budget, allocating budget through forecasting revenues and expenditures, and coordinating budget demands from many agencies. During the budgetary process, the Ministry looks through feasibility studies about pending programs and policies and lays out the budgetary plan from a national perspective. That plan-making process is a push for administrative responsibility by comparing the performance of public agencies.

Ministry of Strategy and Finance monitors the implementation of the budget plan once it passes the National Assembly. For monitoring and evaluation use and furthermore for improving the efficiency of public agencies, the Ministry sets up and enforces guidelines for budget implementation. The Ministry also has the power to adjust and defer the budget plan and even to hold it off. The Ministry's focus continues on evaluating the results of budget spending and of performance evaluations on implemented programs. The Ministry sets up guidelines for preparing for performance plans and performance reports and evaluates the performance of the programs as well as the agency's performance. These evaluations by the Ministry affect the next year's budget plan and the budget allocation.

The Office for Government Policy Coordination is responsible for assisting the prime minister, supervising central government agencies, policy coordination, managing social conflict, public service evaluation, and regulatory reform. The Office conducts government performance evaluation to control public agencies and improve administrative responsibility. The Framework Act on Public Service Evaluation of 2006 requires government performance evaluations to be conducted every April. The 15-member Government Performance Evaluation Committee designs evaluation methods, reviews the self-audit of the public agency, monitors and evaluates the policies and programs, and deliberates and makes final decisions on all related matters.

3. Administrative control by the supreme audit institution

The Board of Audit and Inspection is the supreme audit institution in Korea. The Board is located under the executive but holds an independent position under the Article 97 of the Constitution. Therefore, the independence of the Board's personnel, organization, and budget is honored as much as possible. According to the Board of Audit and Inspection Act, the Board is made up of seven persons, including the chairperson. The chairperson, with the consent of the National Assembly, is appointed by the president, and board members are recommended by the chairperson and appointed by the president. The Board is in charge of auditing of the closing report of the national accounts, maintaining the appropriateness of budget spending through auditing the financial accounts of public agencies selected by laws, and improving administrative operations by inspecting the job done by public agencies and public officials.

The Board undertakes four basic tasks: regularity audits, performance audits, investigations, and forensic audits. First, the regularity audit is the most fundamental task of the Board and is composed of financial auditing and compliance auditing. Financial auditing is to evaluate the accuracy and appropriateness of accounting procedures and financial reports. Compliance auditing is to evaluate whether or not the allocated budget was spent on approved uses and to evaluate if the use of funds followed rules and regulations. Second, the performance audit is to evaluate the effort to achieve the intended goals of policies and programs from the perspectives of cost-effectiveness, operational efficiency, and economic feasibility. This kind of audit has lately been well highlighted in the popularity of the new public management regime. Third and fourth, investigation and forensic audit are to detect the misuse and over-use of public agencies and public officials. Forensic audits use advanced accounting techniques to analyze budget information and then to track down and eradiate corruption. Unlike other countries, the Board in Korea performs the inspection function to uncover wrongdoing by public agencies and improve the administrative accountability.

Public audits by the Board include a broad range of activities from conducting financial audits to providing information for citizens to secure administrative responsibility. The Board is an independent third-party organization to help citizens under information asymmetry, to institutionalize the activities of making accurate information public, and to prevent public officials from committing moral hazards. Summing up, the Board contributes to improving administrative responsibility by satisfying the right-to-know of the public by publishing audit reports, improving sound financial management, implementing lawful administrative actions, and spending the budget appropriately.

However, the fact that the Board is under the executive creates a lot of criticism in terms of its effectiveness and fairness. For example it is difficult to inspect the president and his close aides because of political influence.

4. *Ombudsman for administrative control*

The ombudsman is a program intended to help citizens who suffer violation of rights because of administrative actions or inactions get relief. It also refers to persons appointed by either the executive or the legislature to lead this process. First started in Sweden in 1809, the ombudsman has been adopted in more than 100 countries. Despite differences among countries, it is used as a way to supplement other administrative control measures and to accept public demands for protecting the basic rights of citizens from the threat of discretionary power of public officials. The ombudsman performs the three functions of consultation, problem-solving, and punishment. The consultation function resolves civil complaints by counselling citizens and offering necessary information for protecting and remedying rights. The problem-solving function is, based upon investigative reports on ombudsman cases, to resolve conflicts between citizens and public agencies and to make adjustments in the agency and its policies. The punishment function is to relieve problems in proper process and, if any offence is found, to punish the persons that caused the problem. The ombudsman uses consultation, problem-solving, and then punishment strategies step by step. Citizen participation is stressed in the consultation stage, communication between stakeholders and public agencies in the problem-solving stage, and the effort to share the core idea and tackle the problem is the main focus of the punishment stage.

The Anti-Corruption and Civil Rights Commission is the agency to conduct the ombudsman in Korea. In 2008, the Commission was founded to support the ombudsman and take anti-corruption measures. In addition, other programs – such as administrative trials by the Commission, public agencies' own programs for handling civil complaints, the civil affairs officer in the Blue House, residents' claims for inspection under the Local Government Act, petitions to the National Assembly – play similar functions in Korea.

Cases for the ombudsman are defined in the Act on Anti-Corruption and the foundation of the Anti-Corruption and Civil Rights Commission. Civil complaints have the following components: (1) illegal actions or inaction by government agencies; (2) delays taken place by government officials or the absence of clear standard operating procedures; (3) absurd and unreasonable laws, rules, and guidelines; and (4) other related causes. When a civil complaint is submitted, the Commission can ask related agencies for explanations on the filed complaints; to submit relevant materials and documents to the administrative agency concerned; and to attend the testimony of complainants, stakeholders, reference persons, and relevant staff members. And, this investigator also conducts an on-site investigation at the concerned agency and seeks advice from specialists. Once the investigation is completed, the Commission recommends to the agency concerned a settlement after taking necessary actions or arbitrates the complaint by its authority when the complaint involves a multitude of citizens or has a big social impact. In addition, the Commission recommends to the agency concerned ways to improve on its laws, rules, and policies, which the investigative report suggests.

The ombudsman is a program for administrative control that makes up for the weaknesses of legislative and judicial control on the executive in the era of the administrative state. However, criticisms of the ombudsman are raised in Korea. First, the ombudsman is usually adopted in countries without administrative courts. In Korea, where administrative courts handle administrative litigation, many overlaps occurred. Second, questions about its effectiveness are raised because it only has the power to recommend and disclose without the power to correct. Third, it is an ex-post facto approach and handles cases only after civil complaints. In addition, it can be underused or misused when citizenship is not mature. Lastly, the ombudsman often depresses the passion and energy of public officials.

VII.   Conclusion: administrative control to ensure the administrative responsibility

Diverse tools for administrative control are adopted to ensure administrative responsibility. This chapter introduced most administrative control programs but not unofficial ones such as voting, citizen participation, and establishing administrative ethics and a healthy administrative culture.

The administrative control programs introduced here have their own strengths and weaknesses. Improving the effectiveness of these programs needs to relate programs with each other in creative ways, while making up their weaknesses. Linkages between programs would greatly cut down on inefficiency and improve effectiveness through synergy. The examples are manifold: the ombudsman and administrative appeals, administrative appeals and administrative litigations, audits by the National Assembly, audits by the Board of Audit and Inspection, and self-audits and performance evaluations.

References

Dimock, Marshall. (1951). *Free Enterprise and the Administrative State*. Tuscaloosa, AL: Univ. of Alabama Press.

Hill, Carolyn J. and Laurence E. Lynn, Jr. (2009). *Public Management: A Three-Dimensional Approach*. Washington, DC: CQ Press.

Hong, Joon Hyung. (2010). *Legal Control of the Administrative Process*. Seoul: Seoul National University Press. (in Korean)

Joo, Jaehyun. (2013). *On Administrative Control: A Study about Control Devices for Public Bureaucracy*. Kyunggi-do: Bobmunsa. (in Korean)

Joo, Jaehyun. (2009). Administrative Reform and the Mechanisms of Control over Bureaucracy: An Analysis of the Personnel Reforms under the Roh Moohyun Government. *Korean Journal of Public Administration*, v47n4: 49–78. (in Korean)

Lee, Won Woo. (2011). Characteristics and Issues of Administrative Control in Contemporary Legal Democracy. *Administrative Law Journal*, v29. April 2011: 105–133. (in Korean)

Shin, Minchul and Cho Taejun. (2013). Alternatives for the Development of Internal Control System in the Public Sector. *Korean Public Personnel Administration Review*, v12n1: 169–193. (in Korean)

Yang, Jaejin. (2002). Presidentialism, Dual Domestic Legitimacy, and the Control by the Executive Branch over the Legislature in Korea: Implications for the Korean Administrative State. *The Korea Public Administration Journal*, v11n1: 168–190. (in Korean)

13 Historical review of anti-corruption policy in Korea

Progress and challenges[1]

Kilkon Ko

I. Introduction

According to the literature on the impact of corruption, corruption has a negative impact on economic (Bardhan, 1997; Gupta, Abed, and International Monetary Fund, 2002; Heidenheimer, Johnston, and Levine, 1989; Hope and Chikulo, 1999), political (Girling, 1997; Heywood, 1997), and administrative (Caiden and Caiden, 1977; Werner, 1983) systems. If the proposition that corruption causes economic underdevelopment is true, the counterargument that economic development causes less corruption should be true as well. Despite this logical conjecture, corruption is still a significant problem in Korea, while Korea has achieved rapid economic development from a per capita income of around USD$100 in 1960 to USD $23,000 in 2011.

On the one hand, around 54 percent of citizens responded that government was corrupt in a survey done by the Anti-Corruption and Civil Rights Commission (ACRC) in 2011. Korea ranked 46th out of 177 countries. Korea is even more corrupt than Bhutan whose economy is far less developed. On the other hand, very few policemen or tax collectors receive bribes, which was prevalent before the 2000s. According to the 2013 Global Corruption Barometer (GCB) by Transparency International, around 27 percent of world citizens had paid a bribe in the previous 12 months when they interacted with key public institutions and services. However, only 3 percent of Korean respondents had paid a bribe, making it one of the lowest out of 107 countries. Most domestic surveys asking about the actual experience of bribery are also consistent with the GCB results. This suggests that actual bribery is less serious than citizens' perception would suggest.

Such a different view of the status of corruption in Korea leads to quite an inconsistent evaluation of the anti-corruption policies of the Korean government. The Korean government introduced many anti-corruption policies over the last few decades such as strengthening the code of ethics, promulgating anti-corruption acts, creating anti-corruption agencies, and utilizing a variety of information and communication technologies for monitoring and detecting the corrupt behaviors of public officials. The pessimistic view of the current status of corruption (Choi, 2009; Quah, 2005) tends to conclude that existing anti-corruption policies have failed or been ineffective.

Contrary to the pessimistic view of the effectiveness of the Korean government, this chapter attempts to show that the Korean government's anti-corruption policies have targeted different types of corruption in different administrations. The traditional corruption of low-ranking officials such as taking bribes, misappropriation of public funds, and embezzlement were the major targets in the 1980s. The target has gradually shifted to political corruption and the integrity of the civil service in the twenty-first century. As a result, punished bribery cases and disciplinary actions have decreased significantly, and citizens are not tolerant of political corruption and unethical behavior even if the magnitude is minor. This analysis leads to the conclusion that anti-corruption policies should continue to be revised according to changing economic, political, and administrative contexts that affect citizen expectations of government.

II.   Anti-corruption strategy before democratization: 1961–1987

Korea was under authoritarian governments from 1961 to 1987. In this period, Park Chunghee and Chun Doohwan took political power through military coups. Political rights, including freedom of press and free elections, were not fully protected. Political power was concentrated in a political circle with military leaders at the core. Society was strongly influenced by traditional Confucian culture respecting hierarchy and state authority.

Despite the authoritarian regime, economic development was outstanding. Per capita GDP was around USD$100 in the early 1960s but increased to USD$3,447 in 1987. Such a miraculous economic development was achieved with a feeble market, inappropriate regulations, administrative inefficiency, and excess intervention by government in resource distribution. Corruption in the 1970s could be justified to some extent by the "grease hypothesis." Uncontrolled discretion, vague rules and regulations, and unpredictable administrative red tape generated tremendous transaction costs for businessmen. They attempted to overcome such tedious administrative costs by paying bribes to politicians and civil servants. The low wages of public officials frequently justified their acceptance of bribes, and petty corruption prevailed in many administrative and social transactions. For instance, people had to pay bribes to install telephone lines while "speed money" was paid for education and health services. Informal networks based on school, region, marriage, and kinship were the primary channels for maximizing private interests by sacrificing the public interest. Simply speaking, corruption was a way of life in this period.

Anti-corruption policy in this period can be best described as taking a "political campaign approach." The authoritarian governments launched comprehensive anti-corruption campaigns to offset their democratic legitimacy deficit. For instance, 21,919 public officials (4.6 percent) were punished for offences in 1975 while 4,178 were expelled from the civil service. The number of officials punished increased to 51,468 in 1977, and 8,194 were fired (Oh, 1977). These anti-corruption campaigns usually gained public support even though they were ruthlessly implemented using the monopoly power of the government. One survey conducted in 1977 (n = 2,000) indicated that 79.4 percent of survey respondents believed that corruption had decreased from its level four to five years before due to the political campaigns (Oh, 1977). Such political campaigns did not directly target grand corruption involving high-ranking politicians and bureaucrats. Political corruption was only sporadically and exceptionally known to the public when it did not affect the political interests of the ruling class due to the lack of press freedom.

Economic and administrative development gradually reduced the room for corruption in spite of its prevalence. The number of civil servants officially punished between 1976 and 1987 decreased, as shown in Figure 13.1. Notably, there was an increase in the numbers punished in the early 1980s. The increase in bribery cases was related to a political campaign initiated by the Chun Doohwan Administration, which took power in a military coup and attempted to supplement its lack of legitimacy with economic development and an anti-corruption campaign. Bribery was on a downward trend except for the early 1980s.

Of course, the above trend only reflects serious, officially prosecuted corruption. More relevant statistics include overall misbehavior by public officials as measured by disciplinary actions. As shown in Table 13.1, the number of administrative disciplinary actions also decreased. The total number of disciplinary actions decreased from 7,349 in 1973 to 2,991 in 1987. As there is no reason to believe that the decrease of disciplinary actions was because of a weak will to punish the misbehavior of public officials, it can be concluded that both the most serious punishment (removal) and the most minor (reprimand) decreased consistently in this period.

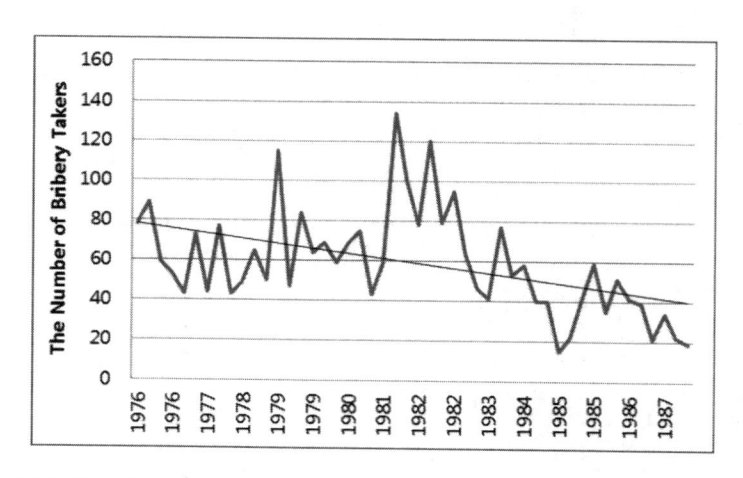

Figure 13.1 Trends in the number of officially punished bribe takers

Source: *Annual Statistical Yearbook of the Supreme Prosecutors' Office.*

Table 13.1 Number of disciplinary actions (1979–1987)

	Removal	Dismissal	Suspension of Duty	Pay Cut	Reprimand	Total
1979	565		11	2,027	4,453	7,349
1980	549		10	1,938	4,273	7,184
1981	425	72	101	1,482	3,023	6,681
1982	484	192	208	1,600	3,423	6,259
1983	399	288	253	1,373	3,048	5,361
1984	304	191	249	1,149	2,635	4,528
1985	248	152	159	963	2,058	3,580
1986	240	200	215	1,212	2,227	4,094
1987	157	129	158	878	1,669	2,991

Source: Yeon (2007).

In sum, the pre-democratization period relied on the political campaign approach. There was no anti-corruption law, independent anti-corruption agency, code of ethics, civil service code of ethics, or protections for whistle blowers. Corruption was punished by some articles of the Criminal Law and the Civil Service Act. Despite the lack of an institutional setting for anti-corruption policy, political campaigns were able to contribute to deterring the exponential growth of petty corruption through regular monitoring and punishment.

However, the political campaign approach was based on political will, especially the will of the president, not laws or institutions. Therefore, it only lasted for a short period. Under these circumstances, an independent anti-corruption agency or anti-corruption law for regulating government-wide corruption was not feasible even though it was widely discussed by academics and policymakers. Consequently, the control of grand corruption committed by politicians became an imminent challenge after democratization.

Another notable implication is that economic and administrative development is positively related to the integrity of public officials. Were the "grease hypothesis" correct, businessmen and public officials would commit more corruption when the economy grows. However, as the Korean administrative system progressed along with economic growth, corruption was able to be controlled to some extent.

III. Anti-corruption strategy during democratization: 1993–1997

Korea experienced a transition to democracy from 1988 to 1992. President Roh Taewoo was elected in a free election, and the administrative and political system gradually moved from authoritarian to democratic. The transition required much trial and error, and political control over the bureaucracy weakened. As a result, the number of punishments increased, as shown in Table 13.2. The total number of punishments increased 37 percent between 1987 and 1992.

In this context, newly inaugurated President Kim Youngsam initiated a comprehensive anti-corruption campaign in 1993. Unlike his predecessors, however, he relied on a legal and institutional approach rather than dictatorship. As his tenure was limited to five years by the Constitution, an anti-corruption campaign based on authoritarian power was no longer a valid option. An institutional approach made after considering the interests of bureaucrats, interest groups, civil society, and other competing political groups was a far more relevant choice for him.

Democracy and the limited tenure of the president caused two significant changes to anti-corruption policies. First, presidents intensified the punishment of corruption early in their tenure. As shown in Table 13.3, the number of bribery cases prosecuted in the first two years of each president's tenure is far greater than in the last two years. Such a difference suggests that presidents usually dedicated themselves to combating corruption, but their efforts faded with their declining political power as their tenure reached an end. Despite the political influence on the number of punished cases, bribery also decreased significantly from the 1990s in the 2000s.

Second, in contrast to the weakening power of the president, citizens were empowered through democracy. Citizens strongly demanded that President Kim prosecute former presidents Chun Doohwan and Roh Taewoo for corruption. These two presidents were eventually given prison sentences even though it was politically burdensome for Kim. Moreover, Kim's own son was prosecuted

Table 13.2 Number of disciplinary actions (1997–1992)

	Removal	Dismissal	Suspension of Duty	Pay Cut	Reprimand	Total
1987	157	129	158	878	1,669	2,991
1988	151	118	140	899	1,838	3,146
1989	292	889	198	1,029	1,989	4,397
1990	247	247	270	1,218	2,674	4,656
1991	175	249	296	994	2,282	3,996
1992	196	266	287	1,027	2,316	4,092

Table 13.3 Average number of bribery cases prosecuted in each administration

	Kim Youngsam (1993–1997)	Kim Daejung (1998–2002)	Roh Moohyun (2003–2007)	Lee Myungbak (2008–2012)
First two years	194.0	203.5	65.0	60.5
Last two years	142.0	95.0	31.0	NA

Source: *Annual Statistical Yearbook of the Supreme Prosecutors' Office.*

for taking bribes before Kim's presidential term ended. These incidents were symbolic examples showing that political corruption began to be a direct target of anti-corruption policy.

The Kim Administration can be considered a period of establishing laws to fight against political corruption. First, Real Name Financial Transactions were employed in 1993 to eradicate the financial black market. This policy was originally designed to reduce illegal financial transactions in the private sector in order to increase tax revenue. The wealthy and politicians held a majority of anonymous bank accounts for evading taxes or conducting illegal transactions before the reform was carried out and ended the practice. In particular, it was discovered when Chun Doohwan and Roh Taewoo were prosecuted that they had hidden more than USD$200 million in anonymous bank accounts. Without a transparent financial system, it seemed impossible to break the illegal ties between corrupt politicians and bribe-givers. The Real Name Financial Transaction policy contributed significantly to abating political corruption even though it was challenged before and after adoption.

Another important institutionalization of anti-corruption policy was the enactment of the Election of Public Officials and the Prevention of Election Malpractices Act of 1994 to replace the Public Officials Election Act. Although it was not effective at punishing, it inhibited political candidates from receiving illegal political funds and buying votes with illegal money. This law became the foundation of the publicly funded election system that was fully institutionalized in the mid-2000s.

Citizens demanded higher integrity from politicians and bureaucrats early in this democratic era, and many laws were enacted to curb political corruption in response. However, on account of the absence of comprehensive institutional settings, anti-corruption policy was not able to eradicate corruption effectively and was still influenced by the political will of the president, whose power was no longer as strong as the presidents under authoritarian governments. Kim's control of the bureaucracy was much more restricted than that of authoritarian presidents. In addition, as the Board of Audit and Inspection and the Prosecutor's Office paid less attention to corruption after the president's political power for fighting against corruption weakened as they had to use major resources for their own tasks.

IV. Comprehensive institutionalization of anti-corruption policies (1998–2002)

The Kim Daejung Administration (1982–2002) faced a new challenge compared to his predecessors as citizen expectations of public integrity had increased significantly. The Asian financial crisis in 1997 brought into question the competence of bureaucrats and the effectiveness of the administrative system. Citizens criticized the government, arguing that the crisis originated from opaque administrative procedures and corrupt practices in the public and private sectors. Corruption was not simply limited to bribery, misappropriation of public funds,

Table 13.4 The perception and experience gap of bribery

Year	Perception (Unit: %)		Actual Experience (Unit: %)
	Prevalence	*Seriousness*	
2000	68.8	75.6	
2001	62.4	70.3	16.2
2004	60.6	77.2	13.8
2005	56.2	71.0	11.6
2006	50.4	64.8	6.6
2007	58.8	69.8	7.4

Source: Korea Institute of Public Administration's annual corruption perception survey.

or embezzlement for these citizens but was related to trust in government. Any misbehavior undermining the fairness and transparency of administration, let alone illegal behavior, was also regarded as corrupt by citizens. The Kim Daejung Administration had to deal with corruption within a crisis of trust in government.

Citizens' expectations of high ethical standards widened the gap between citizen perception and the actual experience of corruption. Table 13.4 shows the results of a national survey of citizen perception of corruption. While most citizens responded that bribery was prevalent, their actual rate of experience giving bribes was very low.[2] This gap also created an elusive perception of the ineffectiveness of anti-corruption policies.

Facing the above challenge, the Korean government initiated comprehensive institutionalization efforts. Previous administrations had used the political campaign approach to draw public support. They also relied on the Supreme Prosecutors' Office and the Board of Audit and Inspection, which are under the direct control of the president, to monitor and punish corrupt bureaucrats. However, these approaches were effective only when the president had strong political power. Hence, the Kim Daejung Administration tried to introduce institutionalized anti-corruption policies. Some major institutionalized policies follow.

The Anti-Corruption Act of 2001 was promulgated by the Kim Administration to create a clean civil service and social climate by efficiently preventing and regulating acts of corruption. The definition of corruption in the law covers both the abuse of public office and illegal behavior. Article 2 defined corruption as:

(a) The act of any public official abusing his/her position or authority or violating Acts and subordinate statutes in connection with his/her duties to seek gains for himself/herself or any third party;

(b) The act of inflicting damages on the property of any public institution in violation of Acts and subordinate statutes, in the process of executing the budget of the relevant public institution, acquiring, managing, or disposing of the property of the relevant public institution, or entering into and executing a contract to which the relevant public institution is a party;

(c) The act of coercing, urging, proposing and inducing any act referred to in items (a) and (b) or of covering it up.

The Anti-Corruption Act was the first law regulating various types of political and administrative corruption. Politicians resisted the Anti-Corruption Act despite the president's strong support for the act when it was proposed by petition from the civil society organization People's Solidarity for Participatory Democracy in 1998. Politicians were concerned that the law might constrain political fundraising as it strictly prohibited money laundering. In addition, other government agencies, especially the Prosecutor's Office, disagreed with the bill, which intended to create an independent anti-corruption agency with the right to investigate and prosecute corruption cases. The Prosecutor's Office did not want to share its power of investigation and prosecution with an anti-corruption agency.

The effort to reduce illegal political funds by enhancing the financial transparency of public and private organizations continued. The Kim Administration believed the opaque private-sector financial system caused political corruption and the economic crisis of 1997. Hence, the government forced companies to adopt international standards of accounting and auditing. Moreover, the government asked public officials to use credit cards for meals and business entertainment expenses as well as for other procurements. This helped the government easily track down and detect any illegal use of funds. Furthermore, auditing of budget expenditures became more systematic through the adoption of information technology and improved accounting rules.

Meanwhile, citizen participation was encouraged as well. Citizens were able to report the corrupt conduct of public officials to the Prosecutor's Office, ministries, or the Korea Independent Commission Against Corruption (KICAC)[3] using diverse and convenient channels such as phone, fax, e-mail, and/or websites. The Anti-Corruption Act also included a clause to protect whistleblowers by providing legal and financial protection, which increased the safety of informants and the confidentiality of information provided. The KICAC also tried to measure the level and causes of corruption of public organizations by performing an annual survey of citizens and publicizing the results. The public and mass media's attention towards corruption increased whenever the results were released.

The institutionalization efforts of the Kim Daejung Administration should not be underestimated. Prior administrations superficially supported the idea of the Anti-Corruption Act and the creation of an anti-corruption agency but did not make any serious efforts as such institutionalization might undermine the interests of politicians. The creation of a legal and organizational foundation politically supported by the president enabled the Korean government to introduce many anti-corruption policies. As shown in the Appendix, most anti-corruption policies modified in the following administrations were initiated by the Kim Daejung Administration. Despite these efforts, citizen concerns over the seriousness of corruption were not significantly alleviated. It took time to change the behavior of politicians and civil servants. At the same time, like his predecessors, President Kim Daejung also suffered from corruption in his family, which tarnished his anti-corruption efforts.

V.   Good governance and anti-corruption policy (2003–2007)

The Roh Moohyun Administration (2003–2007) inherited and expanded the Kim Daejung Administration's anti-corruption policy. Unlike other politicians, President Roh mainly raised political funds using citizen donations and official government election assistance. He also had a fairly loose connection with the conglomerates (*chaebol*), which voluntarily or involuntarily give illegal funds to politicians in exchange for protection or favors for their businesses. Considering that most former presidents had political deficits due to illegal connections with businessmen, President Roh was able to initiate anti-corruption policies targeting politicians.

The Roh Administration's anti-corruption policy was characterized by a holistic approach based on a good governance framework. Rather than using a control and punishment approach, the Roh Administration attempted to reform political, administrative, and market systems to prevent corruption. Historically, most grand corruption cases in Korea were related to receiving funds from private companies for political campaigns and providing favors to donors in exchange. To cut this vicious cycle, the Roh Administration reformed the costly election system. The administration revised the Public Official Election and Anti-Corruption Act in 2004 and made the government fully refund total campaign costs when a candidate garnered more than 15 percent of the vote. Even when candidates received more than 10 percent but less than 15 percent of legal votes, the government refunded 50 percent of total campaign costs. In addition, the revised Political Fund Act codified the general subsidies paid to political parties for their general operating expenses. The amount of the general subsidy was distributed to political parties according to their number of votes in the previous National Assembly election (Article 25, Clauses 1, 3). Moreover, election subsidies were given to parties when a presidential election or various elections for public office were held (Article 25, Clauses 2, 3). In exchange for this refund of campaign costs, the government required candidates to use a single bank account and publicize their accounting documents, and strictly punished violations of the law.[4]

Such efforts led to a significant reduction of election-related corruption. As shown in Table 13.5, the number of people prosecuted in local government elections for violating the Public Official Election Act in 2002 was 5,468 and decreased to 1,803 (by 67 percent) in 2010. There was a 14 percent decrease in prosecutions in the National Assembly elections from 2004 to 2008 (from 3,117 to 2,667 cases).

Table 13.5 Cases prosecuted following local and national elections

Local Elections		National Assembly Elections	
Year	Cases Prosecuted	Year	Cases Prosecuted
2002	5,468	2004	3,117
2006	4,229	2008	2,667
2010	1,803		

Source: *Annual Statistical Yearbook of the Supreme Prosecutors' Office.*

Another target was reforming the outdated anti-corruption administrative system. The KICAC led to the design of a variety of anti-corruption policies regulating public organizations and their management. Evaluation of the integrity and anti-corruption practices of public-sector organizations was one of the main and highly effective roles of the KICAC.[5] Central government ministries and agencies as well as state-owned enterprises had to measure their integrity as part of the performance management system and use the results as a performance indicator. The integration of the KICAC's integrity index into the performance management system led to public organizations developing their own anti-corruption policies. The effort was not just symbolic. Chief executive officers and organizational members put forth ardent efforts to reduce corruption since performance evaluation results were publicized and used for allocating budgets and performance bonuses for public organizations.

Finally, the government emphasized the role of the private sector by protecting whistleblowers and encouraging civil society to monitor the corrupt behavior of public and private organizations. Along with the progress of an e-government system, most public organizations installed a corruption reporting hotline on their websites and compensated whistleblowers.

A notable feature of the Roh Administration's anti-corruption policy is that it was driven not by politicians or individual ministries but by the KICAC, the specialized anti-corruption agency. Although the KICAC could not directly investigate corruption and relied on the Prosecutor's Office, it was able to produce and coordinate a variety of corruption policies and agencies in the central and local governments, as well as in the public and private sectors.

VI. Anti-corruption challenges facing contemporary Korea: 2008–present

A significant change in the Lee Myungbak Administration (2008–2012) was the creation in 2008 of the Anti-Corruption and Civil Rights Commission (ACRC), which inherited most of the KICAC's functions and policies. The creation of the ACRC evoked huge criticism in that its organizational attention was distracted by other policy areas such as processing citizen grievance petitions, establishing and implementing policies for protecting the rights of people, and administrative adjudication.

The Protecting Public Interest Whistleblowers Law was enacted in 2011 during the Lee Administration. Whistleblowers in previous administrations were protected by the Anti-Corruption Act of 2001, but the act defined the method of protection in the abstract. The Lee Administration also attempted to enact the Prevention of Illegal Solicitations and Conflicts of Interest Act, but it was finally promulgated in Park Geun Hye administration in 2015. The implications of the act are very significant. Conflicts of interest are regulated by several laws, such as the Public Service Ethics Act, the Anti-Corruption Act, the Code of Conduct for Public Officials Act, and the Criminal Act in the current system (ACRC, 2012). However, these acts sporadically define the punishment and concrete conditions of conflicts of interest. For instance, it was not illegal under previous laws for a civil servant to receive USD$1,000 from a businessman as a gift not related to his/her official duties. This creates a huge loophole for evading punishment under law. The proposed Prevention of Illegal Solicitations and Conflicts of Interest Act would attempt to penalize the briber and the public official initially whether or not a bribe was related to the official's duties. The Act would also make it clear that taking more than USD$1,000 is illegal whether or not a public official receives a bribe in return for favors. Regrettably, Lee and his successor, Park Geunhye (2013–present), failed to pass the law.

The other notable area of focus for the ACRC is curbing private-sector corruption by increasing penalties against corrupt entrepreneurs. Korean courts have been reluctant to impose severe penalties, even when businessmen are prosecuted because of corruption, especially against CEOs of conglomerates. CEOs have been sentenced to probation in spite of illegal practices. Presidents have tended to give them special pardons even when they are convicted. During the Park Administration, however, the court has been applying the anti-corruption law strictly and is minimizing leniency given to CEOs. The CEOs of SK, Hanhwa, and CJ were imprisoned over illegal transactions.

Despite the above progress, the Lee and Park Administrations, however, failed to initiate more comprehensive anti-corruption policies. They simply followed their predecessors' anti-corruption policies. In particular, the Lee Administration did not show the strong political will to curb corruption. Unlike other presidents, he never mentioned 'corruption' in his inaugural speech, which suggested the weak political will for fighting against corruption. As a result, the total number of crimes (both prosecuted and non-prosecuted cases) by public officials increased from 738 in 2006 to 1,762 in 2012 (see Table 13.6). This trend suggests that corruption cannot easily be eradicated and is even aggravated without continuing efforts by the government.

To summarize, the Korean government has adopted many legal, institutional, and civil society policy tools over five decades' worth of efforts to control corruption, as shown in the Appendix. These policy tools were introduced and changed by different administrations and will continue to change in the future

Table 13.6 Trends in public official crimes by type

Year	Total	Dereliction of Duty	Abuse of Authority	Taking Bribes	Giving Bribers
2006	738	378	218	137	5
2007	717	380	242	93	2
2008	1,100	591	327	173	9
2009	1,192	603	335	244	10
2010	2,176	896	401	839	40
2011	1,574	662	439	413	60

Source: *Annual Statistical Yearbook of the Supreme Prosecutors' Office.*

to target different types of corruption. These policies achieved their goals to some extent and have been revised to target other types of corruption.

VII.   Lessons learned

This chapter reviewed the evolution of Korean anti-corruption policy from 1961 to the present. The level of corruption has significantly decreased even though corruption is still a serious concern in Korea. To some extent, the variety of anti-corruption policies shown in the Appendix can contribute to reducing corruption. Korea now utilizes more information and communications technology to increase the transparency of public administration and reduce opportunities for rent seeking. Few people currently have to pay "speed money" to street-level bureaucrats for education, health, and infrastructure services. Democracy contributes to preventing and mitigating political corruption by increasing political competition and the separation of powers. Citizens are no longer tolerant of corrupt politicians. Mass media, social network services, and the Internet have become powerful tools for detecting, publicizing, and punishing corrupt politicians and civil servants. In this regard, anti-corruption policies, economic development, and political development have at least partially contributed to reducing corruption in Korea.

Despite these achievements, corruption is still a major challenge for the Korean government. People show higher expectations for the integrity of public officials than before. Citizens no longer tolerate previously culturally accepted practices of public officials such as using official power to give favors to friends and relatives. Such high expectations make citizens perceive corruption as more serious. The government has to pursue more comprehensive and strict anti-corruption policies to meet this demand. In this regard, the government has adopted a more holistic approach combining a variety of tools such as codes of ethics, transparency of political funds, creation of specialized anti-corruption agencies, and empowering civil society, as shown in the Appendix.

One notable practice that can be learned from Korea is the emphasis on measuring corruption. The anti-corruption agency (ACRC) measures the level of integrity of public organizations, covering central and local government agencies as well as state-owned enterprises. More than 600 public organizations have to survey their integrity as of 2012, and the results are used on their annual performance evaluations. Although the weight of integrity is only 3 percent, the integration of integrity management into performance management is a promising direction in that it can change the behavior of public organizations that are highly responsive to performance scores.

In conclusion, corruption is neither an incurable disease nor able to be perfectly eradicated by a single policy. Korea has significantly reduced numerous types of petty and political corruption over the last five decades. This achievement, however, is not satisfactory for citizens who expect higher integrity from government. They tend to criticize government for not fixing present problems rather than praising the success of past governments. The Korean government needs to continue to revise its anti-corruption policies and introduce new policy tools to target new forms of corruption to cope with the challenge.

Appendix: contents and characteristics of anti-corruption policies under different administrations

Administration	Principal Anti-Corruption Pledges	Outcomes of Pledges
Kim Youngsam (1993–1998)	• Revision of the Public Service Ethics Act • Enforcement of the real name financial system (Real Name Financial Transactions Act) • Enforcement of the real name real estate system • Enactment of the Public Officials Election and Prevention of Illegal Elections Act (1994) • Introduction of a Public Officials Property Registration system • Installation of the Anti-Corruption Measures Committee • Enactment of the Information Disclosure Act • Revision of the Political Funds Act, Issuing Receipts, Official Report of Revenue and Expenditure of Political Funds (1994) • Revision of the Political Funds Act, abolition of Restricted Funds Donations, punishment regulations, more than 20% expenditure in policy development expenses for government state subsidy (1997) • Reinforcement of the Aggravated Punishment Act (leaking of confidential information by staff, aggravated punishment in the embezzlement of local taxes, extended application to executives of local public enterprises)	• Introduction of a fundamental anti-corruption system from the previous exposure-punishment system to prevent the fundamental source of corruption. • Recognizing and pursuing corruption as the first priority of the state administration • An anti-corruption effort focused on the law and systems • Assessment of previous corruption • Focus on political corruption such as political funds • Application of real-name financial system • Limitations in exercising control on corruption due to various unnecessary administrative restrictions and authoritative administrative practices that did not fade

(*Continued*)

Administration	Principal Anti-Corruption Pledges	Outcomes of Pledges
Kim Daejung (1998–2003)	• Enactment of the Act on the Prevention of Corruption • Enactment of anti-money laundering laws • Enactment of an officials' code of conduct • Installation of the Anti-corruption Committee • Operation of a whistleblower protection system • Public institution integrity measurement • National audit claims • Enactment of the Personnel Hearing Act • Enactment of the Act on Regulation of Punishment of Criminal Proceeds Concealment • Reinforcement of the Aggravated Punishment Act (reinforcement of the amount of bribes and punishment in court) • Revision of the Public Official Election and Prevention of Illegal Elections Act, installation of fraud monitors for election of local officials, presenting candidates' tax earnings and criminal records (2000)	• Solving issues systematically rather than the previous exposure-punishment system. • Anti-corruption policy was pursued generally and systematically in a governmental dimension • The application of various laws and systems • Enactment of laws and installation of a responsible system to prevent corruption • Provision of a whistleblower protection system • Enactment of Personnel Hearing Act • Measurement of integrity • Construction and administration of an anti-corruption system: operating an Corruption Prevention Commission, establishing and operating an anti-corruption plan, a system-improvement recommendation system, integrity measurement system • Public administration information system • Reinforcing real-name administrative system • Ethics system for officials, enacting the Officials Administrative Code of Conduct (2003)

Administration	Principal Anti-Corruption Pledges	Outcomes of Pledges
Roh Moohyun (2003–2008)	• Installation of the National Integrity Commission (previously, the Anti-Corruption Committee) • Installation of the President Affiliated Anti-corruption Authorities Council (2005) • Providing a medium- to long-term anti-corruption road map • Extending the notion of corruption (extorting bribes, etc.) • Assessment of factors causing corruption in terms of laws • Establishment of an integrated information system for anti-corruption • Reinforcement of journalist protections • Blank stock trust system • Limit to allowing denial notice when registering property • Explanation of wealth accumulation process • An exemption law on the confiscation of illegal political funds • Extending the personnel hearing target to former members of the State Council, judges of the Constitutional Court, and the Central Election Commission • Introducing electronic information disclosure • Reinforcement of the Information Disclosure Council based on outsiders • Complete expansion of financial expansion range (2008) • Revision of the Political Funds Act (2004; prohibiting donation of political funds from juridical persons, expenditure of accounting official, disclosing major political fund donators) • Amendment of the Amnesty Act (2007), installation of the Amnesty Commission • Reinforcement of the Aggravated Punishment Act (realizing the weighing of offense, etc.) • Revision of the Public Officials Election and Fraud Prevention Act (2004; extended to five years of tax earnings of the candidate and spouse, etc., mailing tax records, military records, and criminal records to voters) • Revision of the Public Officials Election and Fraud Prevention Act, constant operation of Election Fraud Surveillance Committee, etc. (2008)	• Installation of a general consultative body to promote a national anti-corruption policy • Establishment of a comprehensive anti-corruption plan • Expansion of corruption as a notion of integrity • Introduction of a blank stock trust system to avoid conflicts of interest • Reinforcing personnel hearing and verification system • Reinforcement of information disclosure system • Complete expansion of financial expansion range • Revision of the Political Relations Act

(*Continued*)

Administration	Principal Anti-Corruption Pledges	Outcomes of Pledges
Lee Myungbak (2008–2013)	• Property registration and disclosure of the Monetary Policy Committee, a recommended position • Abolition of the Corrupt Practices Act • Functional integration of former anti-corruption systems such as the National Integrity Commission, the Grievance Settlement Committee, and the Administrative Tribunal. • Significant increase in the recommended target for institutional improvement and its results • Reinforcement of the Aggravated Punishment Act (concurrent punishment of two to five times the sum of bribery in fines or imprisonment in regards to a bribery offense) • Senior official integrity assessment model developed (promoting the introduction of the senior officials' Personal Integrity Measurement system) • Protection of Officials Reporters Act (2011)	• Restructuring the old and inefficient system that induced corruption, impeded the improvement of productivity, and caused public inconveniences that consequently inhibited advancement • National Integrity Commission abolished (replaced by the Civil Rights Commission) • Enactment of the Protection of Public Interest Reporters Act • Diversification of the Disciplinary Committee • Providing office discipline establishment plans (enhanced punishment for drunk driving and sex-related offense) • Providing a plan to extend the period of prescription of disciplinary cause for offences other than monetary offence • Introduction of a relegation system (introduction of demotion between dismissal and suspension, 12/31/2008: State Public Officials Act revised) • Extension of disciplinary prescription to three years (3/21/2012: State Public Officials Act revised) • Prescription of administrative conduct offence extended from three years to five years • Introduction of a disciplinary surcharge system • Improvement in the operation of the Discipline Committee

Administration	Principal Anti-Corruption Pledges	Outcomes of Pledges
		• Disclosing the list and the disciplinary details of enterprises that are affiliated with bribery in the transactions with government offices on the government procurement website, thereby eliminating them from being selected as a public enterprise. • Reinforcement of integrity measurement functions • Improvement of grievance practices and corruption that restrict economic growth • Improvement in the three most corruption-prone areas: public construction contracting/ certification

Source: Based on Chang (2013).

Notes

1 This chapter is based on the article by Kilkon Ko and Sue Yeon Cho (2015), "Evolution of Anti-Corruption Strategies in South Korea". *Government Anti-Corruption Strategies: A Cross-Cultural Perspective.* Y. Zhang and C. Lavena, Routledge: 103–122.

2 The actual experience is still common though most respondents who paid bribes gave less than USD $100. If these respondents are excluded, the bribery rate is less than 1 percent.

3 Once the KICAC receives a report of corruption and concludes that there is an illegality, the KICAC informs the Prosecutor's Office. Then the Prosecutor's Office investigates the case and decides whether to prosecute the accused. Ministries have their own online as well as offline centers to receive reports of suspected corruption, which are examined internally and then reported to the KICAC or the Prosecutor's Office.

4 The person in charge of accounting is sentenced to a maximum of five years in prison or a maximum fine of 20 million won (approximately USD$20,000), when he/she does not properly publicize accounting documents or does not respond to the request of the Election Administration Committee without reason. The results of the election are also nullified.

5 The KICAC had six major roles: i) policymaking, ii) evaluating the level of integrity and anti-corruption practices in public-sector organizations, iii) monitoring corruption and protecting whistleblowers, iv) encouraging public-private

partnerships against corruption, v) improving institutional frameworks by reviewing the relevance of laws and corrupt practices, and vi) inculcating ethical values in society and public organizations by promoting public awareness of the risks of corruption and enforcing a code of conduct for public employees.

References and Further Readings

ACRC (2012). *ACRC KOREA Annual Report 2012*, Anti-Corruption and Civil Rights Commission, the Korean Government.

Amsden, A. H. (1989). *Asia's Next Giant: South Korea and Late Industrialization*. New York: Oxford University Press.

Bardhan, Pranab. (1997). Corruption and Development: A Review of Issues. *Journal of Economic Literature, 35*(3), 1320–1346.

Caiden, Gerald E., and Caiden, Naomi J. (1977). Administrative Corruption. *Public Administration Review, 37*(3), 301–309.

Carney, Richard W. (2009). *Lessons from the Asian Financial Crisis*. London; New York: Routledge.

Chang, Jiwon. (2013). "A Study on Corruption Trends in the Public Sector." The Korea Institute of Public Administration.

Choi, Jin-wook. (2009). Institutional Structures and Effectiveness of Anticorruption Agencies: A Comparative Analysis of South Korea and Hong Kong. *Asian Journal of Political Science, 17*(2), 195–214.

Chung, Y.-I. (2007). *South Korea in the Fast Lane: Economic Development and Capital Formation*. Oxford: Oxford University Press.

Fischer, Frank, and Forester, John (Eds.). (1993). *The Argumentative Turn in Policy Analysis and Planning*. Durham, NC: Duke University Press.

Friedrich, Carl J. (2002). Corruption Concepts in Historical Perspective. In A.J.M. Heidenheimer, Johnston (Ed.), *Political Corruption: Concepts & Contexts* (pp. 15–24). New Brunswick and London: Transaction Publishers.

Girling, J.L.S. (1997). *Corruption, Capitalism and Democracy*. London; New York: Routledge.

Gupta, Sanjeev, Abed, George T., and International Monetary Fund. (2002). *Governance, Corruption & Economic Performance*. Washington, DC: International Monetary Fund.

Heidenheimer, Arnold J., Johnston, Michael, and Levine, Victor. (1989). *Political Corruption: A Handbook*. New Brunswick, NJ: Transaction Books.

Heidenheimer, Arnold J., and Johnston, Michael. (2002). *Political Corruption: Concepts & Contexts* (3rd ed.). New Brunswick, NJ: Transaction Publishers.

Heywood, Paul (Ed.). (1997). *Political Corruption*. Oxford: Blackwell Publisher.

Hope, Kempe R., and Chikulo, Bornwell C. (1999). *Corruption and Development in Africa: Lessons from Country Case-studies*. New York: St. Martin's Press.

Johnston, Michael. (2001). The Definitions Debate: Old Conflicts in New Guises. In A.K. Jain (Ed.), *The Political Economy of Corruption* (pp. 11–31). New York: Routledge.

Kingdon, J.W. (1984). *Agendas, Alternatives, and Public Policy*. Glenview, IL: HarperCollins Publishers.

La Porta, R., Lopez-de-Silanes, F., and Vishny, R. (1997). Trust in Large Organization. *American Economic Review Papers and Proceedings, 87*(2), 334–338.

Lee, Young-ran. (1992). A Study on the Penalty Level of Election Crime – National Assembly Election Law Violation Cases. *Criminal Policy Study, 6*, 109–127.

Lee, Woo-sung. (2001). *How Big is Korean Underground Economy?*, LG Weekly Economy, LG Economic Research Institute.

Lejano, Raul P. (2006). *Frameworks for Policy Analysis: Merging Text and Context.* New York: Routledge.

Lucas, Robert E. (1993). Making a Miracle. *Econometrica, 61*(2), 251–272.

Oh, Seok-hong. (1977). A Study on the Korean Government Reform- Anti-Corruption Policy in the Public Administration. *Korea Public Administration Review, 15*(1), 1110–1140.

Quah, Jon S. T. (2005). *Curbing Corruption in Asia: A Comparative Study.* Marshall Cavendish.

Rose-Ackerman, Susan. (1978). *Corruption: A Study in Political Economy.* New York: Academic Press.

Rose-Ackerman, Susan. (2006). *International Handbook on the Economics of Corruption.* Cheltenham, UK; Northampton, MA: Edward Elgar.

Stone, Deborah A. (1997). *Policy Paradox: The Art of Political Decision Making, Revised Edition* (2nd ed.). New York: W.W. Norton.

Tran, Van Hoa, and Harvie, Charles. (2000). *The Causes and Impact of the Asian Financial Crisis.* Houndmills, Basingstoke, Hampshire; New York: Palgrave.

Uslaner, Eric M. (2004). Trust and Corruption. In J. G. Lambsdorf, M. Taube and M. Schramm (Eds.), *Corruption and the New Institutional Economics* (pp. 76–92). London: Routledge.

Walle, Steven Van De. (2007). Determinants of Confidence in the Civil Service. In K. Schedler and I. Proeller (Eds.), *Cultural Aspects of Public Management Reform* (pp. 171–201). Amsterdam; London: Elsevier JAI.

Werner, Simcha B. (1983). New Directions in the Study of Administrative Corruption. *Public Administration Review, 43*(2), 146–154.

World Bank. (1993). *The East Asian Miracle: Economic Growth and Public Policy.* New York, NY: Oxford University Press.

Yeon, Seongjin. (2007). "The Trend Analysis of Public Officials' Crime: 1964–2005." *Criminal Policy, 19*(2), 115–146.

14 Government innovation

Kwang-Kook Park

I. Introduction

There has been growing demand for government to become more innovative in order to overcome the inefficiencies of bureaucratic government, the low quality of public service delivery, and the lack of transparency since the International Monetary Fund (IMF) crisis in Korea in 1997. Unlike the public sector, the Korean private sector has achieved outstanding and unexpected performance in a short period. Korea is currently ranked 13th in the world in terms of size of the national economy thanks to the great contribution of the private sector. The IT industry, including semiconductors, mobile phones, and electronic goods, has a particularly high reputation for world-class competitiveness.

Nevertheless, many scholars argue that Korea has many difficulties in maintaining sustainable development without government innovation. Byungseob Kim, the former Chairman of the President Committee on Government Innovation and Decentralization identified the need for government innovation in terms of three aspects. The first aspect is related to the improvement of public well-being. There will be high competition between the public and private sectors in the near future over the provision of public goods and services. The second aspect is focused on strengthening the competitiveness of the nation. Competition among nations is intensifying in the era of globalization, which has resulted in the demise of nations that fall behind. The last aspect is the high attention paid to making innovation occur on a daily basis. In order to survive in a turbulent environment, the government should recognize innovation as the prerequisite, not a matter of choice.

Bearing the importance of government innovation, the Roh Administration actively pursued innovation with the goal of building efficient, service-oriented, transparent, and decentralized government during Roh's presidency. His successor Lee who belonged to the opposite party, however, did not succeed in the work of his predecessor who put the highest priority on government innovation with the exception of the field of decentralization. President Park, who took office in 2013, recognized the severity of national problems including growing economic inequality, deepening polarization between the haves and have-nots, and deep-rooted regional conflict between the Eastern and Western regions.

In addition, there have been many serious problems that have appeared recently such as unprecedented climate change, chronic shortages of food and energy, the declining birth rate, and an aging society that have not been solved through the traditional bureaucratic paradigm. In order to overcome those problems preemptively, the Park Administration has tried to revitalize the spirit of government innovation in the name of Government 3.0, putting an emphasis on the values of openness, information sharing, communication, and collaboration.

Several hot issues related to government innovation will be dealt with in this chapter. First, how has government innovation evolved from the Roh Administration to the Park Administration? Second, what are the key elements that theories of government innovation have tried to emphasize? Third, what best practices have been achieved by applying theories of government innovation to Korean governmental agencies over the last two decades? Finally, what policy implications can be drawn through the experiences of government innovation in Korea?

II. The evolution of government innovation in Korea

1. *The Roh Administration*

The Rho Administration (launched in 2003) declared trust, fairness, transparency, dialogue, compromise, decentralization, and autonomy the underlying values the government should espouse. To accomplish those values, the administration tried to set up five types of government: efficient government, service-oriented government, transparent government, decentralized government, and participatory government. The following sections deal with the contents of each type of government in more detail.

1) *Efficient government*

According to the Roh Administration, efficiency can be defined as "a more result-oriented concept that involves the realization of government taking responsibility in a way that enhances the quality of administrative services so that it meets the needs of the people." Bearing this concept in mind, the government has tried to adopt a variety of innovative systems:

i) Building an evaluation infrastructure based on an integrated-result management system where business process re-engineering (BPR) has been regarded as the main instrument for maximizing the value of efficiency.

ii) Developing innovative personnel systems, such as activating personnel exchanges among civilians, government officials, scholars, and politicians, expanding the open employment of interns and experts, and introducing the Appointment and Career Development Program and the Senior Civil Service System.

iii) Creating an efficient service delivery system for the local population, including developing a self-reform system driven by local authorities, reforming the education and training system for local officials, improving the local official personnel system, and strengthening mechanisms for settling disputes between the central and local governments.

iv) Innovating the current tax and finance system, including developing a performance-centered tax and finance system, upgrading format for taxes and financial expenditures, and reforming the management of state-run corporations.

2) *Service-oriented government*

The primary goal of the government is to best serve the public. In this regard, the basic duty of the government is closely related to serving the people, responding the demands of the people, and providing the services that the people really want. Until this time, however, the government was to blame for going in the opposite direction. In order to remedy that defect, the government has tried to introduce three kinds of mechanisms:

i) Developing various services for the people, including reinforcing service standards, improving service equality for the socially underprivileged, and upgrading the supply capacity of related agencies.

ii) Reorganizing the tax system, including improving tax equality and designing a more simple and convenient tax system.

iii) Installing an electronic support system, including constructing a comprehensive welfare system for insurance and medicine and establishing a civil appeals information system.

3) *Transparent government*

No matter how excellent its policies, the government cannot be run effectively if the people do not trust it any longer. Regardless of the type of government, trust and transparency have been the most important social capital components in rapidly increasing national competitiveness. Therefore, the government has tried to take strong measures to reinforce transparency:

i) Reinforcing administrative openness, including expanding the disclosure of administrative information as well as enhancing access and implementing the name recognition system for policies.

ii) Increasing the transparency of personnel management, including establishing an open and fair selection system, diversifying evaluation systems, and introducing a balanced personnel employment system without discrimination.

iii) Preventing abuse of power by local government, including introducing self-regulating control systems such as through reinforcing the responsibility of local government and increasing the soundness of local financial management.

4) Decentralized government

Post-modern society is now becoming more and more complex and diverse, so power and resources should be shared in a balanced way so that all units can make decisions by themselves and take responsibility for their own actions. In this regard, decentralization might be concerned with the delegation of decision-making rights from the central government to local governments in terms of organization, personnel, and budgets. In order to accomplish this goal, the government has taken the following measures:

i)   Designing decentralized organizations, including delegating decision-making authority to local governments and cultivating a horizontal organizational culture within the government.
ii) Promoting the decentralization of personnel management, including expanding the extension of personnel rights and increasing the discretionary employment rights of individual ministries.
iii) Reforming the local finance system, including strengthening local financial autonomy and innovating with regard to local tax systems.

5) Participatory government

As sovereignty comes from the people, the people must have the right to participate in the whole policy process. Nevertheless, the people had been treated as passive participants, not as active participants. As a result, public services provided by the government were not able to respond correctly to the demands of the people. In order to resolve this problem, the government tried to adopt the innovative systems:

i)   Reinforcing the openness of public offices to citizens, including expanding the employment of minorities and building a cooperative culture between labor and management.
ii) Strengthening the value of democracy where the people participate directly in public affairs, including introducing the local referendums, citizen suits, and citizen recall of incompetent public officials.
iii) Establishing a financial information disclosure system where the people are able to participate actively in the financial decision-making process.
iv) Constructing an e-government system, including introducing administrative information distribution, electronic voting, and online public engagement.

2. *The Park Administration*

The Park Administration (launched in 2013) recognized the importance of government innovation disregarded under the Lee Administration (2008–2012) and has embarked on revitalizing it through Government 3.0, which stands for government innovation as a mechanism for increasing national competitiveness.

Despite unprecedented growth over the last 60 years, Korea now faces a variety of social problems, such as a low birth rate, an aging society, and economic inequality and polarization and has tried to overcome these serious problems through government innovation.

The emergence of Government 3.0 can be observed from the four perspectives. First, government management should be run based on the partnership among the public sector, private sector, NGO, and the citizens. Under Government 3.0, particularly, the citizens who once were mere passive recipients are able to play the key role in the policy process. Second, government-held public information related to job creation should be disclosed and shared with citizens as much as they can whenever they demand it. Third, the existing government process characterized by segmented administration between government ministries or agencies should be replaced by the innovative government process that emphasizes communication, collaboration, and integration. Lastly, instead of providing uniform public service that did not consider the characteristics of citizens, customized public service for individual citizens has been in place by reforming outdated organizational behavior and organizational culture that were prevalent in the government. Bearing these changes in mind, the Park Administration declared the realization of transparent government, competent government, and service-oriented government with the feasible action plan.

1)   *Transparent government*

The Park Administration has tried to enhance people's right to know through information disclosure. Information disclosure had been individually managed by the central and local governments. First, the Korean government made public agencies disclose it collectively on the online portal open.go.kr to improve people's access to government information. Second, the Korean government made great efforts to identify and disclose as much public information as possible, such as information about citizens' lives (food and hygiene, security, welfare, local prices, etc.), large-scale projects (public projects, contract information, etc.), and public budgets (local finance, government supervision, etc.). Third, the Korean government has tried to establish a system for disclosure of original texts in order to raise government transparency. This system is not only able to provide citizens information held by the government but also full texts of original documents.

In order to enhance private-sector use of public data, the Park Administration has tried to provide the private sector with highly sought-after data that might have tremendous spillover effects, such as data on weather, traffic, welfare, disasters, safety, education, and finance. Individuals and companies are also able to use information freely by accessing original data and open application program interfaces (API) on the public data portal data.go.kr. In order to assist private sector and citizen use of public data, the government has built a public data governance system, where the Public Data Strategy Committee functions as a control tower for government-private cooperation in the use of public data.

The government has built multiple channels for citizen involvement and communication including telephone, text messages, social networks (SNs, Twitter, Facebook, etc.) as well as an online portal http://epeople.go.kr to strengthen public-private partnerships and collaboration. In particular, policy discussions can be made on the people's online portal through e-hearings, policy forums, and survey functions.

2) Competent government

The Park Administration has embarked on carrying out three ambitious tasks in order to make the government more competent: removing barriers in government, improving communication and collaboration among government agencies, and enhancing administration rationality through the use of big data. The first task of removing barriers is centered on developing and diffusing collaborative work systems. Organizations in the Korean government tried to share information with each other as much as possible. A typical example can be found in the case of the National Health Insurance Corporation (NHIC). The government now substitutes NHIC's medical checkup results for physical examinations for the issuance of driver's licenses, which annually benefits 3 million people and reduces costs by 16.1 billion KRW.

The second task of improving communication and collaboration among government agencies mainly targeted the establishment of an integrated government communication system, strengthening digital collaboration using video conferencing, and cloud systems for the integrated management of work and policy knowledge government-wide.

The third task is focused on increasing administrative rationality by using big data. The Korean government has tried to build infrastructure to allow each ministry and agency to interconnect, share, and analyze necessary public data, which has a greater influence on citizen happiness and well-being.

3) Service-oriented government

The Park Administration set up four main tasks for building a service-oriented government: creating integrated provision of customized services, enhancing one-stop services for business, improving access to services for the information poor, and developing new services using cutting-edge information communication technologies. The first task of providing the citizens with integrated citizen services is called the Minwon 24 platform. The Minwon 24 service portal was developed to provide various types of information in a single window, including medical checkups and license renewal dates.

The second task of enhancing one-stop services for business mainly targets small and medium enterprises (SMEs) by establishing and operating the Integrated SME Management Support System aimed at organizing a government-wide collaborative system. The third task of improving access to services for the information poor aims to develop a welfare delivery system through interagency agreements. It also tries to reorganize local community centers as welfare hubs that deliver one-stop welfare services. The government aims to improve web accessibility for the disabled and elderly by providing various information and communication technology (ICT) hardware. The last task of developing new services using cutting-edge ICTs places a high emphasis on providing new services related to disaster management, environment, public security, among others. Owing to smartphone-based services, citizen quality of life has greatly increased under the Park Administration.

3.   *Similarities and differences*

1)   *Similarities*

Despite the difference in party, the Roh and Park Administrations have the same roots in terms of their emphasis on innovation. First, both administrations had a similar emphasis on citizen-oriented government services and greater use of electronic government. Second, they placed more emphasis on changing bureaucratic culture as well as bureaucratic behavior rather than on remodeling organizational structure. Third, they established new institutions that developed roadmaps guiding government innovation and monitored the whole process of innovation during their presidential terms. Fourth, they recognized government innovation to be a continuing process, not a one-off event. Finally, they ultimately tried to change the paradigm of governmental operation from a bureaucratic-driven to a citizen-driven approach.

2)   *Differences*

Due to the difference in party as well as in the environmental changes surrounding the government, both administrations showed different emphases in the innovation implementation process. First, the scope of innovation under the Roh Administration was much broader than under the Park Administration. The Park Administration has put more emphasis on innovation in the central government whereas the Roh Administration tried to innovate in local government as well as in the central government. Second, the development of web-based applications in the public sector under the Park Administration has been faster compared to the Roh Administration. Third, the Roh Administration's innovation method was more sophisticated than that of the Park Administration because the Roh Administration applied the specific innovation methods called Community of Practice (CoP) and Balanced Score Card (BSC) to governmental organizations as much as possible. Fourth, in terms of governance, the Park Administration is more advanced than the Roh Administration concerning collaborative government, group intelligence, and co-production. Finally, the impetus of innovation under the Roh Administration was stronger than under the Park Administration. The reason is that, while the Roh Administration established an institution in charge of the government innovation on the President's Executive Committee, the Park Administration placed it as a government committee in the Ministry of Safety and Public Administration.

III.   Theories of government innovation

1.   Definition of innovation

It is very difficult to draw an exact definition of the concept of innovation. According to Sorensen and Torfing (2013), innovation "not only involves the generation but also the practical realization of new, creative ideas." As shown in Figure 14.1, innovation can be observed as "a complex and iterative process through which problems are defined; new ideas are developed and combined; prototypes and pilots are designed, tested, and redesigned; and new solutions are implemented, diffused, and problematized."

2.   Types of innovation and sources of innovation

1)   Types of innovation

Drucker (1985) argues that "innovation is the specific instrument of entrepreneurship." Entrepreneurship can occur in every sphere whether technical, economic, or social. Innovation in the economic sphere creates the most important resource of "purchasing power." Drucker noted the importance of social innovation over technical innovation in increasing purchasing power. He introduced two typical examples of social innovation in this regard.

Example 1: The American farmer had virtually no purchasing power in the early nineteenth century. He therefore could not buy machinery. There were dozens of harvesting machines on the market, but however much he might

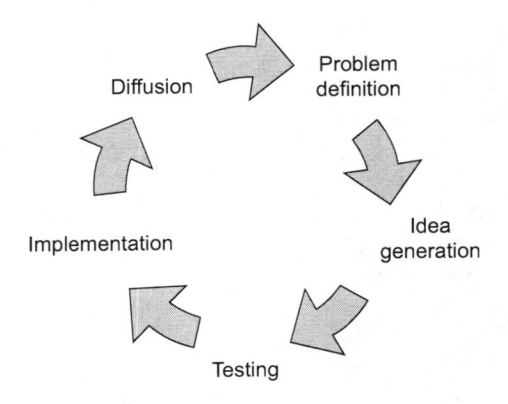

Figure 14.1 The cycle of innovation

have wanted them, the farmer could not pay for them. Then one of the many harvesting-machine inventors, Cyrus McCormick, invented installment buying. This enabled the farmer to pay for a harvesting machine out of his future earnings rather than out of past savings and suddenly the farmer had the "purchasing power" to buy farm equipment.

Example 2: There was not much new technology involved in the idea of moving a truck body off its wheels and onto a cargo vessel. This "innovation," the container, did not grow out of technology at all but out of a new perception of the "cargo vessel" as a materials-handling device rather than a "ship," which meant that what really mattered was to make the time in port as short as possible but this humdrum innovation roughly quadrupled the productivity of the ocean-going freighter and probably saved shipping. Without it, the tremendous expansion of the world trade in the last forty years could not possibly have taken place.

(30–31)

As Drucker showed in these examples, social innovation has had great impact on increasing the productivity of the economy compared to technical innovation. In this regard, social innovation always tries to change mindsets from conventional wisdom to new ways of thinking.

2)   *Sources for innovation*

Innovation might be closely related to change, which always provides the opportunity for developing new products. Drucker argued that "systematic innovation consists in the purposeful and organized search for changes, and in the systematic analysis of the opportunities such changes might offer for economic or social innovation."

Systematic innovation might occur by monitoring seven sources of innovative opportunity across all industries, including the service sector. Drucker (1984) lists them as:

- the unexpected: the unexpected success, the unexpected failure, the unexpected outside event;
- the incongruity between reality as it actually is and reality as it is assumed to be or as it "ought to be";
- innovation based on process needs;
- changes in industry structure or market structure that catch everyone unawares;
- demographics (population changes);
- changes in perception, mood, and meaning; and
- new knowledge, both scientific and nonscientific.

While, in general, the first four sources for innovative opportunity might be linked to the enterprise regardless of business or public organizations, the second three sources might be related to changes outside enterprise, industry, or the service sector.

3.   *Collaborative governance as the government innovation model*

Since Woodrow Wilson proposed that government should be run businesslike in his article "The Study of Public Administration" in 1887, the paradigm of government operations has swayed like a pendulum from authority-based arrangements at one end to market-based arrangements at the other, as shown in Table 14.1.

While authority-based arrangements emphasize the value of democracy, market-based arrangements stress the value of efficiency. Bearing this in mind, while the Classical Public Administration and New Public Administration paradigms underscore the value of democracy, Public Management and the New Public Management paradigms put a higher emphasis on the value of efficiency. As Okun (1975) noted, there might be a "big tradeoff" between democracy and efficiency. In this regard, any choice between the bureaucracy and the market might be an imperfect alternative. To resolve this dilemma, many scholars have tried to seek a third way called collaborative governance, which has been defined as "the process of establishing, steering, facilitating, operating, and monitoring cross-sectoral organizational arrangements to address public policy problems that cannot be easily addressed by a single organization or the public sector alone" (Ansell and Gash, 2008).

Table 14.1 Four institutional forms

1 *Authority-Based Arrangements*	2 *Authority-Based Arrangements*	3 *Collaborative Governance Arrangements*	4 *Market-Based Arrangements*
Government hierarchies (command and control regulations; government agencies)	Outsourcing (principal-agent relationships; long-term contracts)	(Joint provision of services by public, for-profit, and nonprofit organizations; brought together either by mandates or as an emergent phenomenon)	(Self-interest, financial rewards, competition, winners and losers, private property rights)

Source: Jung, Mazmanian, and Tang (2009: 3).

4. *Role of the customer and learning orientation in public-sector innovation*

Despite the importance of public-sector innovation, empirical research on this theme is still scarce. In order to close the gap between theory and practice, Salge and Vera (2012) conducted interesting empirical research with regard to the moderating role of the customer and learning orientation in increasing the effect of public-sector innovation. First, they hypothesized that "the customer orientation of a public service organization is likely to shape the extent to which that organization is able to translate innovative activity into tangible quality improvements." Their results are shown in Figure 14.2.

Looking at Figure 14.2, the analysis shows that the resulting effects of public service quality are totally different in both organizations with high and low customer orientations with regard to innovation. That is the more innovative the activity in organizations with lower customer orientation is, the less the public service quality is. The opposite case is true in organizations with high customer orientation.

Second, from another perspective, Salge and Vera hypothesized that "public service organizations with high levels of learning orientation are likely to yield higher payoffs from their innovative activities than their less learning-oriented counterparts."

Looking at Figure 14.3, the analysis shows that the positive association between public service quality and innovative activity is found regardless of the levels of learning orientation. However, the slope of organizations with high learning orientation is steeper than their less learning orientation counterparts.

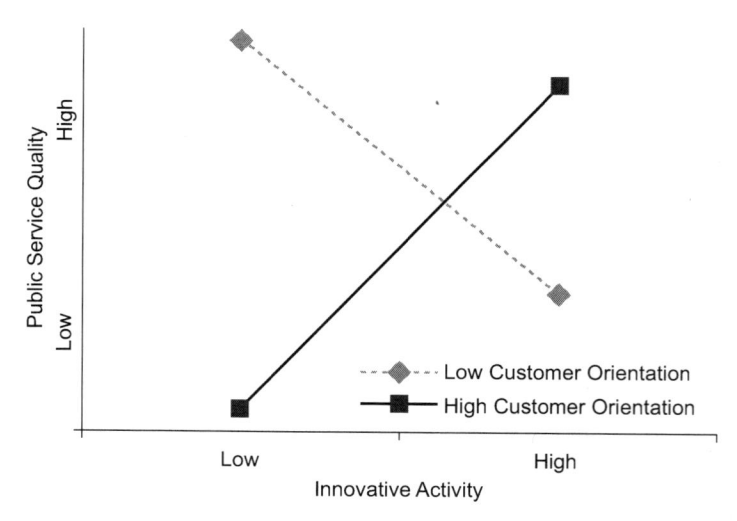

Figure 14.2 The moderating effect of customer orientation

Source: Salge and Vera (2012: 14).

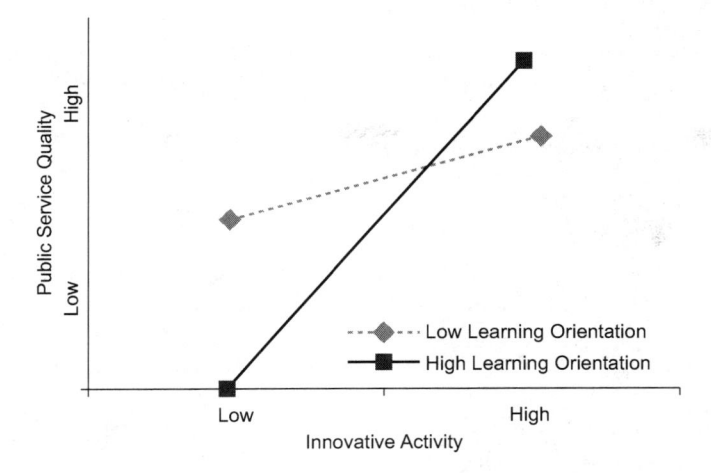

Figure 14.3 The moderating effect of learning orientation

Source: Salge and Vera (2012: 14).

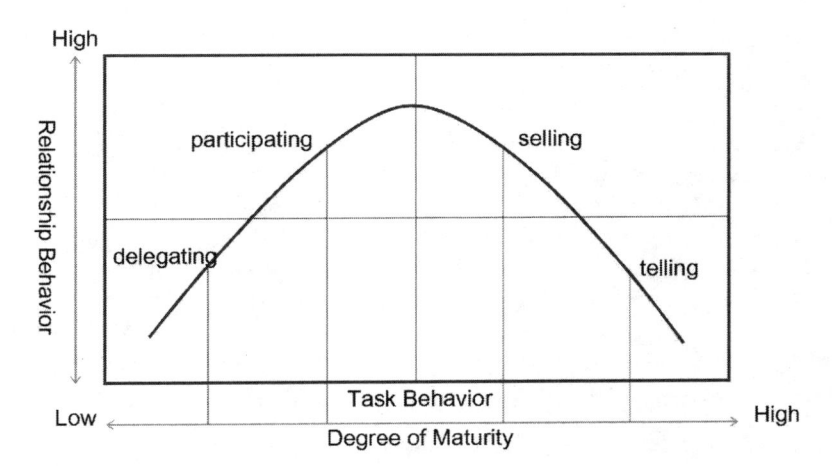

Figure 14.4 Innovation theory to empower subordinates

Source: Hersey and Blanchard, 1982.

5. *Innovation theory for empowering subordinates*

Hersey and Blanchard tried to show how leadership style might change according to the degree of follower maturity. Looking at Figure 14.4, leadership style toward a particular person or group should change when that person or group becomes more mature and willing to work independently. Hersey and Blanchard demonstrate four types of leadership according to follower maturity and corresponding leadership style, such as telling, selling, participating, and delegating.

IV.   Best practices of government innovation

Government innovation throughout the Roh and Park Administrations provided citizens many benefits in a variety of fields of government operation. Two best practices are introduced in this chapter as the most outstanding cases of innovation in terms of transparency, responsiveness, and accountability.

1.   *Corruption impact assessment*

The Corruption Impact Assessment (CIA) developed by the Anti-Corruption and Civil Rights Commission (ACRC) is a kind of legal analysis for investigating and eliminating corruption-causing factors in the stage of drafting all forms of rules and legislation enacted by executive organizations, local governments, and public service-related organizations. Therefore, the CIA can function as a legislative procedure that all executive organizations must follow. That is an executive organization that is going to enact or amend its rules must submit the draft to the ACRC for a CIA. The draft submitted to the ACRC is reviewed, and the ACRC recommends the executive organization remove any corruption-causing factors there may be.

1)   *Background of the CIA*

Most anti-corruption policies or mechanisms prior to the CIA focused on the detection and punishment of violations. However, detection and punishment are not the best policies because they are just concerned with discouraging and threatening possible future crime, not preventing crimes in advance. In the case that the laws themselves are corrupt or contaminated, detection and punishment cannot work as a mechanism useful for reducing corruption. Bearing in mind this fatal problem inherent in the laws, the ACRC has tried to introduce the CIA as a new approach so that it could examine and amend them while rules and laws were still in the draft stage.

2)   *Process of the CIA*

The CIA takes four steps to complete the whole process. These are called request, assessment, amendment, and monitoring and feedback. The first step is the request. In this stage, an executive organization that is going to enact or amend its rules must submit related documents as well as the draft to the ACRC. The second step is the assessment. In this stage, the ACRC reviews the draft and sends the CIA report to the executive organization. The third step is amendment. In this stage, the executive organization may amend the draft according to the recommendation from the CIA report before going to the next legislative stage if there is found to be a corruption-causing factor. The last step is monitoring and feedback. In this stage, the ACRC monitors whether or not recommendations are reflected on the draft. However, the organization is at a disadvantage in an Anti-Corruption Initiatives Assessment if it does not accept ACRC recommendations.

3) *Corruption-causing factors reconsidered*

The CIA has generally used nine criteria to identify corruption-causing factors. As shown in Table 14.2, corruption-causing factors can be divided by the three aspects of demand, supply, and procedure, while each aspect contains three criteria.

Three factors are considered to be important in terms of "Ease of Compliance." The first is the adequacy of the burden of compliance. People may try to avoid compliance by giving bribes when the level of costs and compliance efforts are be appropriate. The second is adequacy of the level of sanctions. Intended results cannot be expected when the content and level of sanctions is not be appropriate. People will not stop violating rules when the sanctions are too lenient, but on the contrary, they try to buy off officials if sanctions are too severe. The third is the possibility of preferential treatment. There must not be any possibility that certain individuals or groups will benefit more from the application of laws and regulations.

Three factors should be mentioned with regard to "Adequacy of Operational Standards." The first is concreteness and objectivity of discretionary regulation. The subject and the scope of discretion should be defined clearly in order to prevent abuse. The second is adequacy of the standards of delegation and entrustment. Standards should be defined adequately and clearly in order to assure the responsibilities of the delegated or entrusted. The third is clarity of financial support standards. It guarantees transparency and fairness in selecting the recipients.

The third aspect is related to transparency of administrative procedures, which involves three factors. The first is accessibility and openness, which guarantee

Table 14.2 Corruption-causing factors

Aspects	Criteria
Ease of compliance (demand)	1) Adequacy of the burden of compliance 2) Adequacy of the level of sanctions 3) Possibility of preferential treatment
Adequacy of operational standards (supply)	4) Concreteness and objectiveness of discretionary regulation 5) Adequacy of the standards of delegation and entrustment 6) Clarity of financial support standards
Transparency of administrative procedure (procedure)	7) Accessibility and openness 8) Predictability 9) Possibility of a conflict of interest

participation by the people and sets up an information disclosure system. The second is predictability, which helps people understand the procedures and predict possible results. The third is the possibility of conflicts of interest. The Korean government has tried to enact laws to prevent conflicts of interest.

4)   Results of the CIA

The acceptance rate for rules increased strikingly from 75.2 percent in 2006 to 93.4 percent in 2013 after adoption of the CIA in 2006. The number of rules with improvement opinions and the number of improvement opinions have been steadily decreasing over the years. In particular, the positive effect of the CIA has been observed since 2012, which might be interpreted as a result of the institutionalization of the CIA, as shown in Table 14.3.

2.   E-government

1)   Business process system

The e-government service of Korea has been oriented towards accomplishing the goal of efficient government. Approximately 362,000 central and local government civil servants in 2013 performed the entire policy process, including documentation, reporting, reviewing, and online approval through the On-Nara Business Process System (BPS). This system has enabled a standardized work process, which has made government decision-making procedures more responsible and transparent. The specific contents of BPS are shown in Figure 14.5.

2)   E-People

The Korean government has also introduced "e-People," where citizens are able to register a variety of complaints through a single online window. Since

Table 14.3 Improvement performance and acceptance rate

Year	Number of Laws for Evaluation	Number of Laws with Improvement Opinions	Number of Improvement Opinions	Acceptance Rate
2006	609	119	359	75.2
2007	1,168	259	737	59.9
2008	1,368	269	496	82.8
2009	1,394	229	508	85.3
2010	1,269	182	403	90.7
2011	1,666	264	505	93.3
2012	1,593	192	508	94.9
2013	1,325	169	357	93.4
Total	10,392	1,683	3,873	

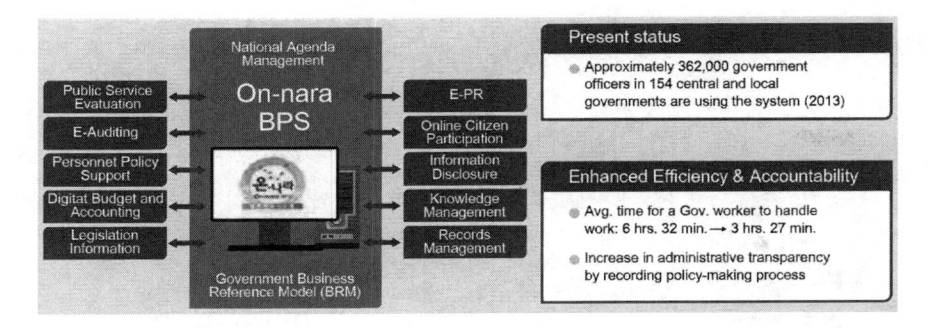

Figure 14.5 The On-Nara Business Process System

Source: Ministry of Security and Public Administration (2014).

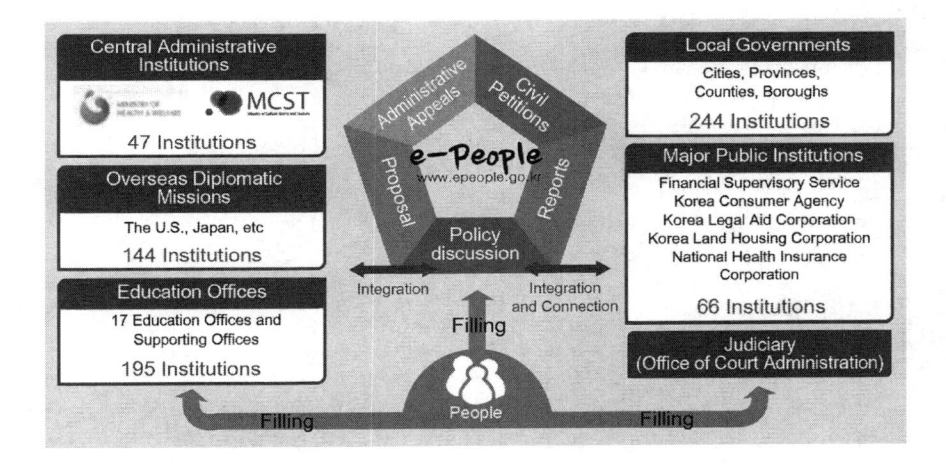

Figure 14.6 The e-People System

Source: Ministry of Security and Public Administration (2014).

e-People is linked to all of the institutions of the central government, citizens can freely contact this system and appeal unreasonable administrative actions, identify needs for system improvements, and address different policy issues. As a result, the number of citizen proposals has dramatically increased from 991 in 2004 to 124,901 in 2010. The specific contents of e-People are presented in Figure 14.6.

3) On-line citizen service portal

This service system allows citizens to apply for services that they want online at any time. Before the introduction of the system, people had to drop by several

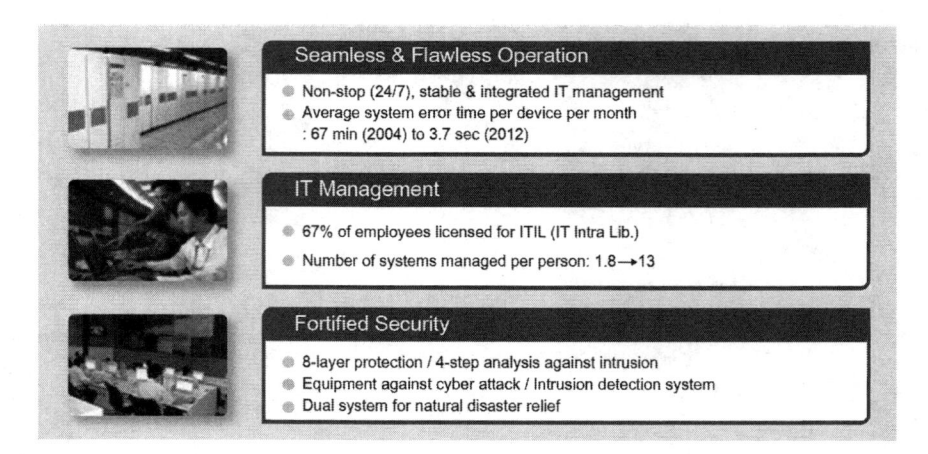

Figure 14.7 The Integrated Government Data Center

Source: Ministry of Security and Public Administration (2014).

administrative agencies to receive services. Approximately 3,000 kinds of services can be processed through the web portal. This system is recognized as a best practice of Korean e-government.

4)   *Integrated government data center*

Korea has built an integrated data center that combines and manages more than 1,200 information systems from 43 government departments. The system makes it possible to provide non-stop, integrated IT management services at any time. The specific contents of the Integrated Government Data Center are illustrated in Figure 14.7.

V.   Conclusion

If the phenomenon of government innovation were an inevitability rather than a temporary fad, it would be expected to be an ongoing process that would be pursued regardless of change of control of the executive branch. Keeping the importance of government innovation, the Korean government has continued to carry out it in terms of democracy, efficiency, and transparency over the years. As a result, Korean government innovation has been labelled internationally as a success story. In particular, Korean e-government ranked first in the UN Global e-Government Survey twice in 2010 and 2012.

Nevertheless, the level of transparency has not been able to improved strikingly despite the intense efforts of the Anti-Corruption and Civil Rights Commission in charge of preventing corruption. However, the introduction of the

CIA has greatly contributed to reducing the level of corruption and is focused on eliminating the corruption-causing factors in advance when enacting laws. This system can be recognized as a product of government innovation in Korea.

Government innovation in Korea is still underway across the nation. Its focus has tended to be on quantity rather than quality. From now on, its focus should shift from quantity to quality, where the happiness of people can blossom without doubt. In the age of globalization, the best practices of government innovation in Korea should spread to the underdeveloped world in order ultimately to increase the well-being of nations that may benefit.

References

Ansell, C. and A. Gash.2008. "Collaborative Governance in Theory and Practice," *Journal of Public Administration Research and Theory*. 18(4): 543–571.

Drucker, Peter F. (1985). *Innovation and Entrepreneurship: Practice and Principles*. Harper Collins e-books.

Hersey, Paul, and Kenneth H. Blanchard, *Management of Organizational Behavior: Utilizing Human Resources*. 4th ed., New York: Prentice-Hall.

Jung, Yong-duck, Daniel A. Mazmanian, and Shui-Yan Tang. (2009). *Collaborative Governance in the United States and Korea*. Seoul: SNUPRESS.

Ministry of Security and Public Administration. (2014). "e-Government of the Republic of Korea," Presented by Nam Kyo Seo in the Meeting of e-Government Delegates, Seoul, Korea. July 23, 2014.

Ministry of Security and Public Administration. (2014). "Government 3.0: Openness, Sharing, Communication, Collaboration," Ministry of Security and Public Administration.

Okun, A. M. (1975). *Equality and Efficiency: The Big Tradeoff*. Washington, DC: Brookings Institution.

Salge, T. Oliver and A. Vera. (2012). "Benefiting from Public Sector Innovation: The Moderating Role of Customer and Learning Orientation," *Public Administration Review*. 72(4): 550–559.

Index